COUNTRY FURNITURE

BY Aldren A. Watson

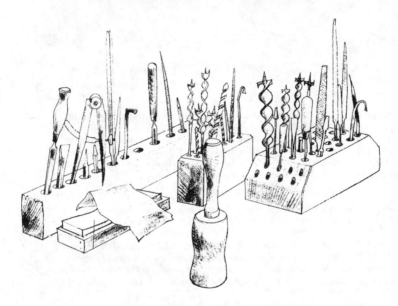

Illustrations by the author

A PLUME BOOK

NEW AMERICAN LIBRARY

NEW YORK AND SCARBOROUGH, ONTARIO

Acknowledgement is made to Doubleday & Co. for permission to quote from *The Cabinetmakers of America*, copyright © 1957 by Ethel Hall.

Published by arrangement with Harper & Row, Inc.

 PLUME TRADEMARK REG. U.S. PAT. OFF. AND FOREIGN COUNTRIES
REG. TRADEMARK—MARCA REGISTRADA
HECHO EN HARRISONBURG, VA., U.S.A.

SIGNET, SIGNET CLASSIC, MENTOR, ONYX, PLUME, MERIDIAN, and NAL BOOKS are published in the United States by New American Library, 1633 Broadway, New York, New York 10019, *in Canada* by The New American Library of Canada Limited, 81 Mack Avenue, Scarborough, Ontario M1L 1M8

Library of Congress Cataloging-in-Publication Data

Watson, Aldren Auld, 1917-
  Country furniture.

  Reprint. Originally published: New York : Crowell, 1974.

  1. Furniture industry and trade—New England—History. 2. Furniture making. 3. Furniture—New England. I. Title.
TS880.W33 1987   684.1'04   86-28533
ISBN 0-452-25923-1

First Plume Printing, October, 1976
5 6 7 8 9 10 11 12 13

PRINTED IN THE UNITED STATES OF AMERICA

for Wendy
who helped put all the pegs in their proper places

Contents

Preface

The country furniture maker was an intriguing kind of person, a type, a special breed in one sense—a man who has been all but swallowed up in the receding perspective of history and social evolution. In a time when garden peas appear to come from a frozen package instead of the earth; when a broken hinge means a new cupboard; when a burned-out fuse cannot be replaced without the services of an electrician; when disposing of wastepaper and garbage has reached the proportions of a national emergency, it is difficult indeed to find grounds for any significant identification with the character and attributes of our forebears. On the whole, modern culture has instructed us poorly, providing only the sketchiest preparation for understanding this man. In many ways he is a stranger, a man who dealt with a dozen problems every day, in the stable, the workshop, or the woodlot—drawing solely on his native intelligence, his skills, and his singular adaptability to find practical solutions. A stranger, but the kind of person it would be good to have known.

Why did he prefer lumber cut in the early winter? Where did he learn about frost-splits? What made him choose cherry wood instead of walnut? How did he come by his woodworking dexterity, his tools, and his knowledge of the characteristics and properties of wood? What kind of a life did he lead? Was it always a struggle with unpredictable prospects for gain? How did his furniture—at times simple to the point of austerity—turn out to be beautiful as well as useful, when his cramped working space was often hardly more than primitive? And why have so many pieces of his furniture survived intact, for so many generations?

These are questions that continue to keep alive the speculation of cabinetmakers, designers, antique collectors, woodworkers, and historians. Attempting to answer them may stimulate not only a more detailed examination of the technical aspects of country furniture, but also a fresh appreciation of this countryman's set of values. For he was a man who lived on the land, close to his family and animals, in constant touch with survival itself, and in circumstances with which we have had little firsthand experience.

ALDREN A. WATSON
Putney, Vermont

ONE
Furniture maker, farmer, woodsman

A rope ferry crosses the river, traveling the quarter-mile on pulley blocks that ride a cable stretched from bank to bank. From the willow-shaded landing the Ferry Road climbs the steep shoreline and then levels off to cross the flat meadow land under the hills. After an uphill climb of another half mile, the road joins the main highway. On the west side is Maple Grove cemetery where upward of one hundred fifty slate headstones are ranged in neat ranks under the trees. Up Main Street, which has been crowned and raked to an even hard-packed surface, frame houses stand under two rows of maples and elms. Ernest Parkman, the town clerk, lives in the third house on the left. He is also town treasurer, the man who quotes facts and figures at town meeting.

Lyman Bailey lives at the next place. He is a widower and has held just about every town office except treasurer. In a few years he will install and operate the first telephone instruments. Right now he has the mail contract, driving the stage between the village and the county seat. His rig is hitched out front.

Warren Willard's blacksmith shop is the next place on the right. Several wagons stand in the big yard out back next to the shop, and a pair of work horses are tethered by the open front doors. They say that Willard, in his fifty-five years, has shod eighteen thousand horses, at the rate of twenty-five to eighty cents each. Often he trades his work for a bushel of apples, corn, or potatoes. He fires his forge with charcoal made right in town.

The street forks by the green: one branch runs past the town hall and on up Kimball Hill, while the other continues north. At one side of the green is the tavern—a respectable inn for travelers, and where townspeople gather to discuss farming, town affairs, politics, or one another.

Corser's store backs up to the brook that runs under a wooden bridge and then tumbles and winds its way down to the river, past a sawmill, a grist mill, a wood-turning shop, and finally another grist mill. Frank Pierce runs the sawmill, producing boards and wholesale lots of chair stock annually, as well as packing boxes. He employs eleven men. James Knight owns the wood-turning shop, but he also saws lumber to order, averaging 250,000 board feet a year. He makes coffins and does some cabinetwork. Zenas Hyde is the proprietor of the upper grist mill, which is a model of convenience that enables him to do an excellent business. He grinds wheat, corn, and other small grains, in season handling better than thirty tons a month. The rest of the year, Hyde, with the help of two hired men, operates a 75-acre hill farm that carries 20 cows, 135 sheep, and 4 horses. Hyde is presently a lister and tax assessor, but has served as selectman, fence viewer, and very nearly—but for six votes—as town treasurer.

The main road winds on upriver, passing the farms of Albert

Townsend, H. L. Scott, Jerome Shaw, Harlan Farr, and Joel Willard (no relation to Warren). Townsend has about the biggest maple sugar bush in the township; Scott is a teamster, hauling wood and timber with his three pair of horses; Shaw specializes in popcorn and tobacco; Farr has both sheep and cattle, and grows all his own feed grains. Last year he made 1,400 bushels of corn and 600 bushels of oats; Joel Willard has what is probably the dirtiest trade of all: he is a charcoal burner, supplying both Willard the blacksmith and Goodwin with hardwood fuel.

All told, the town consists of 17,545 acres, has a population of 1,100 souls, two general stores, two churches, three cemeteries, two blacksmith shops (Willard's and another one which is run by John Goodwin on Ames Hill), and a town hall. There is a brickyard, four district schools, a tannery, and a doctor. The town has a library, housed in the librarian's home.

As for schools, they are all frame construction except for Number 4, which is brick. All of them have but a single room. By law, children between the ages of six and fifteen are required to have three months' schooling annually, either in the summer or winter. In the current year there are 189 summer and 182 winter pupils. Teachers are boarded on nearby farms and receive wages, room and board, and fuel, amounting to about $1,135 a year. The subjects taught are reading, writing, and ciphering.

This was the country furniture maker's village and town—very much the same in Connecticut, Vermont, Massachusetts, New Hampshire, or Rhode Island. The people in such a village lived on the land and were concerned more than anything else with a way of producing food, shelter, and clothing. Whether joiners, farmers, or craftsmen, they were probably quite unaware of the term *versatility*. If they had any thought of success or proficiency, it was for the well-cultivated fields, the fattening cattle, the depth of the sheep's pelt, and a sufficient garden.

If a man in 1780 raised wheat in the spring, corn in the summer, sheared his sheep, worked a couple of days framing a new barn, cut sawlogs in the woods, and then built a table and a set of chairs from the lumber—what would he have called himself? Farmer, joiner, woodsman? Sheep raiser, chairmaker, or builder? Very often the country furniture maker was all of these. At a time when most occupational titles were conferred posthumously, most likely by a clerk who felt obliged to "put down something," the label probably identified only what the man happened to be doing at the moment he died. It seems more sensible, then, to rank him for what he was—a man.

Men of a dozen different occupations turned a hand at one time or another to the making of furniture, but few of them were known as

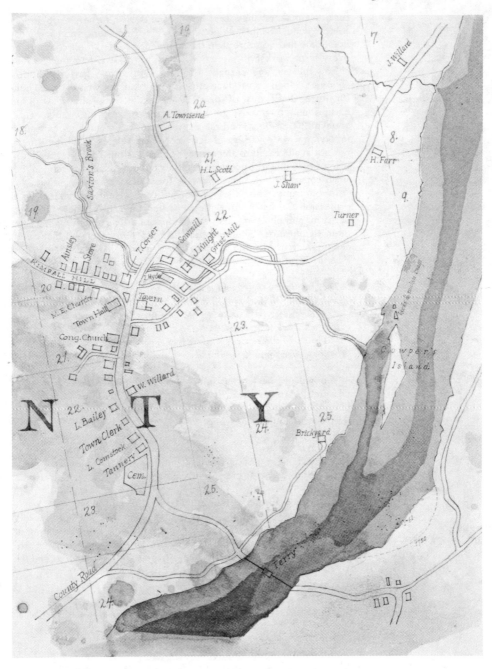

furniture makers: they were housewrights, dish turners, carpenters, joiners, wheelwrights, shipbuilders, carriage makers, and chairmakers. Some had no more than the rudimentary set of tools common in every farm workshop: an anvil, a couple of saws, hammers, a few chisels, planes, and perhaps a square. Others may have had better shops equipped to produce almost every kind of woodwork. Their furniture, built out of practical necessity, was almost without exception anonymous. In a sense, the *lives* of these men were anonymous, too: a natural expression of a complete existence involving a wide variety of activities, each related to all the others but not at all geared to any concept of profession. They practiced not just a single talent, but every one they possessed. Each person in the small community did all the things for which he had an aptitude.

In our time, this kind of versatility is celebrated almost as a profession in itself. But these earlier men had many tasks to perform, and perform them they did, with little if any thought about their significance. Their adaptability was remarkable though, and genuinely warrants the acclaim given it by Charles Bissell in his *Antique Furniture of Connecticut*:

> *They could turn their hand to many trades, such as weaving, shoemaking and tanning, hat making, cloth dressing, blacksmithing, brick making. . . . Then, too, there was the chap who was handy with tools and could turn out a table, or a bedstead—or a coffin.*
>
> *Those who made more furniture than others were usually house builders by trade. They had the tools and were accustomed to working with wood.* *

The village was a self-sufficient community cut off from the surrounding towns by difficult geographic features and poor roads. The inhabitants did everything themselves, and when they lacked people who could—they imported them.

> *The first settlers . . . suffered many inconveniences for the want of mechanics. They sent to Southold for a weaver; to Huntington for a blacksmith, and to Wethersfield for a carpenter.*

The invitation to the weaver is on record in the following words:

> *February 2nd 1653—It is Ordered yt there shall bee an invitation sent to Goodman Morgan of Southold, if hee will come and live here and weave all the Townswork, hee shall come in free from all former charges and the Town will give him 5 and break him 2 ackres of Land.*

—TOWN RECORDS, EAST HAMPTON, N.Y.

*See "Sawdust and shavings" 1: Craftsmen of Suffield, Connecticut; 2: Part-Time Occupations of Furniture Makers; 3: Cabinetmakers in New England, New York City, and Philadelphia c. 1730.

Generally a conservative, hardworking lot, the townspeople could express themselves succinctly, and a number of them achieved a literary polish quite beyond the promise their phonetic spelling suggested. Felix Dominy of East Hampton, New York, was twenty-five when he wrote this essay intended for publication in the local newspaper:

> What I like to see—*I like to see a Man attend to his own business and let his neighbor's alone . . . I like to see a man wear the breeches in his own family . . . I like to see a Carpenter keep his saw in good order and not stand out too often for higher wages . . .*
>
> What I dislike to see—*I dislike to see a Farmer let his fences get down   Keep his cattle on straw, ride a poor horse hard, and dress his daughters in silk . . . I dislike to see a Carpenter set down to whet his tools and at the same time begin a long story—*
>
> *I dislike to see a Young lady display* too *much of neck and* ancles *in company—*

It was not a closed society: the opportunities for economic independence, especially in the northern colonies, were considerable for the likes of a cabinetmaker, shoemaker, housewright, or shipbuilder. Skilled labor was scarce and the wages were generally higher than in Europe. These trades, cultured and expanded by hard work, could and very often did result in the accumulation of money with which a fellow could hire help and start a business of his own. A good man could always find some way to break out of a plodding life of resignation.

Accustomed as these people were to hard physical labor and a strict regimen, they were not organized against having fun. God they feared and God they worshiped, at prayer meeting, at Sunday service, and at home with the Bible. Still, at the end of a tedious day they found energy to load themselves into the buggy or wagon, cross the river, and drive ten miles to a kitchen dance. Arriving almost in time to eat, the assembled neighbors engaged in visiting, gossiping, and prophesying while the children hooted and hollered around the barnyard and orchard. When the supper things had been cleared away, the fiddler perched a chair atop the kitchen table and the dance began. The floor sagged and sprang as the couples turned through the *Virginia Reel, Hull's Victory, Morning Star, Colley's Hornpipe,* and *Molly Hang the Kettle On.* If it were an August evening there were several intermissions, cooled and spiced by liberal amounts of cider, applejack, or rum. The affair might not break up until twelve or one when, tired out laughing, everybody climbed into his rig and headed for home. Hopefully someone had thought to slip the ferryman an extra fee, just to make sure he'd be on hand to carry them back across.

There were other kinds of recreation, too. Among the Dominy family papers are references to a cod-fishing junket to Montauk, a trip to Gardiner's Island that produced a catch of twenty-six fish, as well as numerous expeditions to pick peaches or to go cherrying. A letter to Felix Dominy from David Baker touches on another pastime:

> *Please to give me a detail of your tramp on Montauk, did you get that thanksgiving goose—I guess you had your labor for your pains, Hard work for little Gains—*
>
> *I want to know if you heard any fireing last evening   the boys built a fire with shavings in the street here & in a few minutes the fowl began to come ducks of every description brant & wild geese &c   I shot at the geese once & J   Mulford shot twice at the brant and then our fire was gone it was fine sport I assure you.*

During his term as president of Yale, Timothy Dwight traveled extensively during his summer recesses, recording his impressions and observations in a series of journals. From his *Letters*, written on a trip through New England, is this comment on the inhabitants of Hatfield, Massachusetts:

> *[They are] . . . Men, who devote themselves to their own concerns, usually manage them well. The people of Hatfield are good farmers. Their fields are cultivated, and their cattle fattened, in a superior manner.*
>
> *The inhabitants have . . . been conspicuous for uniformity of character . . .*

And another observation on the town of East Hampton, New York:

> *The village contained at this time [1811] about 120 houses . . . Several of the inhabitants have acquired considerable wealth by commerce and fishing . . . There are now six ships . . . in the whale fishery on the coast of Brazil; each of which is supposed, on average to return annually one thousand barrels of oil . . .*
>
> *. . . a general air of equality, simplicity, and quiet, is visible here in a degree perhaps singular . . . There is, however, no want of social character. . . .*

The Dominys appear to have had that character. They not only made furniture and clocks, but were also very much at home constructing barns, houses, and mills. In one of Nathaniel Dominy's letters are enumerated the specifications for constructing a windmill.*

*See "Sawdust and shavings" 4:   Specifications for a Windmill.

John Henry Belter of New York had some of this same ingenuity, too. Belter devised a lamination process using from three to sixteen thin layers of wood, and eventually applied for a patent on the process:

> *I take sufficiently long strips of veneer and covering the whole of one side with glue, apply it to the short piece and compress the whole either between plain or slightly dished cawls until cold . . . I repeat this process for any number of staves, working rapidly to prevent the glue from becoming cold . . .* *

In the Shaker communities as well, versatility was the byword. Henry DeWitt, who was a mechanic and a joiner in the New Lebanon Community, kept a journal from which these entries were selected:

> Sat 29   *We finished our case of drawers all but staining.*
> Sat 12   *Mended 18 baskets & 3 chairs.*
> Tues 15   *I made a couple of books.*
> Mond 21   *I fixed a saw plate in a bow & cut new teeth & filed it.*
> Fri 1   *I cut a walnut tree for basket bails and rims*
> July   *I turned 604 pins [clothes pins] this week*
> March   *In the* P.M. *I begin to get out some timber for bobins.*
> Sept   *Made a milking stool.*
> Dec   *Made a pair of butternut serge shoes for Polly Reed.*

Every facet of Shaker life was governed by written law that prescribed the conduct and standards of the community down to the very smallest detail:

> *Beadings, mouldings and cornices, which are merely for fancy may not be made by Believers.*

Strictures of this kind may not have encouraged experimentation or the development of new methods, but there was one thing this discipline may very well have created: an enforced attention to fundamentals, which preserved good design, sound construction, and careful workmanship. Though the Shaker cabinetmaker may have been free of commercial pressures and afforded the luxury of leisurely work, he was nevertheless aware of Mother Ann's injunction: "Do your work as though you had a thousand years to live, and as if you were going to die tomorrow."

But the usual country furniture maker did have commercial pressures, as well as time limitations. Still he doesn't appear to have

*See "Sawdust and shavings" 17: Preparation of Glue.

needed any external authority to remind him of good workmanship. Many of these men had served apprenticeships in Europe, or had learned their trade from their fathers. For a time, an apprenticeship of sorts persisted here. It was a natural system that fitted the nature of farm and village life. When not in school, the children were expected to help—in the house or barn, or in the fields and woods. Through this informal family apprenticeship children were trained to be useful. Whether they stayed near home, or married and moved away, they could take with them a means of livelihood.

> *The cycle of necessities first, followed later by the luxuries, repeated itself throughout the Middle West. Journeymen cabinetmakers took to the trails with carts and set out into western New York State, Ohio, Indiana, and south into Kentucky and Tennessee. They carried the simplest of tools with them, not at all the relatively fine equipment that a master craftsman would have at hand. . . . they would wander from place to place to the west or to the south until, reaching an appealing community, they built tiny shops for themselves and became respected craftsmen.*
>
> —J. R. DOLAN

The term *journeyman* originally meant a trained cabinetmaker who worked for a daily wage. His apprenticeship supposedly qualified him to start in business for himself, and many did. Others were more like Dolan's peddlers, moving about and often building furniture to order right on the spot before going on to the next place. And there was another kind of peddler-furniture maker who carted other men's furniture over the countryside in wagons, selling at marked-up prices to generate an income. Lambert Hitchcock was one of the early chairmakers who transacted business with peddlers of this sort, shipping complete chairs into the back country. He also sold bundles of chair parts—legs, stretchers, and slats—that found their way into hundreds of small towns where they were bought by furniture makers, or were assembled on location by the peddler himself, who then sold the finished product. This link gave some of the more remote country workmen a chance to make fancier chairs—with turned legs—than they could fashion themselves. For not every shop had a lathe, even a crude one. Once referred to as *bodgers* [one who begins a task but does not finish it], the English chairmakers made parts on a simple bow lathe, frequently set up right in the forest close to the timber source. Sawlogs were first cut into bolts of the correct length and then split into smaller square sticks. When these were turned, they were then delivered to shops in the villages.

For all his clever handiness with tools and general all-round mechanics, the country furniture maker was still only a human being, no better and no worse than the rest of us. Some obviously knew the way of tools far better than others. These men prospered, if they had a little business sense as well. Others only just scraped by, and no doubt many many more failed and went to farming, or hired out to a craftsman with a better head for business than they had. Some just quit and ran off, like the boy here. Whatever became of you, James Howard?

Ran away the 4th of this instant August from Joshua Delaplain, Joyner, an apprentice lad about 18 years of age. His name is James Howard, is a well fed lad, of a sandy Complexion, has short hair, and had on a full Trim'd Drugger Coat and Breeches, a good Hat, Shoes and Trousers. He can work pretty well at the Joyner's Trade.

—ADVERTISEMENT IN THE *N.Y. GAZATEER*, 1739

We tend to forget that the pieces of early American furniture we call antiques were once brand new, without a scratch, resplendent in their natural wood or bright new coats of paint. They were devoid of any historical patina—merely objects to be slept on, eaten from, or sat in. The construction of this furniture and the woods used in its manufacture reflect the character of those who built and used it. The signs of how this furniture was used are also there for us to read: the well-rubbed knuckle carving on the arm of a chair, the way the spindles are bent and crooked to the shape of the sitter's back, or the slender foot stretcher—once a graceful piece of turning, but now worn flat. This furniture, quite apart from its technical fascination, tells a great deal about the people who were our ancestors.

TWO
Where they came from

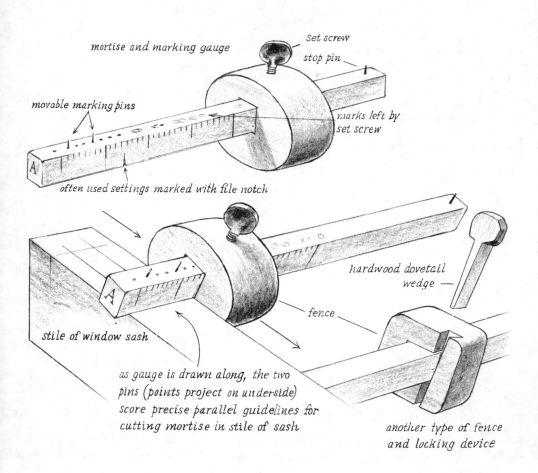

mortise and marking gauge

set screw

stop pin

movable marking pins

marks left by set screw

A

often used settings marked with file notch

hardwood dovetail wedge —

A

fence

stile of window sash

as gauge is drawn along, the two pins (points project on underside) score precise parallel guidelines for cutting mortise in stile of sash

another type of fence and locking device

The term *country furniture* is used to mean furniture built by ordinary people living in rural areas, as opposed to that made in the seaport cities by men we would call professional cabinetmakers.

There are other reasons to put it in a class by itself. The circumstances under which these early Americans made their furniture were unique. They were obliged to make furniture for reasons of survival: they urgently needed it, there was no one else to make it, and no place to buy it ready-made. Starting almost from scratch, they were experiencing the beginning of a new, if familiar, cycle in which they were motivated by primitive impulses stirred by their situation. This had happened before in other, more ancient parts of the civilized world. Furniture had been "invented," manufactured by hand, refined, and its forms developed. The woods most suitable for cabinetwork had survived a period of trial and error, and a complete range of specialized tools had evolved.

But why a new beginning? The first colonists brought with them their attitudes, convictions, and customs: Why not also simply transplant their technologic skills at the same time, picking up in America where they had left off in Europe? It was not that simple, for this *new* England presented a formidable appearance. Things here were just not the same. For one thing, the land was virtually covered with trees—forests that the furniture maker must have recognized as an inexhaustible supply of valuable raw material. Yet before he could use any of it for furniture, acres of that timber would have to be cleared off so he could plant crops. This frustration must have stirred in him a longing for his home country.

There, a man could work in his shop with familiar woods, cut and sawn into boards which he could easily obtain. Expert toolmakers supplied him with everything of steel that he needed. Close by were his customers—neighbors, tradesmen, shipbuilders, instrument makers, and the wealthier class who could afford his best work. The routine of work and living was established.

As he looked about in America, however, the colonist could see very little to reassure him. About the only visible prospect for livelihood was the land, and he wasn't used to that way of life. For a long time there would be slim chance of re-creating that comfortable routine—perhaps never in his lifetime. He could envision no sawmill, no lumber yard, no toolmaker's shop. If he were to have any boards, he would have to make them himself. As he looked over his tools, the probability of producing lumber must have appeared remote, for he discerned that the tool most needed at the moment was his axe. Clear land, build a shelter, and cut firewood to heat it—that would have to be the new order of things, a way of life with few comforts, least of all fine furnishings. As for a market for his product, that wasn't even a consideration: every householder was his own customer.

hanging spice cabinet

Considering the background in Europe from which America's early woodworkers came, we must accept a commonsense explanation for whatever crudity there was in their first sticks of furniture. But at the outset we must believe that the first ships arriving here did indeed carry experienced woodworkers, men of training who could fashion anything of wood, from a bedpost to a sailing ship. In *The Puritan Dilemma*, Edmund S. Morgan says that once John Winthrop's mind was made up to move lock, stock, and barrel to America, it was Winthrop's responsibility

> . . .to see the colony supplied with men trained in all the trades necessary to success. However desirable it was to have none but godly settlers, if the passenger list lacked a necessary sawyer, cooper, surgeon, or whatever, he must supply one somehow. Much of his time went to sifting letters of recommendation, searching out suitable men with suitable trades, and arranging sponsors to pay the passage of those who could not pay their own. . . . Settlers who could afford it carried a number of servants with them, and some of the most essential craftsmen were doubtless transported at the company's expense. [Massachusetts Bay Company]*

That's not to say that some mediocre craftsmen didn't escape the fine mesh of Winthrop's interviewing. Not all woodworkers were mahogany-and-veneer-men; yet to appreciate the country furniture maker and the things he made, we must first refute and discard the widely expressed view which unfortunately now amounts to an assumption:

> The Pilgrims were simple people who brought with them to America only the barest necessities. It is unlikely that the joiners and cabinetmakers among them had the tools to attempt elaborate work; and it is even more doubtful that they had the required skill. Consequently, the furniture they built was crude and utilitarian.

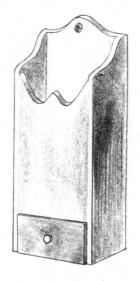

pipe box

The mistake is to assume that what they made in an emergency demonstrated their full capability. They made first what they needed first; it was not until later, at least a generation later, that the furniture maker built what the *customer* wanted. And with this trend toward catering came a confusion and a profusion of crossbred designs, a preoccupation with style, mode, and fashion—influences that can be traced more directly to the whim of the customer than to functional need.

As a class of craftsmen, the early woodworkers were skilled enough to have chamfered a few edges here and there, scraped the

*See "Sawdust and shavings" 5: Early Furniture Makers.

wood a little smoother, or attempted a bit of carving, even to the extent of shaping an octagonal bedpost into a tapered round one. Why too, were nails and screws so seldom used? True enough, iron fastenings were not readily available, and they were costly, but there were nails, and screws also. The woodworker's background and training provide the answer. For example, the interlocking dovetail joint was much stronger and far more durable than a nailed-in bottom of a chest—far better able to carry the weight of the chest's contents. He couldn't help the way he constructed with wood: he made his work to last.

Products of the guild and the apprentice system, these woodworkers were trained, skilled, and disciplined—qualities that were essential to the instruction of their own assistants. Knowing virtually nothing of conditions in America, they crossed the Atlantic with their few belongings and tools. And when they got here some of them probably discovered they had brought the wrong ones. Yet it makes sense to think that a craftsman, contemplating the gravity of the enterprise and the dimensions of the ship, would have taken tools instead of other effects.

But regardless of the size of a man's tool chest and the variety of its contents, never again in his lifetime would he have much opportunity for gracefully turned bedposts and chair legs. If he did indeed manage to survive, at best all he could hope for was that his progeny—the next generation—might revive all the handed-down old skills. Meanwhile he went about the business of making stools, benches, beds, tables, bowls, and cradles. All these articles, nevertheless, persistently announced his good craftsmanship. They were made to last, and they were pleasing to the eye.

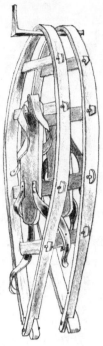

steam-bent snowshoes fastened with tusk-tenons: 18th century

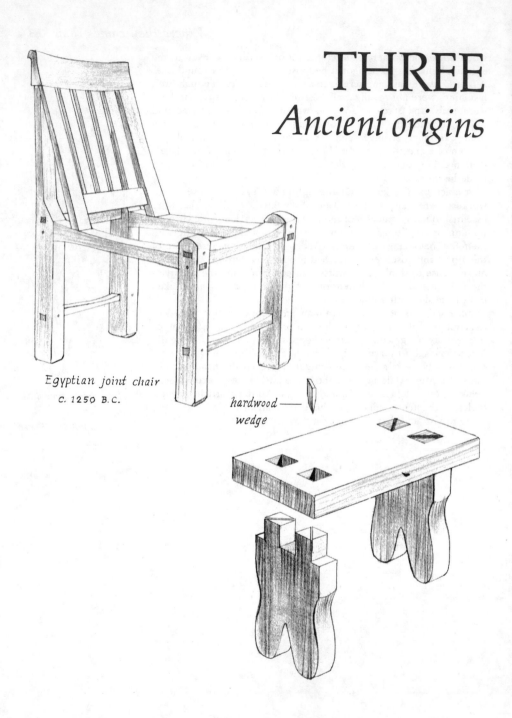

THREE
Ancient origins

Egyptian joint chair
C. 1250 B.C.

hardwood ——
wedge

The woodworking skills practiced by the early American craftsmen stemmed from origins so ancient that the determination of dates becomes not just an academic exercise but an abstraction. Almost identical beginnings occurred in several parts of the world, not always at the same time, but in general taking shape along extraordinarily similar lines. The fundamental techniques of sawing, smoothing, and joining have been known and used since several centuries before the birth of Christ.

The mortise and tenon joint—along with paneling, the very foundation of furniture making—dates at least from 1250 B.C. and possibly earlier, for the Egyptians were using it at that time. Although the invention of the lathe cannot be linked with a specific date, wood-turning was known in ancient Egypt, in Greece, and in the Roman empire, as well as in Asia. The principal disadvantage of early lathes, both pole and bow lathes, was the reciprocating action. The so-called bow of the lathe was mounted stationary over the bed of the lathe, and the bowstring wound round the work to be turned. As the bow was alternately drawn and released, the work rotated first in one direction and then the other, the cutting tool being applied to the work on only one of the two strokes. This sturdy device, with its single moving part, remained in constant use for hundreds of years.

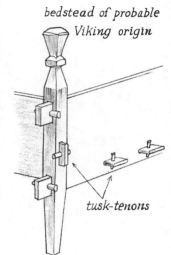

bedstead of probable Viking origin

tusk-tenons

Paneling is an ingenious method of constructing large, flat sections that are light in weight, extremely rigid and strong, and decorative as well. An Egyptian chair from about 1200 B.C. shows more than just a crude understanding of paneling and the mortise and tenon technique. Furniture makers were not alone privy to this knowledge: it was commonly used by shipbuilders, housewrights, and carriage makers. The shipbuilder's mortise and tenon joints were heavier and rougher—no need to make them otherwise—yet in design and function they were the same as those cut by cabinetmakers. The bridge builder's trunnels (tree nails) were oaken pegs a foot or so long and an inch in diameter; yet except for size they were no different from the more delicate pegs used in joining the parts of a table. The dovetail joints, the rabbeted insets, and the molded edges that the cabinetmaker used constantly could just as well have been cut for him by the carriage maker. And in cutting these variants of the basic joints, all woodworkers used tools of like kind, modified in size and scale to suit their particular needs.

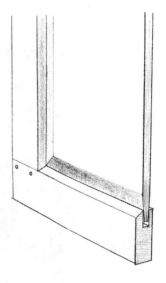

This perfection in the development of tools and methods began and reached its apogee in a historical split second, as if running true to a preordained set of interdependent principles that had lain dormant, awaiting only man's technical development to effect release. Who first used fox wedges in the end of a tenon before it was mated with its mortise? A carpenter? A chairmaker? A carriage

sawing stool

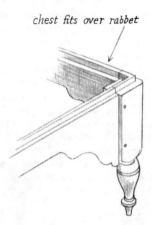

top rail

framing
a door

stiles

muntins

lock rail

grooves to
receive
panels

bottom rail

attaching top to chest of drawers

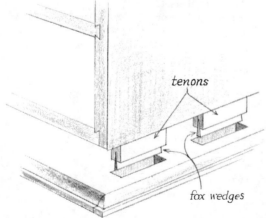

tenons

fox wedges

chest fits over rabbet

maker? Perhaps a house framer first exploited this device for tightening a joint.

It is convenient to assume that furniture making began with the invention of the saw—next to the felling axe, a vital tool. The sheer antiquity of the saw is impressive enough, yet more significant may be the fact that an Egyptian handsaw from 1450 B.C. remains true to the pattern of our contemporary compass saw, the nineteenth-century Swedish handsaw, and many others from several countries. The degree of change in these tools has been so slight that the word deviation would have to be used in place of evolution. It may be noteworthy that the design of the saw handle changed from an open pattern to a fully closed one about 1747 in Sussex, England, but this is more properly an item of curiosity, as it didn't in the least affect the configuration of the cutting teeth.

Likewise the designs and forms of furniture have changed only imperceptibly over the centuries. In most ancient cultures the ruling aristocrat—headman, lord, king, or potentate—sat above his subjects, from which vantage point he could keep an eye on those who squatted around him. Literally speaking, the chair was the seat of authority. In early English history only the chosen few sat in chairs. Whether holding court or merely hosting a feast, the ruler com-

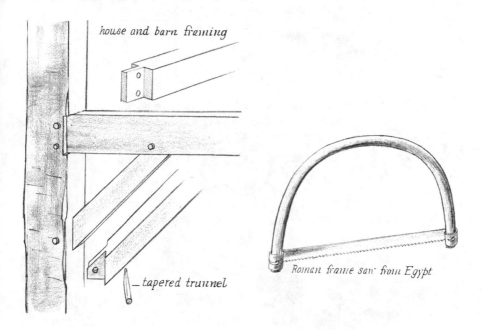

house and barn framing

tapered trunnel

Roman frame saw from Egypt

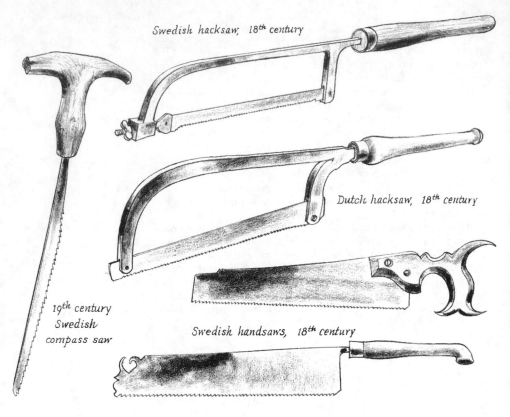

Swedish hacksaw, 18th century

Dutch hacksaw, 18th century

19th century
Swedish
compass saw

Swedish handsaws, 18th century

18th century backsaw with closed handle, used by Samuel Crompton,
inventor of the spinning mule

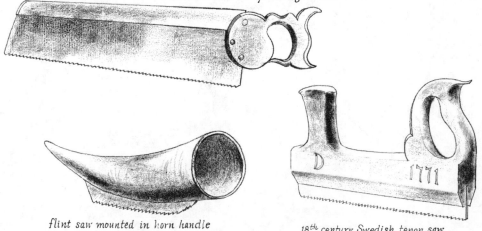

flint saw mounted in horn handle

18th century Swedish tenon saw

manded from his seat of authority, generally a ponderous oak armchair with a high back. It was so heavy that it was rarely moved, and then only by the combined effort of two or three men. The idea that everybody should sit in chairs may have occurred in the heat of some political upheaval, thereby triggering the advent of the *back-stool*, the first chair for commoners. In a token way, the significance of the chair has survived in modern times. A scholar is honored by appointment to a "chair" at the university, and the "chairman" assumes leadership of a department.

On behalf of all furniture forms, the chair reflects the times—good, bad, and indifferent. From the infinite variety of chairs over a period of several hundred years can be selected heavy, cumbersome chairs; graceful chairs with slender legs; stately armchairs; straight-backed spine crackers; low-slung sleepy chairs; and simple, utilitarian seats with no adornment whatsoever. Some are attractive, others are ugly; but all of them constitute good documentation of our changing times. And in point of fact all chairs can be reduced to a simple box form. Fitting slender banisters into the back of a chair made it better looking than a straight, solid plank. But basically the chair was still a box. The first furniture maker to put four separate legs under the seat of a chair wrought a very pleasing change, but

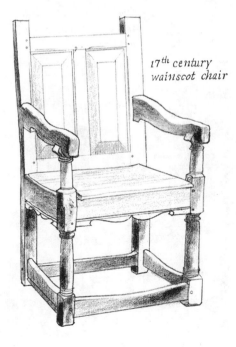

17th century wainscot chair

four-legged corner chair

comb-back Windsor

turned spindle chair
similar to a ladder-back,
from a 14th century
manuscript

17th century carver

*early
Hitchcock*

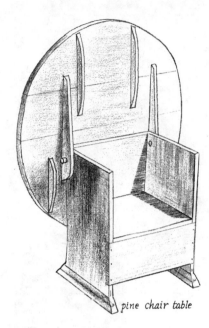

pine chair table

even so, this kind of refinement was little more than cutting away
superfluous wood from the rudimentary box form, although a great
many more refinements followed.

> *The first table top desks were merely boxes with slanting top for writing or,
> perhaps oftener, for reading. Since these desk-boxes had to be lifted, their
> size and weight was necessarily limited. Putting the desk on its own stand
> turned it into a respectable piece of furniture instead of an accessory. . . .*
>
> *. . .It was not long thereafter that the wide and shallow top of such a
> desk was found ideal for use as a base for tall shelves or a cupboard—a
> combination known today as a secretary.*
>
> —HENRY LIONEL WILLIAMS

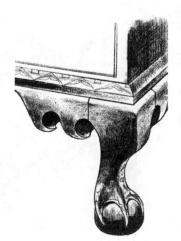

Given the common ancestry of furniture forms, the individual
cabinetmaker carried out his construction with accepted techniques,
though his personal variations created new ideas, either by accident
or intuition. Just how these subtle variations are arranged and
rearranged against the long succession of furniture making may tell
us something about the age of a particular piece, about the period in
which it was made, or about the man who made it. But *only*
something. It would be deceptive to make too much of these

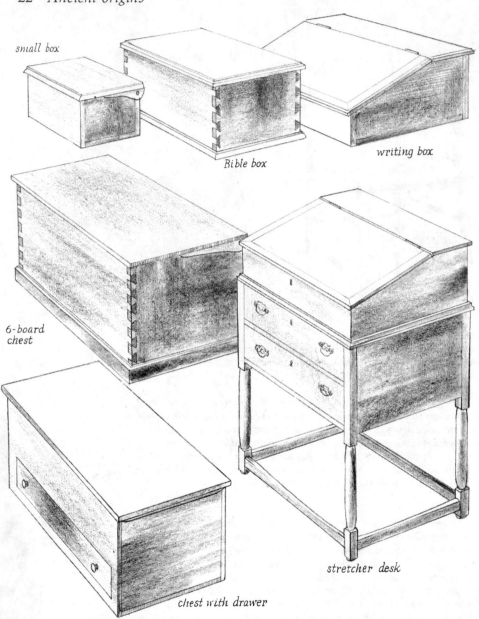

small box

Bible box

writing box

6-board
chest

chest with drawer

stretcher desk

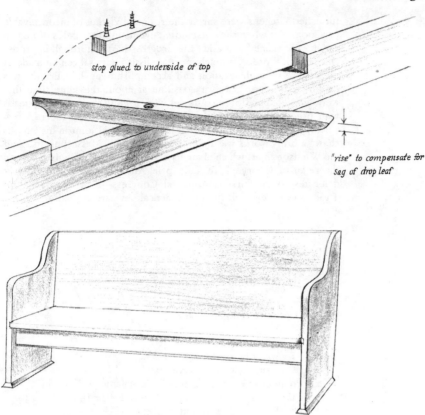

stop glued to underside of top

"rise" to compensate for
sag of drop leaf

indicators since all methods of joinery and woodworking conform
pretty much to an established system.

There was certainly much imitation in America of English and
European furniture: nothing could have been more natural. It would
appear just as natural to picture the country craftsman standing at his
lathe, intrigued by the results of his own experimental handling of
his gouges and skews. Producing mostly for himself, and under no
compunction to copy, he would easily have found these innovations
worth keeping, to be used over and over again. Indeed, as one of the
Shaker elders put it, "We find out by trial and error what is best, and
when we have found a good thing, stick to it."

Looking back at this early period of furniture making, we may be
tempted to see the 1600s and 1700s in America as primitive beyond
imagination; that the people who cooked and lived in those pine-

furnished kitchens were surely the resigned victims of inconceivable privation. Yet when the outstanding events in other fields of human activity are ranged alongside the progress in furniture, all in proper chronological order, a much more realistic appraisal can be made of the degree of sophistication and accomplishment. Leif Ericson was exploring our northeastern coastline at about the same time that woodworkers in a dozen countries were joining chairs and bedsteads with precise craftsmanship and a set of fully evolved tools. A few years before Nicholas Disbrowe closed the final joint in his famous chest, a brass works was being set up in Lynn, Massachusetts. And the Windsor chair, which made its first appearance in England during the reign of George I, turned up in America just in time to seat delegates to the First Continental Congress—a few years before Thomas Godfrey built the first practical navigating quadrant.

TIME LINE

1000 Leif Ericson settled in Vinland, probably on the New England coast.

1588 Published: Thomas Hariot's *A Briefe and True Report of the New Found Land of Virginia*, one of the earliest recorded eyewitness accounts.

1606 Plymouth Company granted charter for colonization.   James I, England 1603–1625

1614 Dutch fur traders established settlement at Albany.

1620 Mayflower Compact signed at Provincetown by the 41 men who made the 63-day crossing with their families.

1629 Nine hundred settlers arrived in Salem harbor, led by John Winthrop.

1632 Dixie Bull and 15 other Englishmen-turned-pirate raided Bristol, Maine.

1642 English ironmaker Joseph Jencks induced to help start an iron and brass works at Lynn, Massachusetts.   Appearance of high-backed settle, a bench with tall arms to ward off drafts

1644   Building of the ship *Trial*
       marked beginning of New
       England shipbuilding in Boston.

       Saugus Iron works established
       on Saugus River, under
       aegis of John Winthrop.

1650   Chair-table with pintle hinges   Nicholas Disbrowe chest,
1656   Harvard College formally   Connecticut valley near Hartford
       recognized Galileo's concept
       of the solar system with sun
       at its center, 23 years after
       Galileo had been forced by   Banister-back chair
       the Inquisition to repudiate   Hadley Chest
       his theory.
1683   Parson Capen House,
       Topsfield, Massachusetts   Sunflower chests by Allis and Belding
1690   Whaling industry begun in
       Nantucket.

       Addition of short legs to the
       chest created early highboy.
1699   English-made, two-section
       sash windows used in Virginia.
1700   Slat-back chair appeared   Rope seats
       simultaneously in New England,
       Pennsylvania, and New York.
1712   Christopher Hussey of   Queen Anne, England
       Nantucket captured first sperm   1702–1714
       whale, altering whale fishing—
       formerly a close-to-shore
       industry.
1725   Cabriole leg in more common use.   George I, England
                                               1714–1727

       Queen Anne style in vogue   Windsor chair
       in America
1728   *New England Weekly* estimated   George II, England
       the cost of living index   1727–1760
       for tradesmen with family of
       eight at £265-18-9 annually.
1730   First practical navigating
       quadrant invented by Thomas
       Godfrey.

1754 Published: Chippendale's
*The Gentleman and
Cabinetmaker's Directory*
1760 Conestoga wagon developed
in Pennsylvania, capacity 4-6
tons. Framed wainscot
construction.
1774 Declaration of Rights
adopted by First Continental
Congress, in Philadelphia
1775 Battle of Lexington: April 19
1776 Thomas Paine's *Common Sense*
1781 Revolution ended

Duncan Phyfe moved from
Albany to New York City
1783 Baltimore to Philadelphia
by public conveyance: 5 days
1787 Tenche Coxe hailed
expansion in America: "We now
make ourselves ships, cordage,
muskets, anchors, nails,
cabinetwork, trunks, windsor
chairs, carriages, and harness."
1789 George Washington inaugurated

First session of Congress

Published: Colle's *A Survey
of the Roads of the United
States of America,* probably the
first road atlas
1792 Colonel Ewel Hale built first
important wooden truss
bridge: 350 feet in two
spans across Connecticut
River at Bellows Falls, Vermont.
1797 John Adams inaugurated
1798 David Wilkinson of Rhode
Island awarded patent for a
machine to cut screw threads
1800 Four-tined table forks began
to replace former two- and
three-tined ones.

George III, England
1760-1820
Thomas Chippendale, England
1741-1779*

George Hepplewhite, England
?-1786*

Goddard-Townsend,
Rhode Island
1725-1858*

Benjamin Randolph,
Philadelphia, retired
1792

Thomas Sheraton,
England 1774-1806*

Samuel McIntire & Son,
Salem 1770-1819*

Duncan Phyfe
1791-1854*

Duncan Phyfe opened cabinet shop
on Broad Street, in New York

Elijah and Jacob Sanderson,
Salem 1775-1825*

*Approximate working years

1801 Thomas Jefferson inaugurated

1802 In Waterbury, Connecticut,
Abel & Porter operated one
of first mills to make sheet
brass for clockmaking,
powered by horses

1804 Lewis & Clark Expedition
left St. Louis.
1809 James Madison inaugurated
1814 William Rush, noted carver
of ships' figureheads, carved
full-sized statue of Washington.
1817 James Monroe inaugurated

1825 Erie Canal opened, linking
Buffalo and New York: 544
miles.
John Adams inaugurated
1829 Andrew Jackson inaugurated
1830 Robert L. Stevens invented
the T-rail, the iron tongue,
and the hook-headed spike:
still used by railroads today
1838 Chauncey Jerome, Bristol,
Conn., began making brass
clocks with standardized
parts, produced 600 a day,
sold for $2 each.
1850 Clipper ship *Stag-Hound,*
designed and built by Donald
McKay, made record run
from Boston Light to the
equator: 13 days.
1851 Published: Herman Melville's
*Moby Dick, or the White
Whale*

*Approximate working years

Dunlap cabinetmakers,
New Hampshire
1769–1843*

Dominy craftsmen,
East Hampton, N. Y.
1760–1860*

George IV, England
1820–1830

1820: Hitchcock started
chair factory in Hitchcockville,
now Riverton, Connecticut

FOUR
Characteristics and properties of wood

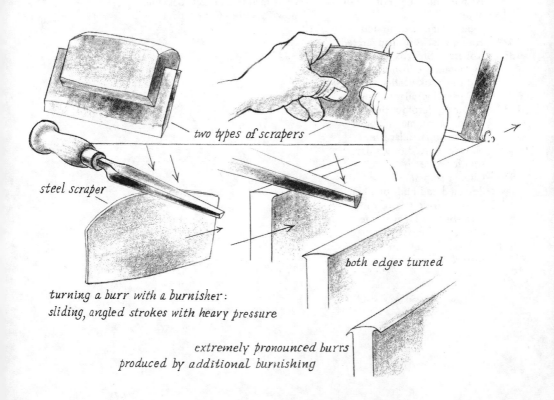

two types of scrapers

steel scraper

both edges turned

turning a burr with a burnisher:
sliding, angled strokes with heavy pressure

extremely pronounced burrs
produced by additional burnishing

Wood is a unique substance: there is no other that the individual craftsman can fashion into such a variety of articles with simple hand tools, and with as little effort. No other material maintains vitality as stubbornly after "death." No other material is so abundantly available the world over, at such low extraction cost. Nor does any other material replenish a supply of its own kind with comparable rapidity, uniformity, or certainty. For all practical purposes, wood is perhaps the only natural material that replaces itself at all. Most of the other valuable raw materials, such as iron, copper, coal, require eons of time to replace the resources consumed in mining. Wood redeposits itself in a matter of generations.

Wood is an organic product. . . . It is on this account that no two woods are alike—in reality no two specimens from the same log are identical.

The various mechanical properties of wood are: (1) stiffness and elasticity, (2) tensile strength, (3) compression strength, (4) shearing strength, (5) transverse bending strength, (6) toughness, (7) hardness, (8) cleavability, (9) resilience.

Wood exhibits its greatest strength in tension, and parallel to the grain: it is uncommon for a stick to be pulled apart lengthwise.

Each growth ring is made up of two more or less distinct parts: the wood nearest the center of the tree is more open textured, and in nearly all species, of a lighter color than the darker, outer part of the ring.

The autumn formed wood is so close that without the aid of a pocket lens, the cavities or pores cannot be distinguished; in the depth of winter the formation of wood practically ceases; with the advent of spring the large diameter tissue is formed; so large are the cells of this tissue that they can be plainly seen with the naked eye in most woods. As the change from the non-porous to the porous tissue is sudden, it imparts to the cross section of the wood the appearance of a ring.

It is virtually axiomatic, then, that rapidly grown wood showing fewer than 8 rings to the inch, yields weaker wood.

—SAMUEL J. RECORD

While England was busy appropriating mast trees for the Royal navy, colonial woodsmen, lumbermen, teamsters, and sawmill operators were felling and skidding trees, and cutting them into heavy timbers, planks, boards, veneer, bolts, shingles, and sled runners from the variety of forest species that grew thick on the New England hills. This apparently endless supply of virgin timber was worked up by woodworkers of every sort into all the tools and implements of a new nation.

*See "Sawdust and shavings" 6: Comparison of Hardness 7: Comparison of Cleavage Strength; 8: Comparison of Moisture and Shrinkage.

If we imagine that the furniture maker was handicapped by a lack of good stuff to work with, an examination of the list of available woods should correct any such idea. It appears he was not limited just to the woods he knew in Europe, though some of these grew here as well. There were some new species too, and he quickly learned their qualities. Some of the exotic woods were missing, but the sheer volume of native timber more than made up for that lack: he could pick and choose, discarding the defective boards and pulling out only the best ones that were straight and true. It was perhaps more accurately a case of his choosing, rather than just using, yet very nearly every indigenous specie turned up in furniture sooner or later. The cabinetmaker, as rationally as anyone else, chose woods which he himself liked, possibly very often influenced by what kinds were on the lumber rack in the loft. In negotiating with a customer, he might make a tactful suggestion that sycamore would be nice. The talk could gently be steered away from cherry—which he didn't have—and brought round to maple, which he did.

Not all the woods that the country furniture maker used are necessarily considered the finest cabinet woods today, for standards have changed and have been influenced by the demands of mass production machine methods. The countryman with his deliberate methods and slow patience could afford to wrestle with a slab of butternut or a cranky piece of elm, using more time than could be justified today.

Much of the early country furniture was made up as solid-wood construction with infrequent use of lathe-turned legs or carved members, and even less veneer work. The curly and figured woods which made the most attractive veneer sheets were popular in the cities and seaports, where higher prices could be charged to pay for the more laborious and costly construction. But the country workman evidently felt himself under no handicap, for he worked in softwoods like pine and found them entirely adequate.

All furniture makers appear to have used all kinds of woods in the same single piece of furniture. For example, Samuel McIntire of Salem, Massachusetts, liked to mix pieces of mahogany with bird's-eye maple and satinwood.* The chairmakers especially habitually combined different woods, often using turned hickory legs in a butternut seat, and topping off the chair with ash spindles and a crest rail of maple. This deliberate choice can be attributed partly to the cabinetmaker's exploitation of the characteristics of each wood, and how it behaved when green or dry. Yet there were other forces at work, too. Sometimes these combinations resulted simply from using what he had on hand, or from a personal preference for

*An East Indian tree of the mahogany family; also in a corrupt sense, any of several smooth-working woods used in furniture.

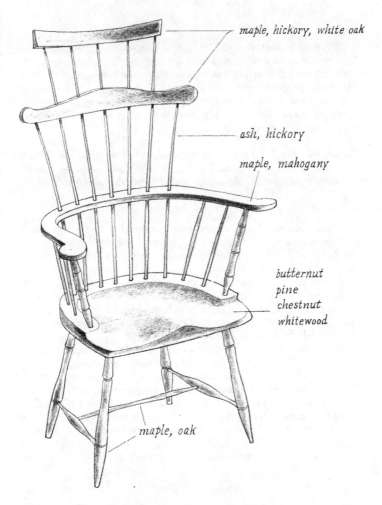

maple, hickory, white oak

ash, hickory

maple, mahogany

butternut
pine
chestnut
whitewood

maple, oak

contrasts of color, texture, and finishing qualities. The chairmaker most certainly knew the value of using both green and dried woods: a seat made of green wood and fitted with well-dried legs could be counted on to shrink tight around the socket ends of the legs, making the final joinery absolutely rigid and durable.

Like Hitchcock the chairmaker, John Dunlap of New Hampshire picked up his lumber from more than one local source and in some instances, when necessity required, traveled personally to find the wood he thought was best suited to the work at hand. Dunlap used maple and birch extensively and made lesser use of cherry. Pine was very commonly used for drawer bottoms and the backboards in cupboards and secretaries. The lack of warping and checking in the Dunlap furniture points to careful choice in selecting lumber—especially where curly maple was used—and to the assumption that the wood was properly dried and seasoned. It is easy to see how much influence the natural beauty of a wood exerted on the average furniture maker for it is exceptional to find any wood that lacks its own particular charm.

> *Sometimes richness of effect is no further attempted than is obtained by the natural beauty of the wood which is employed; and when this natural beauty is considerable, this simple kind of furniture is most highly valued.*
>
> —JOHN PHIN

White oak, ash, and hickory were highly prized by chairmakers because all these woods tended to "whip" far less when working on the lathe, and in the turning of slender parts such as back spindles, this was an important factor.

Regardless of what the furniture was, most craftsmen seemed to look for one universal quality in wood: a certain amount of resistance to the tools that generally insured a cleaner, smoother cut; a quality that was summed up by this: *Any wood that'll bite back when your sawteeth take hold will do for furniture.*

At least seventeen species grew within comfortable distance of the furniture maker's workshop, and for a little more money he could get almost any of the tropical species then being imported from the West Indies, Central America, and South America. Of the native species, one or more of them grew in almost any hillside forest. The ingenious workman adapted not only to the available woods, but also to whatever means were required to get the lumber out of them; sometimes snaking out his logs with his own team, or trading labor with a neighbor who had some trees he wanted.

WHITE ASH

> *The timber principally used in . . . carriages is the ash. This is not an elastic, but rather a tough and fibrous wood, capable of altering its form by the application of pressure, and therefore when not in large masses requires iron plates to secure it.*
>
> *By boiling it becomes very pliable, and may be formed into almost any shape, provided it [the piece of wood] is not too thick. For this purpose it is better to use steam than water, as water is likely to dissolve and carry off the gluten which unites the fibres.*
>
> —JAMES W. BURGESS

Heavy, hard, and exceptionally tough, white ash is fairly easy to work, although chairmakers as well as carriage makers discovered its propensity for throwing up splinters, particularly when the wood was bent to excessive curves. It has a grayish white color, straight grain, and a slight resemblance to hickory. It was used for chair spindles, banisters, and back slats, as well as for an occasional lathe-turned piece. Ash stoutly resists decay and rot when exposed to the weather, though not as dramatically as locust. This quality put it as number one or two for farm implements, tool handles, and the running gear of wagons and sleds.

Boards cut from older, slow-growing trees in a crowded forest show a noticeable cross-figure called *curly ash*, which was exploited in much the same way as veneer patterns. And Burgess describes another peculiarity of the white ash:

> *Some trees which have grown on hillsides much exposed to constant winds present a remarkably wrinkled appearance through their whole length, and it is scarcely possible to plane their timber smooth; this is the toughest of all ash timber.*

He also maintained that the best ash wood came from trees that were felled when the sap circulation was at its lowest ebb, as the pores are open then. The second-growth wood* is especially valued for its superior weight, strength, hardness, and stiffness—all prime characteristics for carriage work. Ash has been called the tree that's so tough ". . . it will sometimes pull out its own tongue when it's

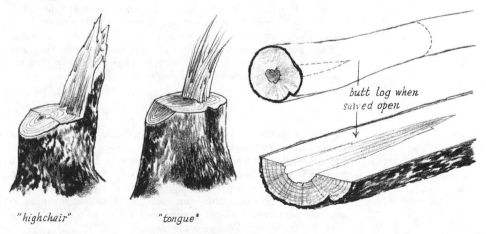

butt log when sawed open

"*highchair*"   "*tongue*"

*Forest trees that come up naturally after the removal of the virgin timber either by fire or logging.

felled." The sinewy muscle of ash runs with the grain, a feature that can cause the heartwood center of a tree to yank loose just as it starts to fall. A jagged "tongue" is left on the stump, and a corresponding long, thin cavity in the best part of the tree—the butt log. Woodsmen say, "When cutting ash, saw fast at the last."

White ash warps and twists very little, but it does have a tendency to check and split during air drying—a drawback that was largely overcome by stacking the new boards in a shaded place, or by sealing the ends of the boards with paint.

BASSWOOD

Also called *whitewood*, basswood is often loosely used to describe the wood of the tulip tree. It is light, soft, and tough—a wood with very little graining. The tree grows tall and straight, although it is not uncommon to find a gentle bend in the trunk near the ground. Generally free of knots, it was much used by the chestmakers of the Connecticut River valley, and by chairmakers, who prized it for seats.

BEECH

A relative of the oak and chestnut, beech is sometimes called *ironwood*, but this term can have little significance other than referring accurately to it as one of the strongest woods—heavy, hard, with a good resistance to shock, and reasonably well suited to steam bending. From time to time faulted as a wood that was "subject to the worm," beech nevertheless works down to a fine surface and finishes well; has a fine, uniform texture, and does well on the lathe. It was used in a great many kinds of solid-wood construction, and later as a stable base wood for veneering. Beech was also used for tool handles, woodenware, and in cooperage.

BIRCH

Special care must be given to birch during the drying and seasoning process, for it has a tendency to shrink more than other woods, and to end-check, or crack open, near the ends of the boards. Still, birch was a very popular wood, despite its drawbacks. Furniture made of it was exported to Europe and England where it gained favor as a natural finish product. The term *mahogany birch* was invented to describe birch that had been treated with a dark stain that accentuated the natural similarity to mahogany.

Carriage makers made good use of the wide boards the birch tree yielded, planing them smooth and fitting them into the frames as floorboards. But birch has a brittle nature that made it unsuitable for steam bending—a quality that also called for caution in nailing close to the ends of boards.

BUTTERNUT

Much weaker than its relatives hickory and walnut, butternut or *white walnut* was nevertheless used in chairs, tables, benches, and other furniture. It has a texture coarser than walnut, and larger pores, but it was easy to work and quickly acquired a mellow patina from exposure to the air and sunlight.

RED CEDAR

The range of the red cedar once covered nearly all the United States including the New England area. Great quantities of cedar furniture were at one time manufactured for shipment from New England to the southern states. The heartwood was a bright, strong red with sapwood streaks of cream or pink. The wood was heavy and hard—a slow grower—but it lacked stiffness and strength, and had a very bothersome habit of splitting when nailed. But in spite of these failings, there are quite a number of "seeder desks" and other pieces listed in furniture makers' inventories.

Virginia cedar was thought to be nearly as good as Bermuda juniper, but the Carolina variety was considered the best. As a moth deterrent for the lining of storage chests, boards at least $3/4$ of an inch thick are needed, with as many knots as possible, for that's where the highest concentration of aromatic oils—the moth repellent—was deposited.

CHERRY

A very dense, close-grained wood with a natural depth of color, cherry ranked as one of the choicest cabinet woods, along with maple, walnut, and mahogany. The heartwood is usually reddish tan, and the sapwood a narrow band of creamy pink, which in older trees may be nearly white. Like all fruitwoods, cherry grows slowly but never attains spectacular diameters. In spite of the characteristically narrow boards from the cherry tree, these modest dimensions didn't stand in the way: cherry boards were used for almost all kinds of furniture:

> . . .a *two-drawer stand of cherry with mahogany veneered front, a three-drawer bureau similar in some details to the stand, and an oval tiptop table made by Linsley [Harvey J. Linsley of Woodbury, Connect-*

icut]. Standing today . . . is a house where lived the Trowbridge family. A large cherry tree was cut down on this property and the wood taken to Linsley's cabinet-shop, where it was made into the above furniture.

—ETHEL HALL BJERKOE

In the main, the country craftsman made up cherry as solid-wood furniture, while in the cities the occasional wavy swirls and infrequent feather-crotch patterns were set aside for veneer work. In his detailed study of the Dominy craftsmen, Charles F. Hummel says that the cherry drop leaf table listed in one of his inventories is the only piece of veneer furniture that can be attributed with certainty to the Dominy family of cabinetmakers.

As with all hardwoods, cherry needed sharp tools to work it, yet because of its grain and texture, very little scraping or smoothing was required to bring the surface to finish: a good sharp plane or chisel left a glass-smooth surface. With age cherry acquired a rich purple-red hue, and a patina that rapidly improved with every scrubbing and rubbing, not to mention the frequent, inadvertent applications of polish in the form of bacon fat and butter!

The resistance of cherry wood to all the edge-cutting tools suggests a consistency harder than wood—something more like metal.* Tapping a piece of well-seasoned cherry on the end-grain produces a ringing resonance.

CHESTNUT

This was not the horse chestnut, but the variety known to furniture makers as "sweet chestnut," a specie that grew in abundance in the Northeast until about the turn of the nineteenth century, when a blight appeared in the form of a fungus *(endothis parasitica)*. Spreading quickly and thoroughly, the blight soon decimated the extensive stands of chestnut, and stood off all attempts to revive the growth. Before this destruction, the majority of chestnut trees selected for lumber were first girdled and allowed to die before felling. The tree grew tall and exceptionally straight, providing main-trunk logs that yielded wide boards for cabinet and furniture work. Typically shot full of worm holes, the wood nevertheless remained perfectly sound. It had a handsome warm yellow color that in time mellowed without

*Teak—and to some degree maple—has some of that texture-of-metal. In the jungle where teak grows there were few roads, no diesel logging trucks, and no rail lines. The only way to get the dense, heavy logs out of the tropical forest was by way of the rivers. Teak will not float when green, or fresh-cut. To obtain merchantable teak then, the trees were girdled and allowed to die on the stump. When they had dried out enough to lose weight and gain buoyancy, they were rafted together and taken downriver.

the assistance of any finish or wax. F. Lewis Hinckley says that "the wood held little attraction in the production of early American furniture, except for some use in concealed structural purposes," a fact that is verified by the frequency with which Newport, Rhode Island cabinetmakers made it into drawer bottoms and sides. In this function as structural wood it was rigid, strong, and durable, though it could be slabbed off, or split, with a single stroke of the axe. This may be considered a redeeming feature, for many a cupboard and chest was made entirely of chestnut boards—doors, panels, and drawers.

Years after the chestnut blight had passed, leaving countless stands of dead timber, these once proud trees were transformed into trainloads of telephone poles: poles as straight as arrows that outlasted several modifications of telephone lines, and lasted years longer as fence posts around the farm. Set in the ground untreated, chestnut survived the weather almost untouched by rot and decay.

ELM

Although Hinckley states that elm timber "was not utilized in Colonial or Federal times," it may be that he referred to its use as a building timber, where exposure to the weather was an obvious drawback, for elm does poorly outdoors. Yet it has a stringy, tough, coarse, and uneven grain with frequent subversive twists that were no great hazard in plank flooring in dry places.

Elm was definitely a furniture wood. There are innumerable references to elm chair seats, and its wood was considered perfectly utilitarian by wagon makers, who made it into wheel hubs, or naves. The tree often grew various burls with erratic and attractive patterns which blossomed out in veneer sheets. Elm veneer often showed serious defects, but these small areas were successfully patched with inlay pieces, even on new furniture.

HICKORY, SHAGBARK HICKORY

This excellent wood was said to be the hardest and strongest of our native timbers—a statement that some might rather see applied first to white oak. In spite of the temptation to split hairs, however, hickory well deserves the honor: it is a slow grower that when fully dried and seasoned has the feel and appearance of bleached bone, and superior wearing qualities. In the time of country furniture at least, hickory headed the list of woods particularly well suited to steam bending, sharing this distinction with white oak and ash. Ash may have been put at the end of the list because of its propensity for splitting on the outside, or tension side of a bend, especially when the wood used was very thin. Its springy resiliency made hickory a fine wood for chair legs, slats, and spindles—structural members that could be turned or worked down quite slender without risk of losing strength. Yet when dry the wood was so hard that nailing was difficult, and it was not the easiest to "work in the requirements of cabinetwork." Hickory was used extensively in wagon work for axles, and the simple moving parts of farm implements and vehicles.

The number of carriage and wagon makers in this period had reached enormous proportions. Their advertisements crowded such magazines as *The Carriage Monthly,* alongside countless ads for carriage tools, iron parts, hub-boring machines, patented folding buggy frames, and innumerable devices calculated to speed up the manufacture of horse-drawn vehicles. This industrious effort of course speeded up the consumption of hickory trees too, and was the subject of a speech by B. F. Von Behren, delivered at a meeting in Chicago in 1905. Quite unaware that the advent of the automobile was imminent, Von Behren lamented: "Hickory trees are becoming extinct in these states. The shortage in this article, which is the most essential component of wooden vehicles, probably will make necessary a general raise in prices of all wooden vehicles unless the supply is increased, and it can only be done by growing the timber."

Depletion of the hickory stands was only one alarming aspect of the situation. Obtaining hickory of satisfactory quality was gaining attention as well:

> *While the area of the country where good hickory is obtained is more extended than where the elm and hub stock is found, it is true that the very best [hickory] grows in the same localities, and under much the same conditions of soil and proximity to the sea as in the case of the elm; but the region where fairly good hickory is found extends further down the seacoast, much of the good spoke timber now being obtained in Virginia and North Carolina while the stock of New Jersey and Connecticut was largely exhausted years ago, and can now be obtained in these localities only in small and scattered lots.*
>
> —H. H. LOCKWOOD, IN A LECTURE BEFORE THE TECHNICAL SCHOOL FOR CARRIAGE DRAFTSMEN AND MECHANICS, NEW YORK, 1905

LOCUST

The best carpenter with the biggest hammer can't sink a nail into dry locust, which may be why they say "locust will last two years longer than stone!" Having many of the characteristics of hickory—extreme hardness, springy toughness, and superior durability even in the weather—locust was used for chair seats and other parts where nails and screws were not needed. The wood has a taffy tan color when fresh-cut that turns to a grayish yellow when it is dry. Aside from its furniture uses, locust worked well for the running gear of wagons, though its weight was something of a disadvantage. Locust tends to end-check but the ends when trimmed off remain stable. This superb wood didn't escape the notice of wooden shipbuilders either: used to make the tapered trunnels for fastening ships' timbers, it maintained the strength of iron while retaining flexibility. Farmers made sturdy fences with locust posts that stood solid for fifty years and were reset bottom end up to last another fifty.

MAHOGANY

One of the smoothest working furniture woods, mahogany shrinks very little, tends less to warping and twisting than many other woods, and is hard enough for almost any job. Ship and boat builders found it adaptable to their purposes: a mahogany plank twenty or twenty-five feet long bent easily over the frames of a longboat and required no steaming other than at the forward end where it had to be twisted and fastened to the stem.

A native of Africa, South America, and Central America, as well as the Caribbean countries, various mahogany woods have been imported to the United States since the 1600s, a large proportion of the early lumber coming from the West Indies.

Mahogany: To be sold by Samuel Williams, in Fourth Street, near the sign of the Indian Ocean, 25,000 feet of Jamaica, Bay, and Providence Mahogany, In logs, planks, or boards, suitable for Cabinet and Chair Makers, house and ship work, printing presses, &c. Also, Red-Cedar, Walnut, Poplar, Cherry-tree, and Gum Boards—Any young beginners wanting a stock of seasoned wood, may be supplied at the shortest notice, upon very low terms, from town or country.

—INDEPENDENT GAZATEER, JAN 15, 1791

It was widely favored by all branches of the woodworking trade. The heartwood of some mahogany had a substance that repelled parasitic larvae, in a way similar to cedar. The grain is open, the wood strong, and is easily worked with hand tools. Honduras mahogany was considered superior to the Spanish variety which was generally unfit for most cabinet and carriage work.

With great buttressed roots extending twelve or fifteen feet above ground level, the trees were felled from a staging built above this swelling. In order to reduce the weight of mahogany logs so they would float, the trees were cut into lengths and squared up as finished timber right in the forest. Each owner marked his own timbers and skidded them to the nearest river, usually at night to spare the oxen unnecessary exposure to the tropical heat. The logs of various owners were rolled into the river bed—dry during the summer—where they awaited the flood stage of the rainy season. They were carried downstream and eventually loaded onto ships, the entire process taking up to a year.

Mahogany grew to an immense size—as much as one hundred fifty feet high, with a massive butt log measuring ten or twelve feet across. Often growing as isolated individuals no more than two or three to the acre, these huge trees yielded logs weighing fifteen tons or so, and produced boards that were free of knots and as wide as forty-eight inches.

Carved mahogany showed a crispness comparable to chased metal, a characteristic that could be seen in the high polish imparted by the smoothing plane. So dense is the wood, and therefore so accurately could mortise and tenon joints be cut, that fitting the tenon to its mortise often created an air compression that made assembly difficult. For this kind of exacting joinery, woods such as teak, ebony, rosewood, walnut, mahogany, maple, and other dense woods—whether rare, imported, or from local forests—were much more satisfactory to work than the softwoods. Since density is usually associated with closeness of grain, much cleaner sawcuts were possible in these woods, and far less dressing with the chisel or plane than with pine, for instance. From the standpoint of both time and workmanship, this is a great advantage, especially as the surfaces of a tenon are so narrow and short that dressing them up true is a tedious and ticklish task.

While usually straight-grained, individual mahogany trees reacted to the variations of weather, location, and growing conditions: some grew shorter than others, or exhibited peculiarities such as burled or feather grain, crotch patterns, and other interesting figures of special interest to the veneer craftsman.

MAPLE

Known by the names rock maple, hard maple, and sugar maple—the tree whose sap is boiled off to make syrup—maple has always been at the top of the list for furniture, cabinetwork, patterns, tool handles, wooden machine parts (such as spinning bobbins), shipbuilding, and dozens of articles so well known as to need no mention. The wood is heavy, very stiff and hard, and resists shock and bruising perhaps better than any other wood. Like cherry and teak, it has that "resistance-of-metal" quality.

Growing oddly sometimes in all kinds of twists and burls, the maple produced beautiful figures and patterns that quickly were colloquially called curl'd maple or curly maple, bird's-eye maple, and burled maple—freak grains that the veneer cutter found ideal.

*Whoever has got any curious
Maple Tree knots to sell may hear
of a Purchaser from the Publisher.*

—*BOSTON GAZETTE,* APRIL 30, 1739

Even today, the gnarled old sugar maple that has seen fifty or sixty sugar seasons come and go, standing alone in the fence row, is sought after by lumbermen who will run the risk of striking half a dozen sugar spouts buried deep in the three-foot-thick butt log, just to get a few hundred feet of wavy grained boards.

There are very few statements about wood that can be made categorically: one about maple may be the only exception. It was used by every furniture maker living in the climate where the tree grew, as almost any inventory list will bear out. Spelling the name by the phonetic method then in current usage, "mapol bords" appeared in written records consistently. And this handsome, creamy-colored wood was made up mostly as solid-wood construction, behaved well on the lathe, and could be worked into the tightest mortise and tenon joint possible. Dense, almost as hard as hickory, and having a "resonant timber ring," maple was unquestionably a wood fit to grace the country furniture maker's coat of arms.

OAK

In the time of King Henry VIII of England, the oak that went by the name "park oak" was thought to be the best for cabinetmaking, for ". . .Oftentimes have I seene of their workes made of that oke so fine and faire as most of the wanescot that is brought from Danske [Denmark], for our wanescot is not made in England."

Before the invention of the pit saw, good boards were made of oak by splitting off flat, shingle-thin slabs with a broadaxe or froe. A light blow started the split and the oak's helpful propensity for splitting along the grain did the rest. The boards produced by this process of *riving* were rough and varied considerably in thickness from one end to the other, not to mention from edge to edge. Yet they retained maximum strength because none of the longitudinal fibers were severed. All the oaks—and there are many varieties—have this penchant for splitting. In some instances a handicap, this splitting was turned to advantage in the making of early clapboards—tapered flat boards used in sheathing the sides of buildings. The term *clapboard* [from German *klaffen,* to split] comes from the old practice of sawing oak logs into bolts and then splitting them end-to-end, cleaving off a thin, tapered board with each stroke of the froe. As the radial lines converge naturally at the center of the bolt, boards made this way were thick on one edge, and thin on the other.

a "glut" for splitting plank

For centuries white oak has been the recognized choice of furniture makers, wagon and carriage makers, coopers, and especially shipbuilders. Once dried and seasoned, white oak thrives on moisture, whereas most of the other oaks react in exactly the opposite way: they quickly begin to deteriorate and rot. Shipbuilders at an early time discovered that white oak, which they used green unless it was for construction above the waterline, was greatly hardened by contact with salt water. This led them to pack the spaces between a ship's frames with salt—a technique known as *salt blocking.*

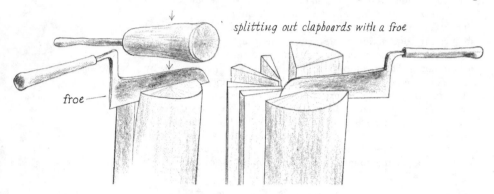

splitting out clapboards with a froe

froe—

This fine wood was used not only for paneling, but for table tops, chairs, stools, chests, window framing, house timbers, floor planks —any place where strength and durability were required. The carriage maker found white oak excellent for wheel spokes, preferring the wood from oak saplings, which ideally he cleft to the proper dimensions instead of sawing them. The term *wainscot* is derived from *wagenscot* [Middle Low German *wagen* wagon + *schot* wooden partition], the side panels of wagons, but now refers only to wall paneling extending from floor to chair height because such paneling is constructed in the same way—and from the same stuff—as early wagons.

WHITE PINE

Here, without much dispute, was the prime wood of the country furniture maker. The pine grew just about everywhere, and in great profusion, its top branches often reaching to one hundred twenty feet above the ground and its trunk swelling out to sixty inches in diameter. Lumber from these trees was straight, even-grained, and with a pleasing color that ranged from creamy white into pinks and browns. After air drying and seasoning pine was light in weight, yet quite strong enough for nearly every kind of furniture work with the

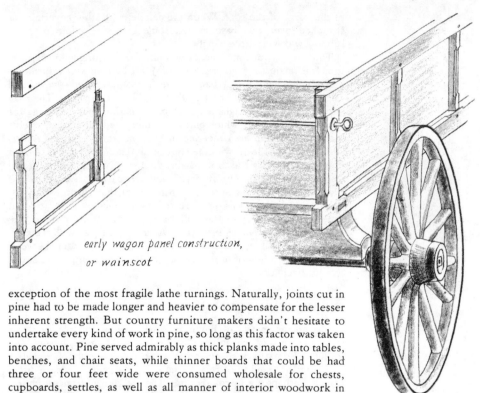

early wagon panel construction,
or wainscot

exception of the most fragile lathe turnings. Naturally, joints cut in pine had to be made longer and heavier to compensate for the lesser inherent strength. But country furniture makers didn't hesitate to undertake every kind of work in pine, so long as this factor was taken into account. Pine served admirably as thick planks made into tables, benches, and chair seats, while thinner boards that could be had three or four feet wide were consumed wholesale for chests, cupboards, settles, as well as all manner of interior woodwork in house construction. It is difficult to imagine the almost inexhaustible supply of pine that was at hand. The fine old houses were built of almost solid wood, with interior partitions of two-inch plank set edge to edge to form the foundation for nailed-on split-oak laths.

Pine tree wood of the eighteenth century was habitually known as "old pine," a much harder article than modern white pine. With age and exposure to the air and sunlight, it acquired a hard surface skin as well as a beautiful mellow patina. Old pine showed prominent annual rings, which when worked with a plane or chisel appeared to have a resinous tackiness and an aromatic smell. A piece of this antique wood—freshly cut into today—gives off a faint whisper of that aroma again. This pine had a tendency to dent and bruise easily. Handling new boards required care, especially in clamping it up in the vise on the bench: pieces of scrap wood were usually put on either side of a board in the vise.

Carriage makers too valued pine for their work. The roof frames were usually boarded over with half-inch pine boards that easily bent to the curve of the roof. When the dampened leather covering was stretched over this base, a handsome and serviceable roof resulted—with very little weight.

The country furniture maker was not the only one who eyed and took the majestic pine tree.' Major John Dunlap was a furniture maker who lived about half a mile from Mast Road—which still carries traffic in the town of Goffstown, New Hampshire. The road got its name from England's practice of marking and reserving for the Royal Navy all white pines that measured more than twelve inches at the stump. A meeting in Portsmouth in 1748 set aside a certain parcel of land, with the stipulation that "All white pine trees fit for His Majesty's use for masting the Royal Navy growing on said tract of land be hereby reserved and are hereby granted to His Majesty, his heirs and successors forever for that purpose."

Enforcement of this law created more than a little friction, especially between the sawmill owners who supplied men like Dunlap, and the King's surveyors. A single pine tree with the girth and height suitable for a British ship of the line represented several hundred board feet of prime lumber, and to the furniture maker this was his livelihood.

SYCAMORE

In the ancient world of Egypt and Asia Minor, the sycamore, or sycamore fig was probably the plane tree of Scripture, legend, and folktale. Primarily a shade tree that provided storybook travelers with welcome and cool relief, it also bore a fruit that was edible, though perhaps not up to other figs. The North American sycamore, defined as any plane tree of the genus *Platanus,* is a taller tree with a unique bark coloration consisting, particularly in older trees, of yellow gray patches mixed with dappled moonlight areas. Its toolworking characteristics are not especially noteworthy, and its uses were rather limited, yet chair parts were made of sycamore, and it found its way into tool handles, butchers' blocks, and cooperage staves. It has good shock resistance, is moderate in weight, stiffness, and hardness, and appears to have had no disadvantages in strength. When worked it took on a lustrous smooth surface with an almost soapy patina. In England sycamore was used for veneer work and inlays, where the interesting fiddle-back figures showed up well.

WALNUT

The best walnut came from the slower growing trees deep in the woods where they were in competition with other species. These trees yielded dense, straight-grained wood ranging in color from a light buckskin tan to rich, purply browns not infrequently streaked with dark lines. Individual walnut trees that grew out in the open—the walnut is primarily a lone tree in any case—grew much faster and so produced coarser wood. No great loss without some small gain, wood from these walnuts showed much more interesting variations of grain, pattern, and figure, from irregular forks and crooks to odd twists and burls—the veneer maker's perfect stuff.

When properly dried and seasoned, walnut was unmatched for hand toolworking. It held its shape well, without much tendency to warp and twist. Despite the exceptionally good veneer that certain trees produced, the country furniture maker used walnut almost exclusively as solid-wood construction material. When veneering became more popular and cheaper, walnut logs were cut more and more into thin sheets, a single tree yielding an astonishing amount of them:

About 1835, in a small Missouri town, a man put his family in a covered wagon and started the long trek to the Pacific coast. After several weary months they reached their destination, the banks of the Columbia in western Oregon. Among their treasured possessions was a tiny tree, carried from Missouri, which they carefully planted in the rich bottom land of their new home. Many years went by, ninety-three to be exact, and one day the descendants of the original pioneer were persuaded by a timber buyer to sell the walnut tree that, as a sprout, had made the long journey from Missouri. . . . It produced nearly 90,000 square feet of veneer, which sold in its entirety to a furniture factory for approximately $20,000.

—MALCOLM H. SHERWOOD

Legend has it, too, that in several small villages near Frankfort, Germany, a young farmer contemplating marriage had first to produce proof of having planted a specified number of walnut trees, highly regarded as shady resting places for the traveler. It is not known for certain why the walnut was chosen, unless it was for the fact that flies and other insects are repelled by the tree.

Saw it, plane it, smooth it a bit with the scraper, and walnut was finished. Naturally stable even without any finish, walnut nevertheless finishes admirably to a velvety surface, pleasing to the eye and to the touch.

The countryman who could point to even half this number of woods seasoning on his lumber racks would have considered himself rich indeed in the raw material of furniture. But Lambert Hitchcock himself could not make so much as one single split spindle without first seeing the tree felled, worked up into sawlogs, drawn to the mill, and ripped into boards.

FIVE
Sawmill to workbench

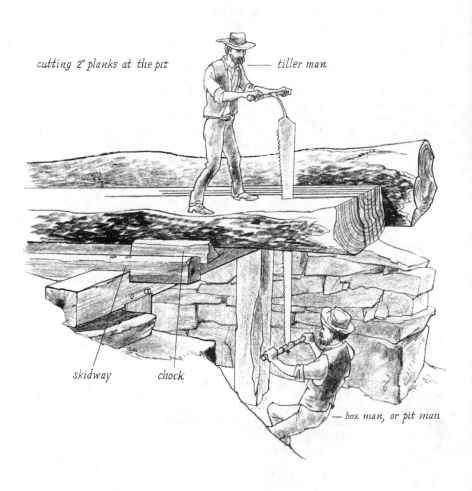

cutting 2" planks at the pit — tiller man

skidway   chock

— box man, or pit man

Since very early times sawlogs have been made into boards by the pit-saw method—a rudimentary lumbering technique that produced remarkably good boards and planks. The saw was a long, wide, coarse-toothed rip blade with a wooden crossbar handle at either end attached to the blade through iron eyes. Two sawyers were needed to operate this instrument. One stood on top of the log, which was chocked up firmly on a wooden staging over a pit dug in the ground. The other stood in the pit under this framework. Working in these awkward positions, the two men laboriously sliced off boards, one at a time, the top sawyer mostly just pulling the blade back up, while the pitman performed the bulk of the work on the downstroke—assisted by gravity and the rake of the saw's teeth. This method and this same type of saw persisted even after water power had been harnessed to the task, albeit the water-driven saw now had several blades instead of just one. The blades were locked into a wooden frame side by side, the whole assembly oscillating up and down, but ripping several boards simultaneously. With such a rig one man and a helper—often a boy—could cut four thousand board feet of lumber

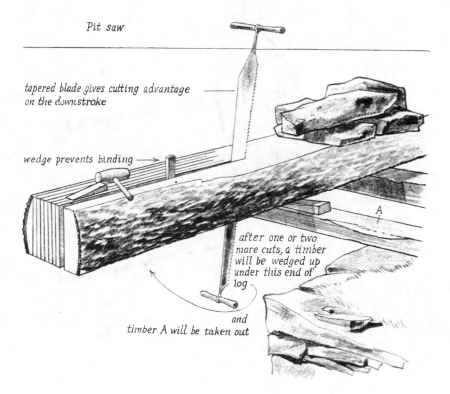

Pit saw

tapered blade gives cutting advantage
on the downstroke

wedge prevents binding →

A

after one or two
more cuts, a timber
will be wedged up
under this end of
log

and
timber A will be taken out

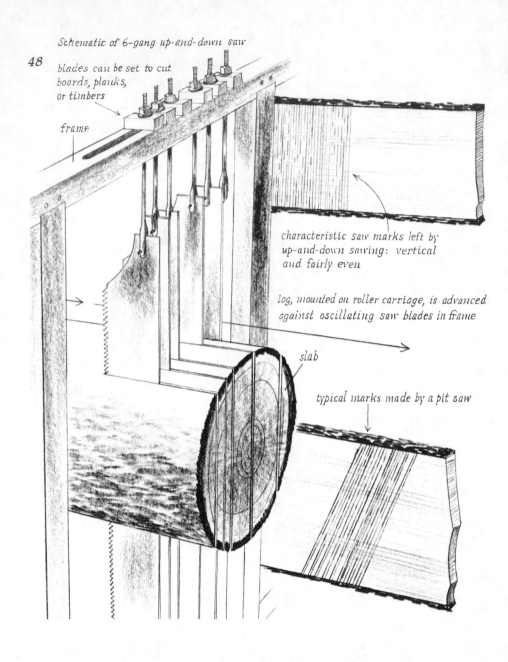

Schematic of 6-gang up-and-down saw

48

blades can be set to cut boards, planks, or timbers

frame

characteristic saw marks left by up-and-down sawing: vertical and fairly even

log, mounted on roller carriage, is advanced against oscillating saw blades in frame

slab

typical marks made by a pit saw

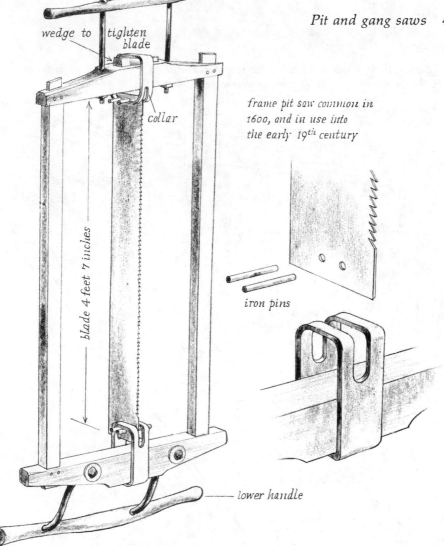

wedge to tighten blade

collar

blade 4 feet 7 inches

frame pit saw common in 1600, and in use into the early 19^(th) century

iron pins

lower handle

in a ten-hour day. This was a prodigious innovation that immediately affected the economy, for it brought the price of lumber down within reach of many more consumers.

In one form or another, this technique continued on a commercial scale well into the late 1800s when the coincidental development of the steam engine and the invention of the circular saw together created the first fully powered sawmill. Actually, the up-and-down

log scale used in the woods to calculate the approximate number of board feet of lumber in logs of various diameters and lengths

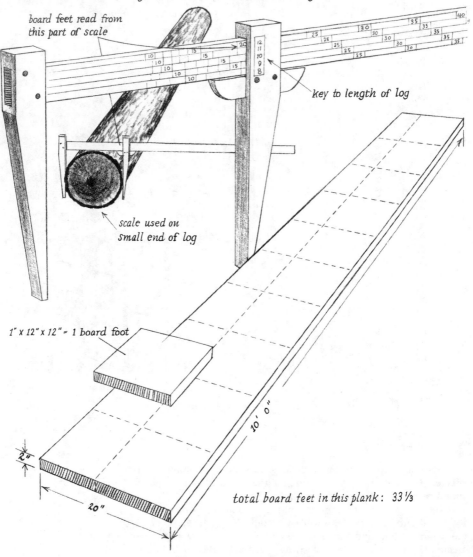

board feet read from
this part of scale

key to length of log

scale used on
small end of log

1" x 12" x 12" = 1 board foot

2"

20"

10' 0"

total board feet in this plank : 33 ⅓

principle has never become obsolete: as recently as 1945 the English
firm of Speare and Jackson was exporting cases and cases of such saw
blades to remote forests in Africa, South America, and Central
America where difficult and isolated terrain continued to frustrate
the introduction of more modern methods.

There are two basic methods of sawing lumber, whether by the
pit-saw system, or by modern band saw. The first and most
economical one is known as *plain sawing*: the four sides of the log are
sheared off to remove the bark and cut down to flat wood. Then the
log is simply sliced up, one board after another, without changing
the position of the log on the saw carriage. Plain sawing is cheaper
because it is faster, and the amount of waste is negligible. From the
furniture maker's standpoint, however, lumber of much better
quality results from the method called *quarter sawing*. By this method
the log was first sawed into quarters, rotating it each time on the
carriage. Each quarter was then sawed into boards according to one
of several patterns, the object being to have the saw cuts run as
nearly parallel as possible to the medullary rays, or radiating lines.
Boards sawed by this system did not warp as much. Moreover, they
tended to be harder, more durable, and less liable to twisting. This

cask of English sawblades, 1826

value	£	100	- 0	- 0
freight		1	- 1	- 8
duty		0	- 10	- 0

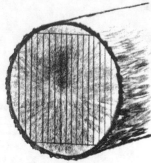

plain sawing

"silver grain" is practically free of cellular structure—one of the chief factors that affects shrinkage. Quarter sawing wasted more wood than plain sawing, and required more labor because the log had to be rotated on the carriage many times in order to keep the correct face next to the saw. A great deal of marginal wood went onto the sawdust pile, but at that time waste had not reared its threatening head. There was plenty of timber. Furthermore, the larger the diameter of. the log, the easier it was to justify using quarter sawing.

Lumber was generally cut long in advance of its fabrication by the furniture maker, and its ultimate working qualities were affected by several factors, one of which was the time of year the tree was felled. Most farmers who cut their own firewood planned on taking the horses into the woods in early winter as soon as the sap was out of

quarter sawing

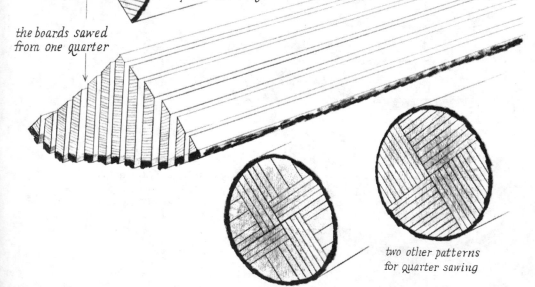

*one of the more common quarter sawing patterns
in which on the majority of boards
the annual rings are at right angles
to sawed surfaces, or very nearly so*

*Quarter sawing was a logical, simple method for any of the
up-and-down rigs*

*the boards sawed
from one quarter*

*two other patterns
for quarter sawing*

the trees and there was a scattering of snow on the ground for the dray. Cordwood cut under those conditions would then have six or eight months in which to dry, and because it was dry the wood produced far more heat per pound of wood than an equal amount of green wood.

The only proper time for cutting down trees for wagon timbers is the month of February, because trees are then out of sap . . . with pores and cells closed [which therefore makes] the timber more compact and long lasting. In . . . November, December, and January the trees are wet and sometimes sap-frozen; but in February milder weather sets in, and the sweeping winds will dry out the timber.

—M. T. RICHARDSON

Dry stuff was what the furniture maker wanted—had to have. In seasoning wood, the direct effect of the loss of moisture is a stiffening and a strengthening of the wood fibers, and in the making of furniture, the facts of stiffness and strength are essential. For furniture work it was thought desirable to have the wood dried to a fairly uniform moisture content slightly under 15 percent. Green lumber, full of sap, and with stringy fibers, was almost impossible to work; had he been limited to that sort of stuff, the cabinetmaker could hardly have made much of note. In a modern dry kiln, a green board can be forced to a more or less dry condition in a very short time. But in an earlier day there was only one way to dry lumber—in the open air. It was a slow process indeed, often requiring up to seven years, depending on the species and local weather conditions. One old-fashioned rule-of-thumb put drying time at one year for every inch of board thickness. Perhaps an exaggeration or a bit of folklore, yet time was of little consequence so long as you got a head start on the drying process, and kept new lumber coming in every year. Air drying is still considered a very satisfactory method, because the moisture level drops very slowly indeed, allowing the structure of the wood to adjust gradually. In this way, many of the severe stresses exerted by the modern dry kiln, and the defects they often produce, may never take place at all. In fact, the survival of so much of the fine old furniture may be due, at least in part, to lumber that was dried in the open air.

As moisture leaves the wood, it leaves the cell cavities first, and the cell walls next. As the cell walls lose moisture they contract, and contraction hardens the wood. A wooden bucket filled with water may be used as an example. The interior is the cell cavity, the wooden staves are the cell walls. Empty out all the water, and the cell walls—still soaked and wet—are left to dry out. If the bucket dries out enough, cracks will appear between each stave—the contraction.

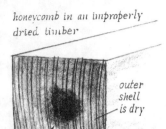

honeycomb in an improperly dried timber

outer shell is dry

core is still wet

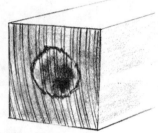

outer shell separated from core

A further observation on the drying process indicates the importance of *uniformity* of drying:

In drying wood, no increase in strength results until the free water is evaporated and the cell walls begin to dry. *Once completely dry, soaking the wood in water merely fills the cavities and intercellular spaces, but has no effect on the mechanical properties.*

As wood dries, the cell walls shrink until they are quite thin, or almost entirely gone. Uniform drying throughout the stick is therefore important, to maintain constant strength.

When uneven drying progresses, especially in air drying, an outer dry shell develops, isolating by a sort of "case hardening" the center part of the stick, which cannot dry; or at best dries exceedingly slowly, taking perhaps years. Not uncommon for the core, when it finally does dry, to then pull away from the outer shell, causing what is known as "honey comb," or "hollow horn."

—SAMUEL J. RECORD

Carriage makers were also quite conscious of the importance of well-dried lumber, and almost every book on the subject stresses that there ". . . should be a goodly stack of well-seasoned timber" on hand. Not infrequently, wheelwrights seasoned their own stock in specially built sheds where the new timber could be stored out of the direct sunlight, but at the same time exposed to free ventilation.

Commenting on the proper handling of thin boards such as those used for paneling, Burgess urged that it be dried ". . .in the same way, and in addition the ends . . . be secured to prevent splitting. Panel stuff undergoes another . . . seasoning after it is planed up and then put aside in a moderately dry place, with slips of wood between each board. . ." permitting a good circulation of air.

In a house heated only by open fireplaces, the moisture content of the air was very much higher than we are accustomed to today, and furniture wood was not subjected to any radical changes in humidity. Although the burning firewood released heat, it also returned moisture to the air, thus maintaining wood in a healthier condition —and the people probably as well. Green lumber retains a surprising amount of moisture—both sap and water—which when it evaporates reduces not only the volume of the board, but also the weight. This is the process of shrinkage, much more pronounced, and much more bothersome to the furniture maker in the cross grain than in the length.

Boards dried by this slow process were constantly exposed to the fluctuating levels of humidity, losing moisture on warm days and gaining some on rainy days. In effect, by the time the boards were taken inside, they'd be nearly immune to new changes in atmospheric conditions. Checking, warping, twisting, and shaking had all taken place outdoors under optimum conditions, bringing the lumber to air conditions almost identical with those inside the shop, which was a long way from zero moisture content.

The woodworker, whether carpenter or furniture maker, had one final drying stage at his disposal. For example, when all the frame pieces for a paneled door had been cut, fitted, and made ready to join, they were generally all loosely knocked together, but not taken up tight nor the pegs driven in. The whole assembly was then put away in a dry room, either laid out flat on a pair of horses, or stood up leaning flat against a firm support such as a wall. There it was left for a time—a length of time determined by the craftsman's intuitive judgment as to how long this "second seasoning" should be.

There were three principal ways of storing green lumber for this air drying. Probably the most common was the flat stack method which is still used today, and can be seen in any sawmill or lumber yard. A layer of boards was laid flat on three or four heavy supporting timbers spaced out flat on the ground, with air spaces an inch or two wide left between each board and its neighbor. On top of this layer went three or four "stickers," or narrow strips of lumber waste—usually edgings. These stickers were laid down directly over the timbers underneath, to prevent the boards from sagging. Then

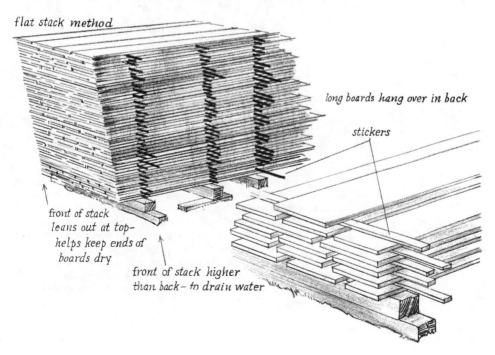

flat stack method

long boards hang over in back

stickers

front of stack leans out at top-helps keep ends of boards dry

front of stack higher than back- to drain water

another layer of boards, a layer of stickers, and so on. The stack was built up in this fashion, layer on layer with stickers between each, the height of the stack limited only by the arm-reach of a man standing in the bed of a wagon. M. T. Richardson recommended that lumber be stacked to dry on the north side of a building, out of the direct sunlight, and suggested that to insure really top grade lumber "timber will be much improved by putting some in a blacksmith shop around the chimney and close under the roof, to be smoked, which makes timber very hard and lasting." It's well to remember that Richardson was writing about carriage making, and his reference is no doubt to spoke wood. This smokehouse method would only have been practical for rather small pieces of lumber, for the average blacksmith shop was too cluttered with its own bric-a-brac to accommodate stock of any appreciable size.

Pole piling was an easier method of stacking lumber, since it required a less elaborate foundation and no stickers were used. Besides, lumber could be stacked this way with far less labor, and was also thought to accelerate the rate of drying. The crisscrossed boards stood very nearly on end, shed rainwater quickly, and therefore showed little staining caused by puddling that could damage flat-stacked stuff. Furthermore, any boards that were inclined to warp and twist did so without delay, because there was no clamping action or pressure from the upper part of the stack: there was no upper part.

By the third method—end stacking—lumber was stood on end leaning against a flat and substantial support, either the side of a building or a specially built framework. This was essentially the same as pole piling, except that individual boards could be taken out without handling the whole pile. Whatever the method, better lumber was obtained by drying it under some sort of shelter, ideally one with at least two sides slat-boarded to keep out the direct sunlight while permitting generous circulation of air.

When the lumber finally came off the drying stack, it went through two more stages before it was ready to be made into furniture. In old-time sawmill practice, the bark edges were seldom trimmed off at the time the log was sawn into boards. This operation was generally not done until after the lumber was dry, and ready to be sold. Then the bark was trimmed off on an up-and-down saw not

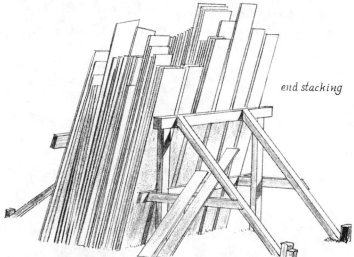

end stacking

unlike the big one at the mill. The accuracy of this work was not much more refined than the workings of any of countless portable sawmills today, with the wobbly carriage traveling back and forth on poorly aligned tracks, and a circular blade that most likely was improperly set and filed right on the arbor.

The final task of truing up the edges and smoothing the surfaces was left to the woodworker to do. For a considerable period of time before the advent of the power-driven planer, the furniture maker did this job with his wooden joiner—a heavy plane of rock maple about three feet long and three or four inches square in section. He

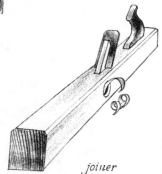

joiner

made innumerable passes from one end of the board to the other, shaving off the ragged fibers and smoothing out the obvious humps and hollows. No matter how hard he tried, though—and we don't know if he even did—hand planing produced a surface a great deal less precise than the flat-milled effect left by a machine planer. And a good bit more attractive to look at.

For all his supposed lack of sophistication, the furniture maker had remarkably good stuff to work with. When he sent his nephew or his apprentice with the team to the local sawmill to fetch "a lode of cherrytree bords," more times than not he could be pretty sure of getting his money's worth. To make certain, he could—and many times did—go along with the wagon to pick over the lumber, one board at a time. For there were a number of defects and imperfections that only a practiced eye could spot.

common distortions in wood
that affect its quality as cabinetmaker's stuff

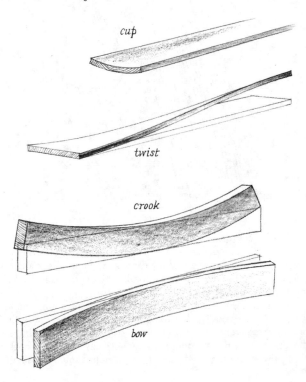

cup

twist

crook

bow

Some of these flaws can be seen in the standing timber, but others generally do not become visible until either the tree has been felled and logged up, or the logs sawn out at the mill.

The presence of *knots* didn't necessarily spoil a board for furniture. Loose knots are the sort that separate from the surrounding wood and tend to fall out as the wood dries, leaving holes. The other variety—bound knots—were acceptable in lumber that was to be used in inconspicuous places, such as for the backs of bureaus, chests, or drawer bottoms.

Checks, or *checking*, showed up most often in close grained woods like birch, beech, and maple, generally quite soon after the boards were sawn. Exceptionally hot drying conditions aggravated this condition by drying the ends of boards much faster than the centers.

Wrenching of a tree in high wind often created pockets, openings, or separations that followed round the annual rings. These *wind shakes* cannot usually be detected in a standing tree, although in the felling a shake may be extended so that it spoils much lumber.

The external signs of decayed or rotten areas are quite obvious while the tree is standing, and generally indicate rather extensive *staining* of the wood inside. If the staining is confined to a local area without migration to the sound wood adjacent to it, a good sawyer could often salvage nearly all the wood in a valuable butt log.

Confined to the conifers, *pitch pockets* are openings in the grain structure (parallel to the annual rings) that contain pitch. When affected logs are sawn into boards, these pockets are sliced open, leaving open pockmarks scattered at random over the surface of otherwise perfectly good lumber.

Splits result from torn wood fibers, caused by careless handling of logs in the woods, or in transit to the sawmill. An incipient split in a standing tree can be extended by the grinding and twisting of high winds that rack the main trunk—the part of the tree that provides the most valuable logs.

Frost-splits are generally seen as radial cracks extending from the outside of the tree toward the center, and are nearly always down close to the base of the tree. It is thought that a temperature of 14° Fahrenheit or less is required to start a frost-split, but observations cited by Samuel J. Record indicate that these other points must be considered also:

1) *Frost-splits can occur at temperatures* higher *than 14°.*
2) *Most splits take place just before dawn, i.e., when the air and the soil are at the lowest temperature of the night.*
3) *They are rarely heard of at noon, in the afternoon, or in the early evening. But they are heard! The sound is like that of a rifle shot.*
4) *They most always occur between two roots, or the collars of two roots.*

5) They seem to occur most often in old, stout-rooted, broad-crowned trees.
6) Trees growing in wet locations are most susceptible.
7) Most frost-splits occur less than three feet above the ground.

Certain trees may develop internal stresses and strains, from causes unknown, but often in the valuable butt log part of the tree just above the felling notch and the back cut. When the axe or saw severs these stressed fiber tendons, the suddenly released tension explodes with immense energy up into the trunk, following the grain. Although there may result a fairly deep crack in trees over twenty-four inches in diameter, this did not necessarily render all the lumber worthless.

If the furniture maker felled his own trees and hauled the logs to the sawmill with his own team, he assumed responsibility for all such risks, and suffered the loss from damaged timber on his own account. On the other hand, a man could avoid all such hazards and simply select his stuff from the mill yard, leaving the matter of risk in the hands of the mill owner.

Aside from these tangible defects, odor, color, grain, texture, and "a feel for wood" all told the countryman something about the suitability of wood. The furniture maker, it appears, had a nose for all this, and—to judge from inspection of any well-made antique today—his nose worked quite well: the joints are tight, the pegs not loose, the typical chair showing no rack to speak of, unless of course it has been standing too close to a steam radiator.

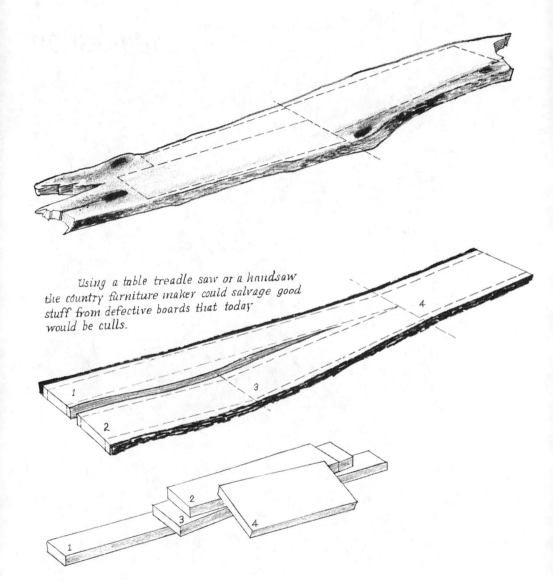

Using a table treadle saw or a handsaw
the country furniture maker could salvage good
stuff from defective boards that today
would be culls.

SIX
The workshop

sawing thin boards with a 3-gang frame saw

It is improbable that any country workshop was built to preconceived specifications or a set of plans, though the furniture maker may have considered the ideal arrangement for one in his mind's eye. And at some point he may have thought: *This bench can be moved against that other wall—it will make space for another window and some tool racks. Come summer an ell can be added on for lumber storage, and the boards will dry out more evenly.* No man can work day after day in a shop without periodically rehearsing changes that he knows would make it more convenient. The country workman had more practical notions on this subject than he had time to carry them out, for there were other pressing demands on his time and energy. He had two or three cows, a team of horses, a wagon and other farm implements, and there was always something to be made, mended, or replaced— in the house, the barn, or outdoors. These were duties just as essential to his way of life as his woodworking tools and his trade of furniture making.

The countryman led a busy, jack-of-all-trades existence, the bulk of it outdoors, from which can be assumed that most of his furniture making was done in the winter when farm work waited, snowbound in hibernation. True enough, there was outside work even in winter—firewood to be cut and drawn. Didn't he know that well enough? Struggling with ice-cold chains and stiff harness on a zero morning, he knew he couldn't handle carpenter's tools with his ears in muffs and his hands in mittens. His workshop, his wood, his tools, and his hands—all had to be reasonably warm.

And the warmest place, in most cases it seems, was the back room right against the wall of the kitchen. A good warm place where an extra fireplace could easily be tapped into the kitchen chimney. The typical rural homestead was a line of buildings strung out from the road to the barn, the whole structure comprising small rooms, sheds, and additions that proved their worth the year round: eventually they all filled up with seasonal equipment such as sugar buckets, butchering tubs, wagons, sleds, and quite often, just ordinary junk. This train of buildings also provided a handy way to get from the house to the cow shed without floundering through the snow—not an inconsequential consideration. If he'd had his druthers, the country furniture maker might have chosen to take over and remodel two or three of these connecting sheds. But heating them would be a serious problem, so the best solution seemed to be a warm, if small, cubicle within pie-smelling distance of the kitchen.

scribing compass

It was indeed a small shop, and crowded. There was little chance to organize the work areas. Building a chest of drawers ordinarily required an ample space where the pieces could be assembled flat, without taking up all his workbench; but space was limited. Still, some surprisingly complicated pieces of furniture were made in

meager surroundings like this. One man admitted that when he had a
board longer than eight feet, he had to carry it out into the yard to
turn it around! Yet the same board turned up finally as part of a
dovetailed hope chest for one of his marriageable daughters.

The William Cannon shop in Sandisfield, Massachusetts, was a
good example of the back room farm shop. It was a room twelve feet
wide and twenty-two feet long with a fireplace and a door at either
end. And it was equipped with a thick oak plank workbench thirty
inches deep, running the full length of one wall. A woodworking
vise was attached to the end of the bench nearest the window, and
an iron box vise at the other. There was a small anvil in one corner, and
near it a low, heavy-framed bench where most of the farm repair
work was done. Another shorter bench stood along the opposite
wall. Short lengths of lumber shared the space under the bench with
usable scraps of iron and wood, and Cannon had built some
overhead storage for long boards by running ceiling joists across the

room level with the eaves and braced up to the rafters. Simple flat shelves for small tools ranged along the walls at random, fitted in between beams and windows. Saws and large tools hung from pegs in the wall over the bench. Rows of similar pegs, and sometimes spikes along the ceiling joists accommodated patterns, garden tools, an extra six-foot crosscut, chains, and a host of miscellaneous hardware that might some day—or possibly never—be needed. The shop was cluttered: human nature devises a thousand excuses for chucking things into the nearest corner "just for now."

Then again, some furniture makers outgrew the confines of the farmhouse. An ambitious man whose productivity and circumstances afforded him the chance might see commercial possibilities in his particular cleverness with tools. His local reputation for making especially nice chests of drawers could stir his confidence to seriously consider expansion or specialization. This meant giving up some of his other farm work, or at least turning it over to the care of his wife, but he could arrange to keep his land holdings, carry on with his crops, his lumbering, or his mill operations. He couldn't disband these occupations, for they brought in cash and goods that he needed, but the actual labor of these enterprises could be entrusted to hired help so long as their supervision rested with someone of authority in the family.

For the countryman, a decision like this was in the nature of a grave undertaking, because it affected the entire family and the whole routine of life. Naturally, the regular work would have to go on uninterrupted while he set out to look at the idea from all sides. It would take many many months of figuring and planning, and considerable ciphering. Perhaps he'd spend a year and a half—even two years—working out the details. Meanwhile, as he went about his daily work and chores, he'd be evaluating the men he knew of, seeing what each man was qualified to do, and constantly mulling the notion over in his head:

> *Our oldest son Thomas can do good work now at the bench. Frank is a good joiner and a hard worker, too. Though the man he works for in Hartsville seems to be enjoying the larger share of the profits. Frank has not the head for a business all his own, though he is my own brother, I must see what he thinks of this. Moses Blanchard is not doing well, though he has the use of the Whitney mill just for the taxes, his chairs are rough. Four days a week with me, with someone watching him, I could have twice the work. Thomas and I could make something of that nice stand of ash, as well. He could deliver chairs down country and take also a small load of frame stock for the boat yard in Wethersport.*

From such recurrent imaginings of a spacious, better-equipped shop, and of increased cash, more than one free enterprise furniture maker began to skirt the idea of expansion into a full-time trade. Whether the shift came about gradually or was accomplished in a single burst of upheaval, there would be an immediate need for more space—say two or three times what he had now. Could more of the house be used in some way? Would the addition of two large rooms in an ell provide the necessary space, or would a completely new building have to be erected? There was much in favor of this scheme: one room could be built over the other to save on heat, and the loft space would make good lumber storage.

The final solution might have resembled the cabinet and clock shop of the Dominy family in East Hampton, New York. Their dwelling was the nucleus of a fair-sized workshop, which with some remodeling and the addition of new rooms for a small forge and clock shop accommodated a lathe and a great wheel to drive it, thereby greatly increasing their capacity. Their renovated house-

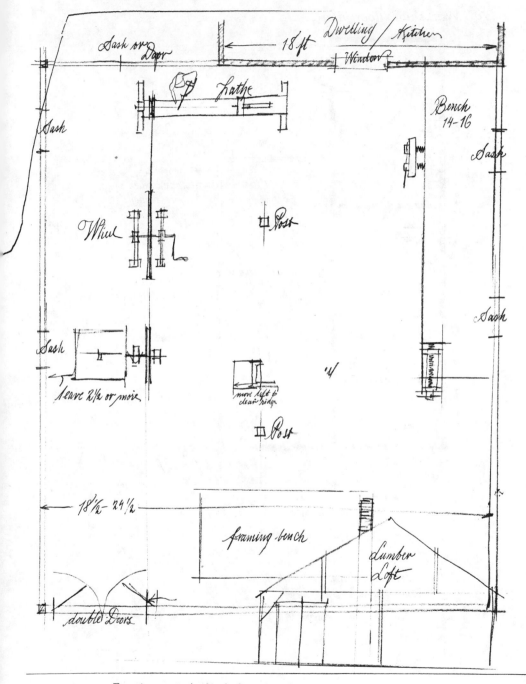

Furniture maker's sketch for proposed
workshop addition to dwelling

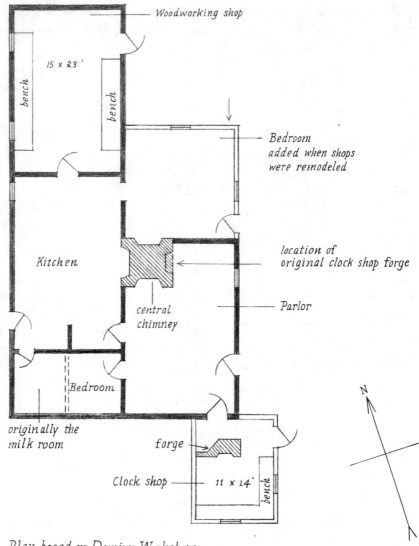

Woodworking shop

15 x 23'

bench

bench

Bedroom
added when shops
were remodeled

location of
original clock shop forge

Kitchen

central
chimney

Parlor

Bedroom

originally the
milk room

forge

Clock shop

11 x 14'

bench

N

*Plan based on Dominy Workshops
in East Hampton, New York*

Scale: $\frac{3''}{32}$ = 1 FOOT

Original dwelling shown by heavy lines

workshop by no means represented the ultimate in design, but it was far roomier, lighted with numerous windows, on the whole well laid out, and easily big enough for all the men in the family enterprises.

An enlarged cabinetshop like this, assuming the enterprising energy of a talented family, could handle virtually any sort of furniture or cabinetwork, as well as clocks and their wooden cases.

For reasons of income, geographic location, the affluence of customers, or simply personal inclination, some country furniture makers decided to take the step into what was more properly a professional status where all his income—or most of it—was derived from cash and not kind. For others, whose fires of ambition may have been more intense than the heat of action, moving cautiously into a specialty such as chairmaking may have been sufficient. But it's not unlikely that the majority of countrymen carried on as before,

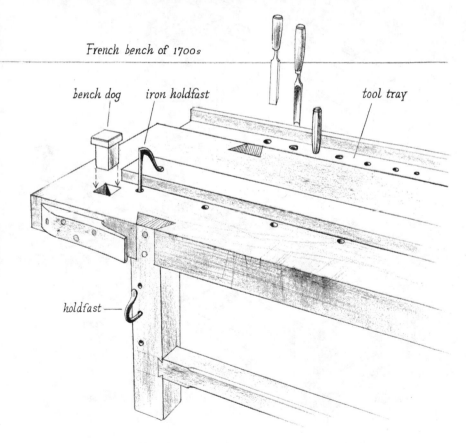

French bench of 1700s

bench dog   iron holdfast   tool tray

holdfast —

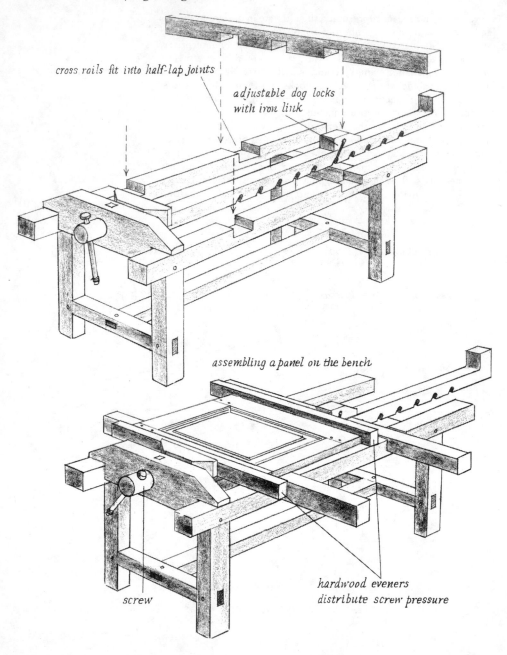

cross rails fit into half-lap joints

adjustable dog locks
with iron link

assembling a panel on the bench

screw

hardwood eveners
distribute screw pressure

working alone and part-time in small shops that produced a relatively small volume of work.

In making either change—to expansion or to specialization—the countryman-turned-cabinetmaker must have been surprised at other changes he probably hadn't anticipated: from a man who once enjoyed the simpler existence of making things himself with his own hands to one who now spent many hours balancing books, buying and trading lumber on a large scale, filling the shoes of a salesman, harmonizing the problems of a crew of hired men, and generally working in the manner of a businessman.

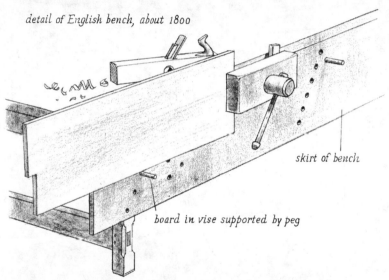

detail of English bench, about 1800

skirt of bench

board in vise supported by peg

As time went on and the ideal arrangement of workshop equipment received more attention, several woodworkers of notable ability collected their ideas in handbooks, usually expressing them in most positive terms:

Benches should be down the sides, with vises about three feet from the windows. They should be at least 2 feet 6 inches apart, as considerable space is needed when fitting and knocking framing together in the bench-way.

The air quickly becomes vitiated in a workshop where a number of men are working, and an overheated room full of stagnant moist air soon takes away any inclination to work.

—RICHARD GREENHALGH

the so-called German bench

tool tray

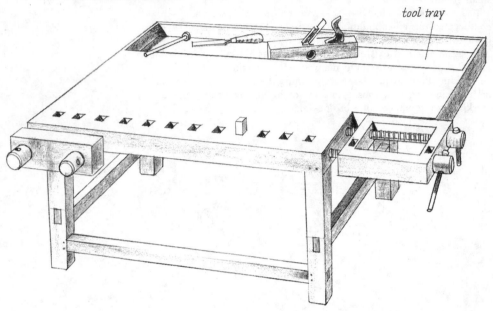

45° planing vise for cleaning up mitered joints

bench

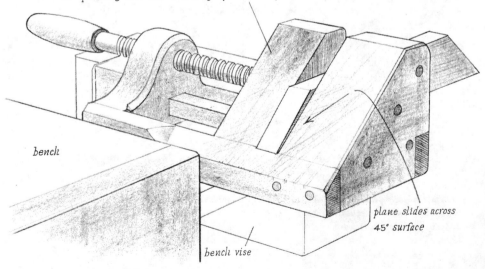

plane slides across
45° surface

bench vise

The German bench is the best for the cabinet-maker. . . . In Germany, the work-bench has had more consideration bestowed upon it than it has in our country; and the result is a bench far surpassing ours, at which the workman can quickly and firmly secure his work in any position.

—RICHARD BITMEAD

These were nice refinements, but they came on the scene too late to be of any real use to the average country furniture maker, whose workshop tended to remain largely the result of making do with what was at hand.

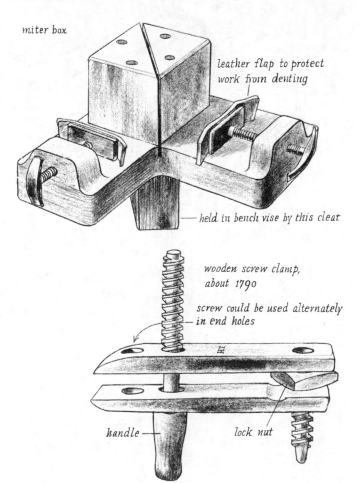

miter box

leather flap to protect
work from denting

— held in bench vise by this cleat

wooden screw clamp,
about 1790

screw could be used alternately
— in end holes

handle —

lock nut

a Shaker workbench

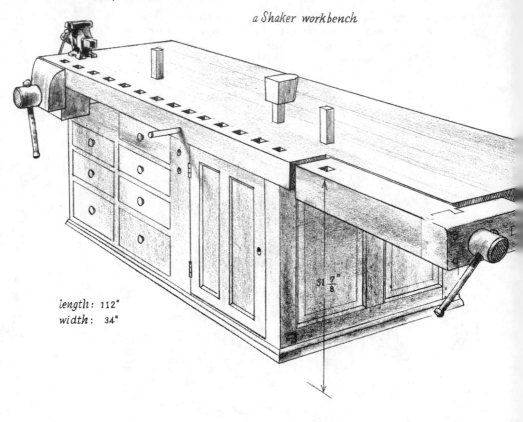

length: 112"
width: 34"

$31 \frac{7}{8}$"

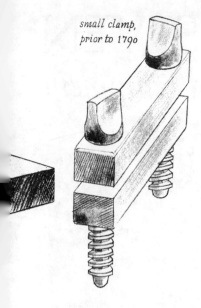

small clamp,
prior to 1790

clamps and wedges for edge-joining boards

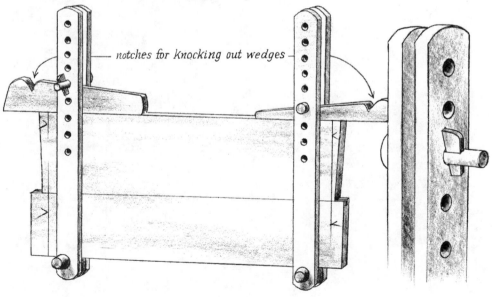

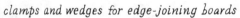

— *notches for knocking out wedges* —

SEVEN
Bench tools and equipment

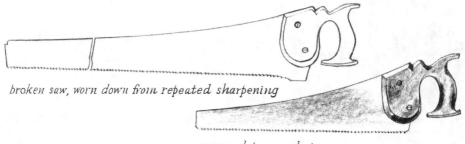

broken saw, worn down from repeated sharpening

reground to new shape

the broken piece, ground to new shape, fitted with handle : a "new" tenon saw

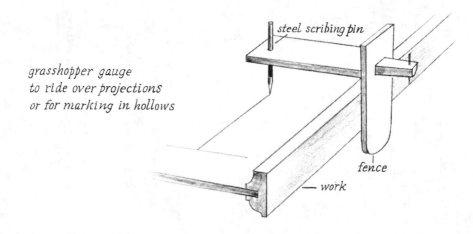

*grasshopper gauge
to ride over projections
or for marking in hollows*

steel scribing pin

fence

— work

The country furniture maker worked with a set of tools that was strikingly similar to that used by ancient craftsmen in 3000 B.C.:

> *Specimens of tools . . . have been collected in the United States, chiefly in Pennsylvania, but a short study of them will soon convince us, that though made in America, they were not invented there, but represent long-existing types of world-wide use, brought thither by the Colonists; hence, that the collection is neither local nor national, but international and of general ethnologic interest.*
>
> —HENRY CHAPMAN MERCER

They were almost identical to tools in common use throughout the civilized ancient world. Whether a saw had eight teeth to the inch or ten; whether one chisel was an inch longer than its mate—the form of the tool was the same. Aside from the recent introduction of electric power there have been no fundamental changes in the function of woodworking tools—only minor variations that can scarcely be called innovations.

These minor variations came from the hands of every craftsman: when he bought tools he had to make and fit his own handles, for toolmakers ordinarily sold only the steel. When a saw broke off, the frugal cabinetmaker smoothed up the end and went on using it. If he needed a very slender saw blade, he ground one down to size. His tools were as much an expression of his craft as the furniture he made with them. Using choice, close-grained woods such as hickory, maple, beech, birch, and the fruitwoods—apple, cherry, and pear— the woodworker fashioned not only most of his tool handles, but many of his planes as well. There was a strong leaning toward beechwood planes: they were considered smoother to work, and less tiresome to handle—and this feeling persisted even after the introduction of steel framed planes. Some craftsmen—the Dominys, for example—made their own irons as well.

We're tempted to call these personal and individual peculiarities by the name of evolutionary change, perhaps because of a conditioning to modern tool manufacture which is geared to speed, uniformity, perfect finish, and sameness—qualities singularly lacking in old tools. Old they were: no pair of tools were exactly alike, but an examination of the tools of a Dunlap, a Dominy, a Jeremiah Cresson, or a Duncan Phyfe creates the impression that these tools were fully as sophisticated as their modern counterparts.

For example, the country furniture maker had access to an extremely wide choice of planes, each designed for a specific task: compass planes, molding planes, joining planes, and smoothing planes. The fore and jack plane appear to have been one and the same, the terms being used interchangeably, although in the six-

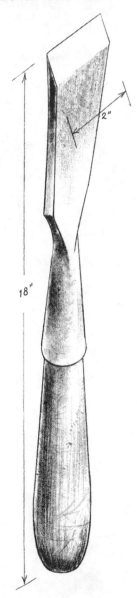

2"

18"

shipbuilder's chisel

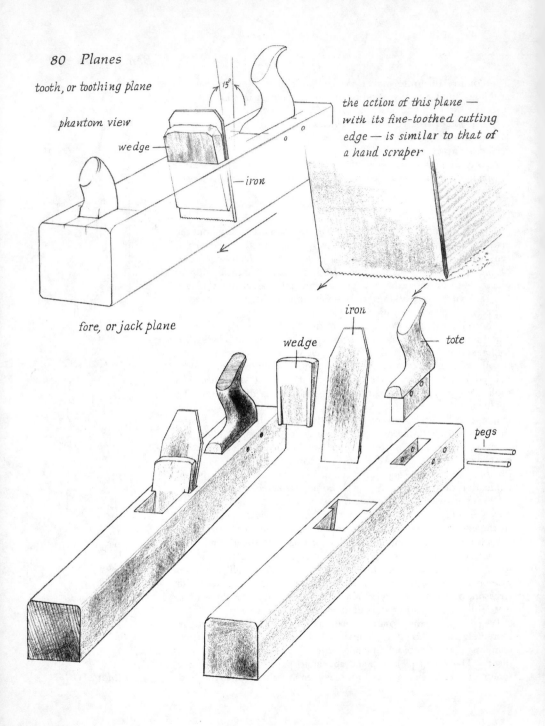

80 Planes

tooth, or toothing plane

phantom view

wedge

iron

15°

the action of this plane —
with its fine-toothed cutting
edge — is similar to that of
a hand scraper

fore, or jack plane

wedge

iron

tote

pegs

teenth century the term *fore plane* was perhaps the more common. It was called a fore plane because it was used before coming to work with either the jointer or the smoothing plane—to take rough sawn boards down to a preliminary degree of smoothness. The blade, or iron, was slightly convex. The surface it left was more or less ridged, as anyone can tell by running the fingers over the backboard of a chest or a clock case.

His smoothing planes were just that, designed to *scrape smooth* following the natural surface contour of the wood instead of removing it down to a perfect, milled-precision surface. Since every piece of wood was hand-fitted, there was no reason why boards had to be mechanically precise in thickness, other than the furniture maker's own standards.

When water power, then steam, and factory methods were harnessed to the finishing of boards, output was vastly increased. Fewer men could make more boards in less time and for less cost. But the saw blades, ganged together and driven by these new kinds of power, were of the same basic pattern that had been used in saw pits since early times. Nor did this acceleration in the production of the woodworker's stuff immediately affect his handmade product. It was not until much later—when these concepts of machine manufacture caught up with the demand for more and cheaper furniture—

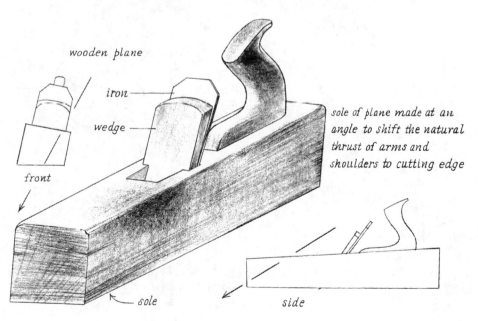

wooden plane

iron

wedge

front

sole

sole of plane made at an angle to shift the natural thrust of arms and shoulders to cutting edge

side

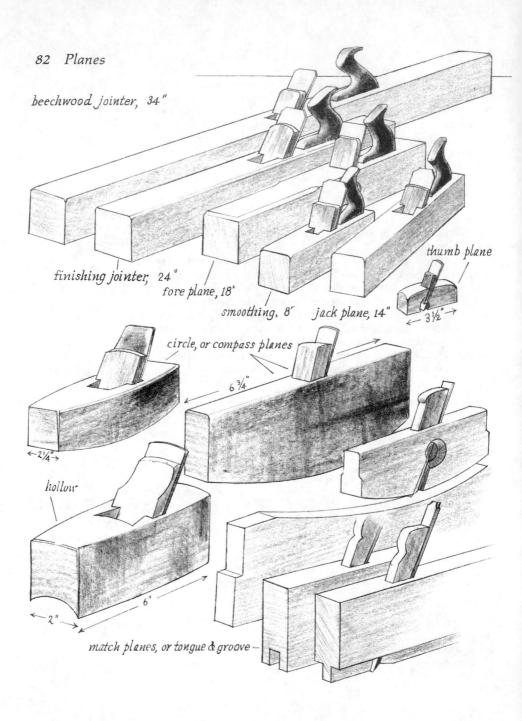

beechwood jointer, 34"

finishing jointer, 24"

fore plane, 18"

smoothing, 8"   jack plane, 14"

thumb plane

3½"

circle, or compass planes

6¾"

← 2¼" →

hollow

← 2" →   6"

match planes, or tongue & groove

that handmade furniture came to be regarded almost as a performing art instead of an everyday utilitarian function.

At the same time, shipwrights, carpenters, chairmakers, house builders, joiners, and even bridge builders were all working with tools so much like those of the cabinetmaker that only minute differences can be seen. The joiner's mortising chisel differs from a carpenter's chisel mainly in the thickness of its shank and the angle of the cutting edge. The shipwright's big, hefty, long-handled chisel is for all the world like an out-sized carpenter's firmer. And the

continued on page 88

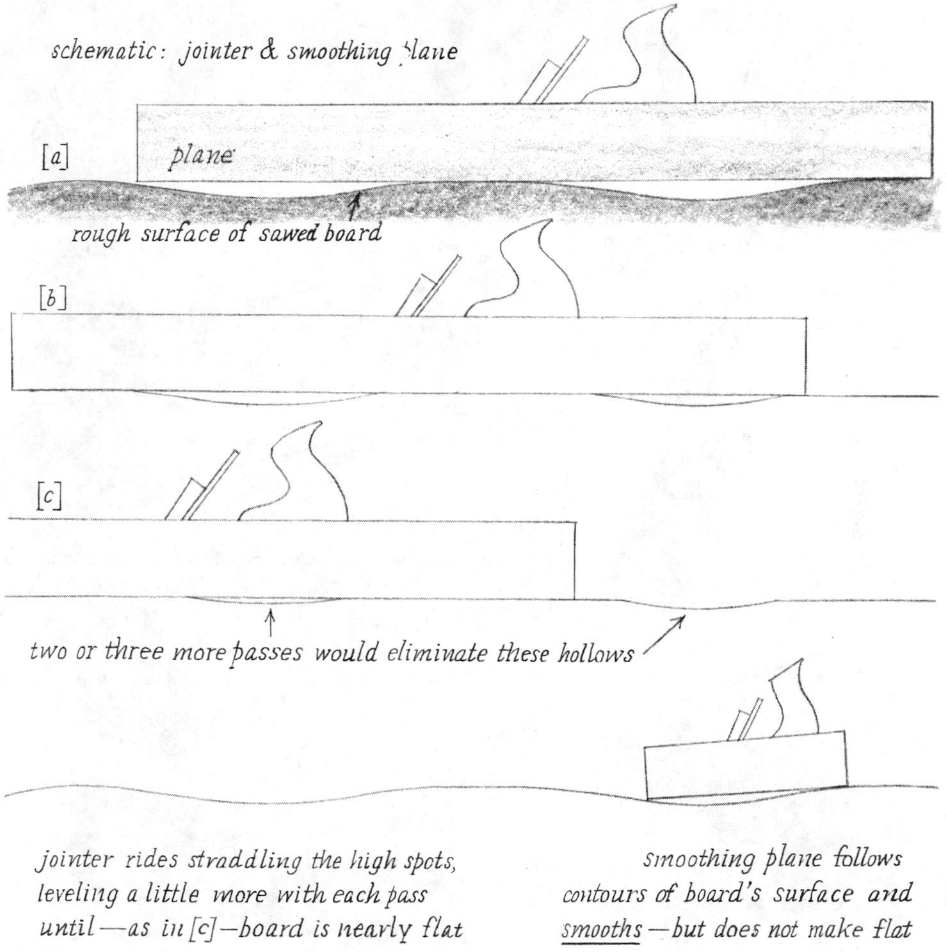

schematic: jointer & smoothing plane

[*a*]

plane

rough surface of sawed board

[*b*]

[*c*]

two or three more passes would eliminate these hollows

jointer rides straddling the high spots, leveling a little more with each pass until—as in [c]—board is nearly flat

smoothing plane follows contours of board's surface and smooths—but does not make flat

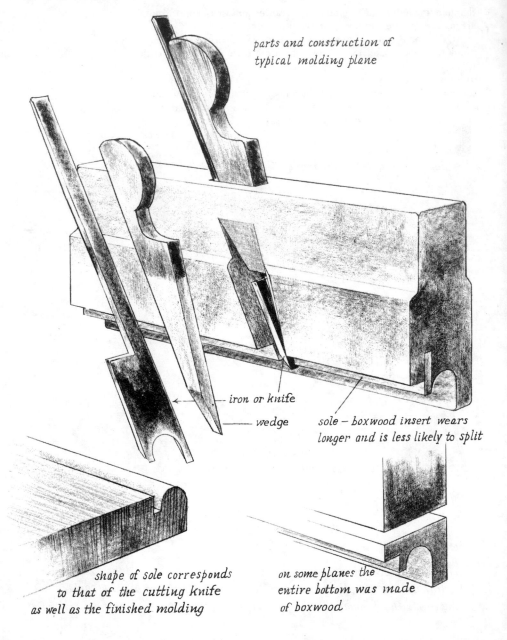

parts and construction of
typical molding plane

iron or knife

wedge

sole – boxwood insert wears
longer and is less likely to split

shape of sole corresponds
to that of the cutting knife
as well as the finished molding

on some planes the
entire bottom was made
of boxwood

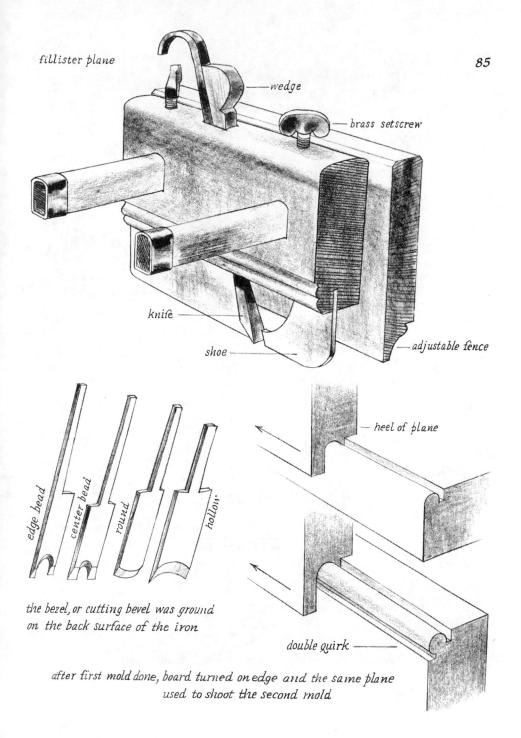

wedge

brass setscrew

knife

shoe

adjustable fence

edge bead

center bead

round

hollow

heel of plane

double quirk

the bezel, or cutting bevel was ground
on the back surface of the iron

after first mold done, board turned on edge and the same plane
used to shoot the second mold

wide molding, requiring removal of considerable wood, often run with "two-man" plane using manpower or water power

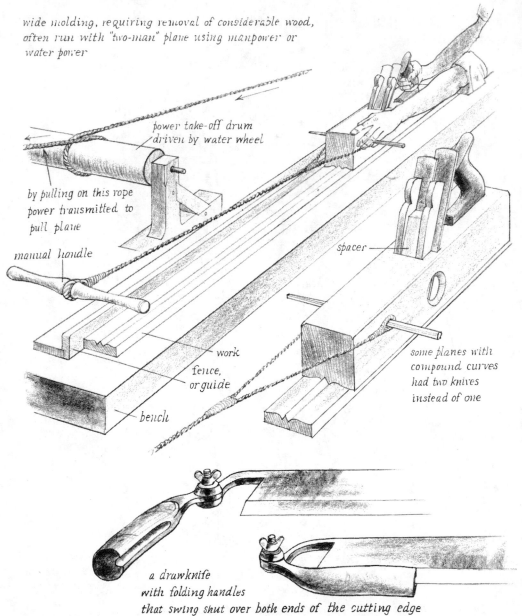

power take-off drum driven by water wheel

by pulling on this rope power transmitted to pull plane

manual handle

spacer

work

fence, or guide

bench

some planes with compound curves had two knives instead of one

a drawknife with folding handles that swing shut over both ends of the cutting edge

a versatile tool used to rough
out or shape — where a considerable
amount of wood   was to be removed

tang of knife

through late 1700s tangs were
bent over on end of handle

later, tangs were cut off
and headed

handle drilled with spiral bit
and then reamed with a hot iron
to make a tapered bore for the tang

various-sized augers used by chairmakers were virtually the same as those used to frame a barn or a covered bridge.

In effect, any ancient cabinetmaker—in another incarnation— could have worked quite comfortably at the Dunlaps' bench, or the Dominys', or in the small, backroom workshop of any countryman. For that matter, he could find his way around a modern shop— confident of recognizing every tool in the place.

Private papers and public records provide numerous inventories of personal effects left behind by deceased furniture makers—lists that give a fair idea of the tools these men worked with. It's risky to attach too much significance to these lists, however, for there are often as many tools missing as there are recorded. Tools are nice things to have, and since they're easy to pick up, have a way of vanishing. A cabinetmaker who died in 1787 might very likely have been bedridden for as much as a year prior to his death. Quite a few of his tools, especially the smaller ones that are so often absent from inventories, may have been loaned in that time—willingly or otherwise. Once in the hands of a borrower, there they might have stayed for months—or forever.

Drawing hard and fast conclusions from these inventories is an interesting if misleading game unless some thoughtful deductions are attempted. For example, the inventory of Benjamin Burnham might be accepted at face value, in which case Ethel Bjerkoe's comment may be correct:

This list showed that he was at least a chairmaker, and possibly a cabinetmaker, although from this meager list of tools it must be supposed he could not have made anything like a chest, unless a very rude one.

> *4 augurs*
> *1 frow*
> *2 bits*
> *3 pair of chisels*
> *   gouges*
> *723 foot of pine*
> *100 pine planks*
> * 45 doz chair rounds*
> * 1 table*
> * 8 chairs*
> * 3 chests and cupboard*
> * 2 chests and box*
> * 2 chests*

On the other hand, the question could be asked: Was this in fact a *complete inventory*, tallied by a conscientious clerk? It might have been the work of a neighbor—and a well-meaning one—who came to the widow's rescue and did the best he could. Suppose we guess that Burnham's planes, saws, and some of his chisels and bits were missing—borrowed, lost, or lifted. This conjecture is the more believable because every woodworker, no matter what his particular trade, needed those basic tools. He *must* have owned them. What happened to them?

And what about those seven chests? Who can be certain what was in them? Did Burnham make them to sell, or were they from his own kitchen and parlor—stuffed full of his personal effects? What happened to their contents, for surely they were emptied. There might have been several parcels of tools inside!

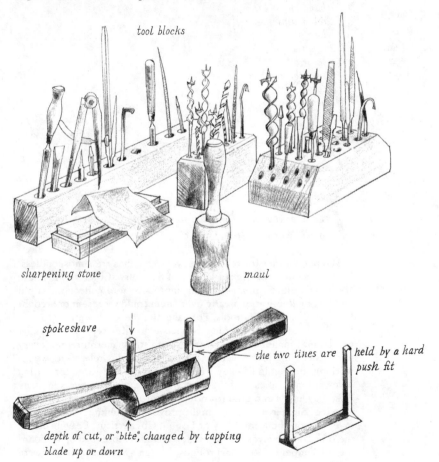

tool blocks

sharpening stone

maul

spokeshave

the two tines are held by a hard push fit

depth of cut, or "bite", changed by tapping blade up or down

The will of Zachariah Sanford is almost as cryptic. Probated in Saybrook, Connecticut in 1732, it listed the tools in his collection as:

11 rope hooks
3 spindles
2 hooks
2 burning irons
3 swigle knives
5 Turning Chisells and gouge
Joyners plow
4 small plains
2 hand plains
2 cove plains
long plain
2 squares
chair bit
3 small bitts
3 chisels
2 gouges

broadaxe

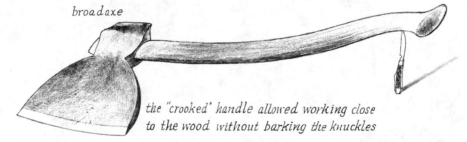

the "crooked" handle allowed working close to the wood without barking the knuckles

The possibilities for reading between the lines are almost endless. In the inventory of Medad Parker of Salisbury, Connecticut, there are exactly eleven items—not an impressive tool collection, you'd say. Yet by implication nearly every item could represent or account for a whole handful of tools. For example, the single entry "Joiners Shop" could mean anything from five to fifty separate tools. A word-stingy man indeed who wrote that list. Furthermore, not every item listed in these inventories was necessarily related to woodworking: Benjamin Cheney's *holing ax* was probably used for cutting holes in fence posts, and the item *grindstone*, which appears in many lists, may have been used for nothing more exciting than sharpening a scythe. Similar deduction might prove enlightening if used on the inventory of Ebenezer Tracy of Lisbon, Connecticut. Leaving out all the other data it gives, the fact that it includes more than 6,000 board feet of lumber, 6,400 chair rounds, and an assortment of hardware

gouges

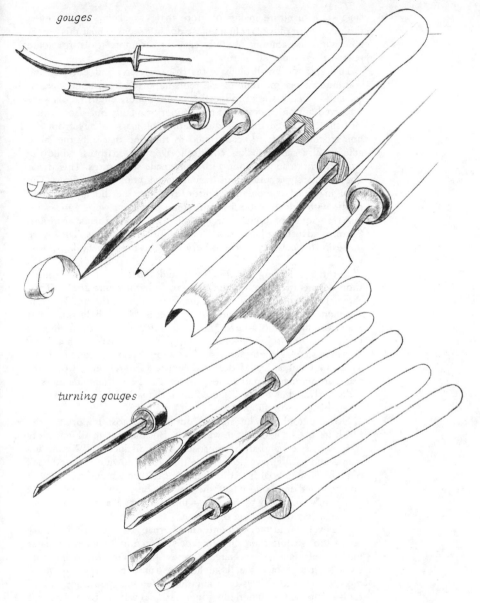

turning gouges

suggests a furniture maker of more than casual importance, even though the list of tools at first glance doesn't seem to bear this out. A man with that amount of stuff certainly had more tools: for some reason they're not all there.

The first settlers brought tools from England and Europe, and continued for some time to use tools imported from both sources, for good steel was not produced here until later. English tools were imported not only because of their superior quality but also because British trade regulations required the colonists to buy from the home country. We're accustomed to thinking that only the more affluent city cabinetmaker could afford imported tools, while the country workman got along with homemade substitutes. This idea is not completely accurate, but it does have a grain of truth in it. The rural man had comparatively little cash, but he did have trading credit with the local blacksmith, some of whom were good tool-makers. Some of them, but not all. One wood turner in South Carolina advertised his loss of "a parcel of turning tools. They were made in this country, and are very clumsy, and may be known by that."

Yet the surviving Dunlap tools and those from the Dominy shop—some of them homemade—are anything but crude. They show craftsmanship as fine as English toolmakers, who undoubtedly supplied Americans with their tool patterns. Nevertheless, the first American-made tools never really threatened the strong import trade. For one thing, overland shipping costs were so high that distribution was quite limited. For another, as Secretary of the Treasury George Dallas declared before Congress in 1816, hardware, ironmongery, and cutlery were in a class of manufactures so little cultivated as to leave the country almost totally dependent on foreign sources of supply.

No one tool can be singled out as the most important: the furniture maker needed the whole lot. But the saw, in all its variety of shapes, sizes, and styles approaches that distinction. Without it a man could hardly have done more than chop down a tree and hack out a few rough boards. At first little more than a metal spatula with notches filed into one edge, the saw has been through a complex evolution—long ago to be sure—that produced a type for every conceivable woodworking operation.

The everyday farmer-carpenter had perhaps the more rudimentary set of tools, while the cabinetmaker's collection included a greater number of planes, saws, augers, screw bits, and various finishing tools such as scrapers and keyhole instruments. The joiner used more planes and chisels than anything else, and the turner's lot of tools comprised innumerable gouges and skews, not to mention his most vital piece of equipment—a lathe. Therefore, in a very large

Inventory of Ebenezer Tracy, Lisbon, Connecticut: 1803

   148′ *mahogany*
  2148′ *cherry board*
   491′ *do. birch and beech [do. means ditto]*
   111′ *mangrove do.*
   516′ *pine do.*
  1503′ *do white wood*
   579′ *do maple*
   707′ *do chestnut*
   571 *oak joists*
    52 *moulding planes*
    27 *Joiners planes*
    76 *Chysils, gouges, &c*
    14 *fine and coarse hand saws*
    50 *Iron squair*
    50 *hold fast*
        Bench dog
        Glue kettle
     2 *lead pots*
        varnish pot
    12 *lbs glue*
        Stone yellow
     2 *low bureaus*
     1 *long table 7′*
     2 *Pembroke do*
     3 *Candlestands*
    50 *clock cases*
        highpost bed
     2 *do*
     2 *Common beds*
        Chest Drawer
   103 *Chairs of different sorts*
        Copal varnish
        marble paint vat & grinder
     6 *lbs emery*
    12 *gross screws*
     4 *drawer locks*
     3 *setts bureau trimmings*
    35 *escutcheons*
    50 *sundry paints*
        Sideboard unfinished
        Table
  6400 *Chair rounds & legs*
   277 *Chair bottoms**

*See also ''Sawdust and shavings'' 9, 10, 11, and 12: Cabinetmakers' Inventories.

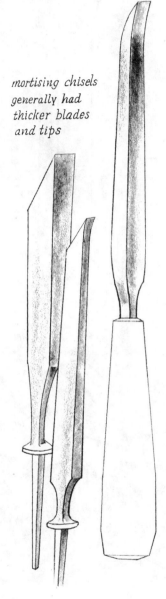

*mortising chisels
generally had
thicker blades
and tips*

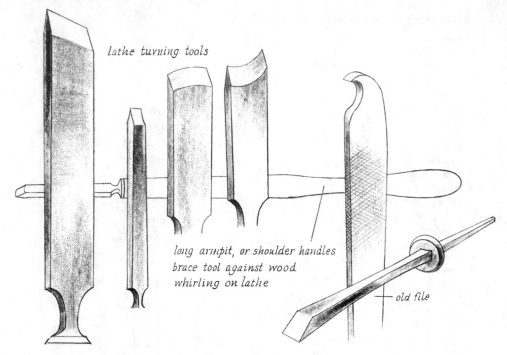

lathe turning tools

*long armpit, or shoulder handles
brace tool against wood
whirling on lathe*

old file

chisels   gouges   veiner & plow

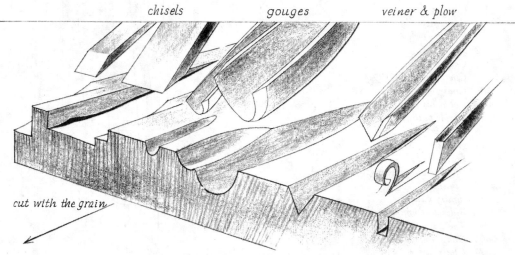

cut with the grain

shop where cabinetmaker, joiner, and turner all worked side by side, the comprehensive list of tools would have been rather immense, comparable to this one:

List of a Chest of Joiners Tools to be Shipt pr Wm Neale for acco' of Wm Wilson (being for Richard Johns)

12 pair of Hollows and Rounds [planes]
1 Oge of 4/8 [molding plane]*
2 Astricles one 4/8, One 6/8 [molding planes]
2 Picture frame Planes
2 Bead Planes one 3/8 the other 3/16
3 Rabbit Plains viz One 1½ In escou [skew] the others square
  One an Inch, the other ½ Inch
1 Side Rabit Plain
1 Astrical & hollow to work in Quirk
1 Moving Filister without Arms
1 Left handed Filister of 2/8
2 Pair of Groving Planes with the Tongue brass,
  the one 4/8 the other 6/8
1 Plow with 2 Set of Irons [molding plane]
1 Sett of bench Plains wth a jointer
1 Half Upright Foreplain & Smoothing D^o
1 Strike block & one tooth plane wth 2 Irons of different Cut
1 Stock [bitstock] with 1 Set of Gouge, 1 of Center & 1 of
  Alis' Nose Bitts Alis the maker's name
1 handsaw 2^feet 2½^In long ⎫
1 Panel D^o same length ⎪
1 Tenant Saw [tenon saw] ⎪ *all of White's best sort*
1 Sash Saw ⎬ *with a good Saw Sett*
6 Small key hole do ⎪
6 Small key hole saws ⎪
8 Mortois Chizells ⎭
12 broad & narrow Firmers
12 broad & narrow Gouges with the Steel the Inside
3 Scribing Gouges with the Steel the out Side of 3/8 & 5/8
3 doz Moores best plain Irons 2 @ 2½ In
3 doz Handsaw Files fine cut
1 Pair Pinchers
1 Pair of Nippers for Cutting Wier
1 Joiners Hatchet
1 Turkey Stone Clear of Knotts

  Let the Beach be well season^d the chizels & gouges be handled, The plains in good order—Let all things be of the best & the Chest neatly fitted.

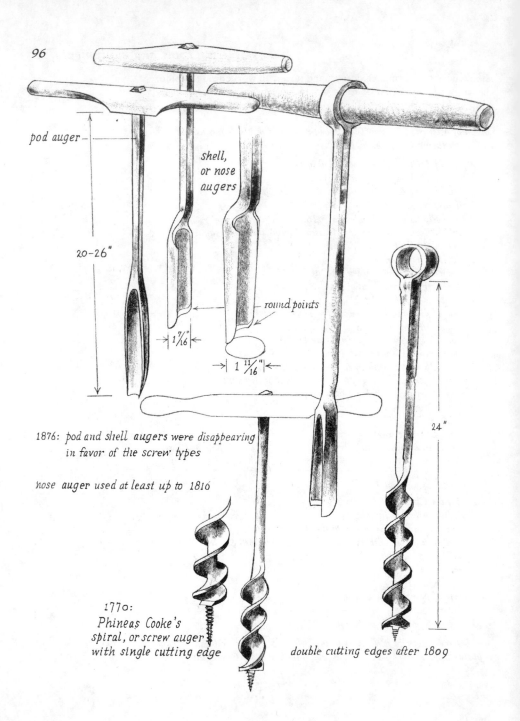

pod auger

20–26"

shell,
or nose
augers

round points

1 7/16"

1 11/16"

1876: pod and shell augers were disappearing
in favor of the screw types

nose auger used at least up to 1816

24"

1770:
Phineas Cooke's
spiral, or screw auger
with single cutting edge

double cutting edges after 1809

Augers were also indispensable, the *nose auger* producing far more leverage because the cutting scoop was offset. The extremely long-shanked type was used by house builders, and even longer ones were necessary in the shipyard for boring through timbers up to two and a half feet thick. These were generally made in the yard's blacksmith shop by welding the auger head to a shank several feet long. Some augers were made with an iron ring on the end through which a wooden bar could be inserted for greatest leverage.

In the early 1800s Cutler & Company of Sheffield, England, made augers in eleven sizes ranging from one half inch to two inches in diameter. Although Phineas Cooke had invented a *spiral* auger about 1770, pod and shell augers—which are variations of the nose auger—were in use well into the 1870s. It is next to impossible to date exactly when an old tool was abandoned in favor of an improved one: some cabinetmakers are still using these old style augers today. Cooke's auger closely resembles our modern bit screw, though its gimlet point—forerunner of the heavier point on modern bits— proved to be too fine and frequently broke off. Cooke's model had but a single cutting edge, in contrast to the double-lip bits which came into use soon after 1809.

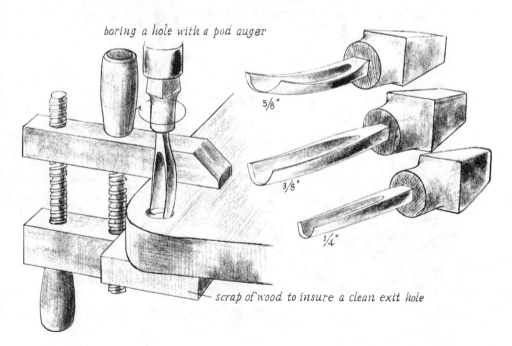

boring a hole with a pod auger

5/8"

3/8"

1/4"

scrap of wood to insure a clean exit hole

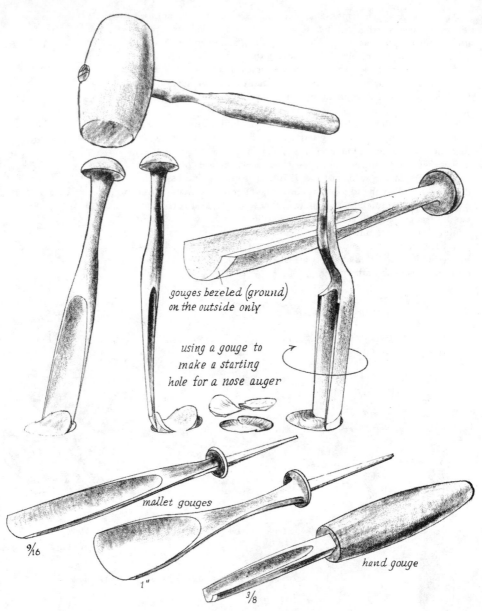

gouges bezeled (ground) on the outside only

using a gouge to make a starting hole for a nose auger

mallet gouges

⁹⁄₁₆

1"

³⁄₈

hand gouge

These augers are difficult tools with which to bore holes, and a considerable dexterity is required to use them, as James Smith makes very clear in his *Panorama of Science and Art* (Liverpool, 1815):

> *The largest of the boring tools for wood is the* auger. *The oldest construction of the auger, which is yet in common use, in various parts of the country, cannot be wrought till a small excavation has been made, which is mostly done with a gouge, at the place where the hole is to be; and till the auger arrives at a considerable depth, the motion of it is very unsteady.*
>
> *Everyone . . . knows by experience that he never can so completely exert his strength in this operation, as when he bores down perpendicularly, with his body leaning over his work . . . the unsteady and irregular motion of the auger . . . at its first entrance into the wood, occasions the holes to be bored very crooked, often larger without than within, and very wide of the direction aimed.*

Files and rasps were valuable in furniture making too. The file is much more than a smoothing tool—though it is that. Essentially, it is a cutting tool with rows of geometrically arranged burrs, or cutting edges, pierced into the flat paddle of steel.

> *A farrier's rasp is an excellent tool for preparing a rough piece of wood for the lathe. Where only a small quantity of material is required to be removed it will be found to be more convenient than the axe or paring knife.*

—JOHN PHIN

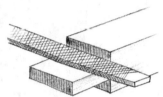

fitting and smoothing a tenon

Files were made of first-rate steel. By a method that John Jacob Holtzapffel describes, the workman sits with the heel of a small anvil almost between his knees. The file blank—which was first greased— is held tightly against the top of the anvil by two leather straps, pressure being exerted by the workman's feet. The first cut is made nearest the off-end of the blank with a special chisel—always wider than the file to make a clean cut—held approximately at an angle of 55° to the perpendicular. The cutting edge of the chisel is slightly blunt, since the object is to *indent* the steel of the blank—not actually to cut it free. The angle of the chisel makes a cut that pushes the steel up into a sharp ridge. On half-round files, two or three joined cuts were necessary to reach over the curved surface.

Files were ideal for finishing the surface of end-grain wood such as the narrow edges of a dovetailed drawer front. The joiner found files just the thing for smoothing molding rounds, cleaning out inside curves, rounding corners, and often as a substitute for glasspaper (a forerunner of sandpaper).

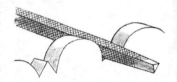

smoothing up in a tight corner

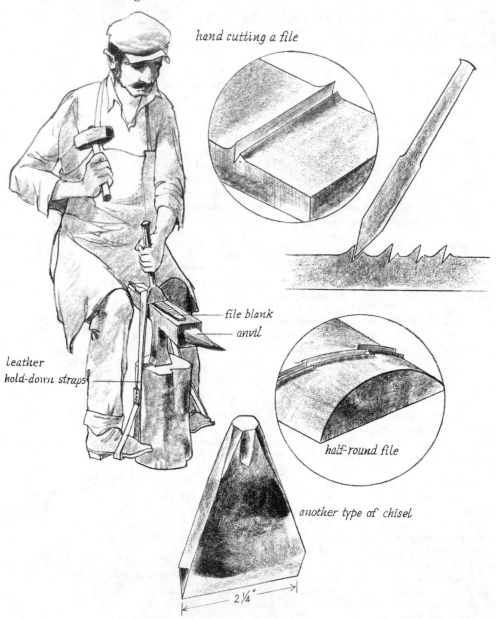

hand cutting a file

file blank

anvil

leather
hold-down straps

half-round file

another type of chisel

2¼"

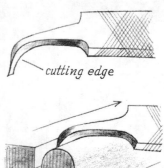

cutting edge

For smoothing fine bead moldings, the tang of an old file could be sharpened (with another file) and then bent in a matching hook. This improvised tool did as nice a job as a piece of freshly broken glass, which by the way should be deemed a "tool" in its own right. And files were useful, too, in making patterns or wooden templates. These were generally sawn from quarter-inch pine or basswood, and carefully shaped and faired up to exact contours, a job that a file did better than anything else. On large patterns such as those for chair seats, thin battens were nailed across the grain to prevent their splitting and warping. A hole bored in one corner provided a simple means of storing the pattern, hung on a peg in the wall. From these templates which were more accurately carved than cut, parts of furniture could be easily duplicated, though not in the sense of interchangeability that we are familiar with today.

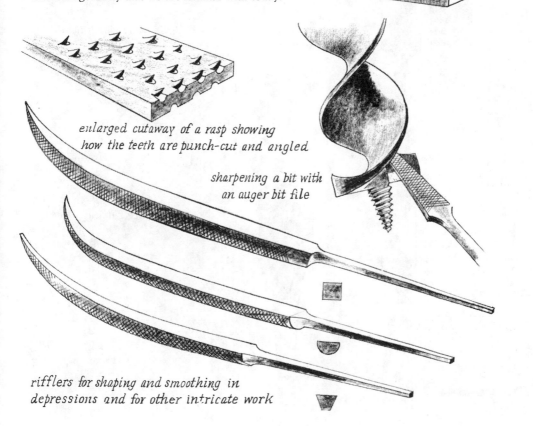

enlarged cutaway of a rasp showing how the teeth are punch-cut and angled

sharpening a bit with an auger bit file

rifflers for shaping and smoothing in depressions and for other intricate work

Files were of course used for sharpening axes, cold chisels, screw bits, gimlets, and many other small tools. But for keeping a keen edge on a tool made of steel—chisels, plane irons, and the like—only the lumbering grindstone, running under dripping water and turning ever so slowly, could do a lasting job. Most shops had one, and they were well cared for:

> No grindstone should be exposed to the weather; it injures the woodwork, and the rays of the sun will harden the stone, so that in time it will become useless; neither should it be allowed to run in water, as the part remaining in it softens and wears away faster than the other portion. The water should be dropped or poured on. . . . By attending to these rules cabinet-makers will be saved much vexation and expense.

—RICHARD BITMEAD

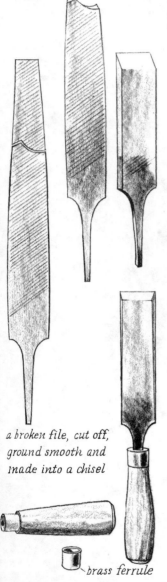

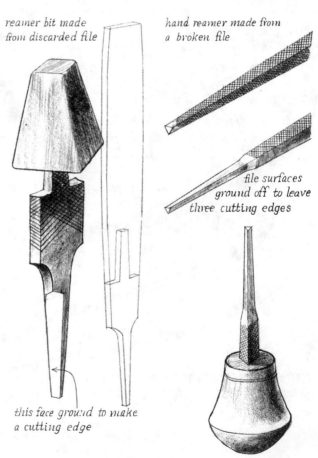

reamer bit made from discarded file

hand reamer made from a broken file

file surfaces ground off to leave three cutting edges

a broken file, cut off, ground smooth and made into a chisel

brass ferrule

this face ground to make a cutting edge

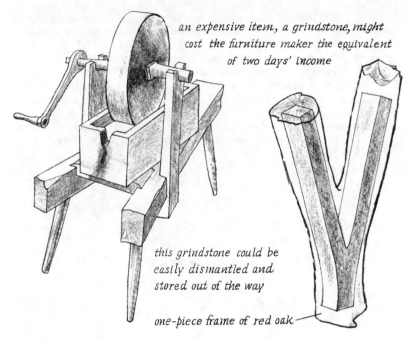

an expensive item, a grindstone, might cost the furniture maker the equivalent of two days' income

this grindstone could be easily dismantled and stored out of the way

one-piece frame of red oak

This may be the reason that many antique grindstones are worn out-of-round, and why they are often equipped with a tin can suspended over the stone, dripping water slowly. When completely used up—their burrs worn flat or filled with wood—worthless files were converted into kitchen knives, scrapers, chisels, reamers, countersinks, and a dozen other home-invented tools that required good steel.

files of various shapes, or patterns were made in several sizes and cuts

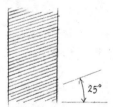

25°

single cut:
one series of parallel cuts at an angle of 25° to the mid line

double cut, or crosscut:
two series of crossing cuts, one finer than the other

float cut:
coarse single cut, or rasp

The file has even found its way into the English language with other connotations, and into literature as well. A rasping voice has its own special timbre, and it was William Thackeray who said, "Will is an old file in spite of his smooth face."

For the furniture maker who manufactured chairs or any other pieces with turned legs or members, a lathe was naturally essential. It was a relatively complicated and expensive piece of equipment, and the companion mechanism, the great wheel, was in the same category. With these two pieces of equipment, however, a chairmaker could really make chairs at a great rate, and to fine tolerances besides.

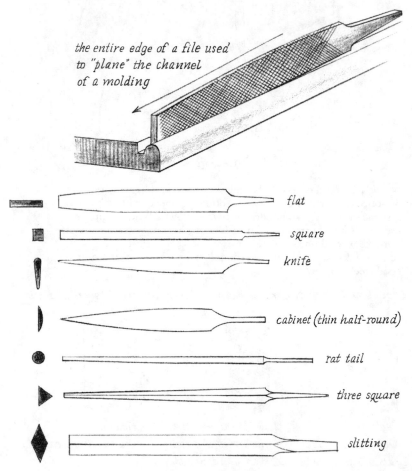

the entire edge of a file used to "plane" the channel of a molding

flat

square

knife

cabinet (thin half-round)

rat tail

three square

slitting

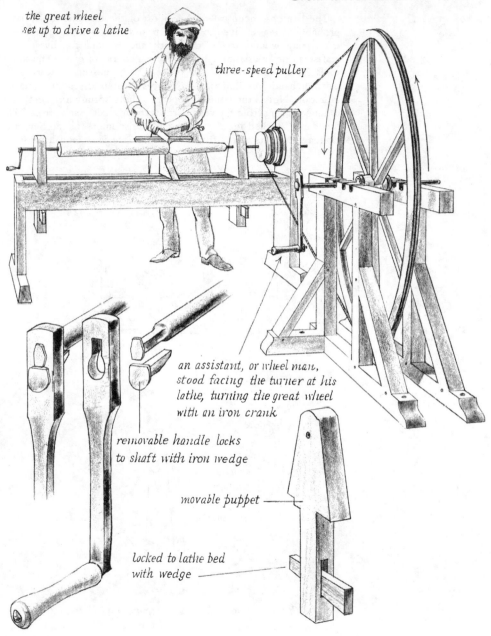

the great wheel
set up to drive a lathe

three-speed pulley

an assistant, or wheel man,
stood facing the turner at his
lathe, turning the great wheel
with an iron crank

removable handle locks
to shaft with iron wedge

movable puppet

locked to lathe bed
with wedge

The lathe has been called the oldest of the machine tools, most probably owing its invention to the primitive bow drill, driven by a taut string wound round the work and rotated rapidly by the craftsman or an assistant. In the normal course of events, machine tools have come about by a process of harnessing power to an existing hand tool function—a process that is essentially one of imitation. Not so the lathe. It appears to have sprung into being as a unique concept from the very start. Egyptian chairs dating from 2000 B.C. have "turned legs." Yet this is a misnomer, for the Egyptian language had no words for *turning* or *turned work*, and it must be

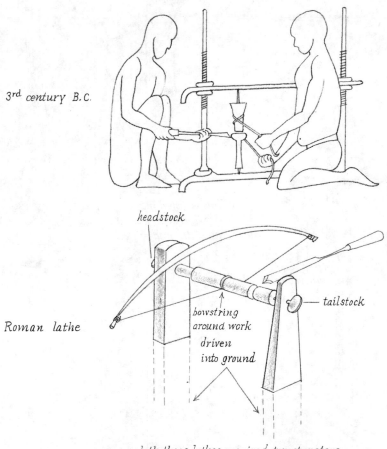

3rd century B.C.

headstock

tailstock

Roman lathe

bowstring
around work
driven
into ground

both these lathes required two operators

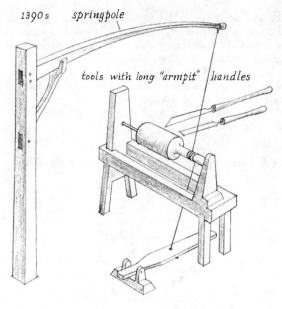

1390s   *springpole*

tools with long "armpit" handles

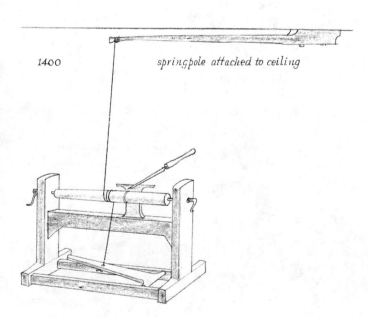

1400   *springpole attached to ceiling*

supposed that what appear to be turned legs are those that were worked down round from shaped or carved legs. A tapered piece of wood was planed off with a spokeshave or conventional plane, and the edges of the facets then smoothed round.

The lathe was evidently in use in the eighth century B.C. and possibly as early as 1000 B.C. An acceptable piece of evidence is an Etruscan bowl from about 700 B.C. that bears marks typical of lathe tools. By the second century B.C. lathe work was fairly common in most of Europe and the Near East.

clockmaker's turn, made of brass and driven by a small bow

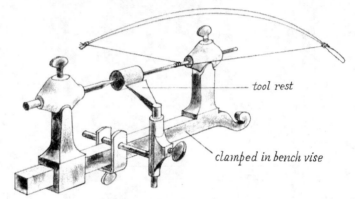

tool rest

clamped in bench vise

French instrument maker's bow drill

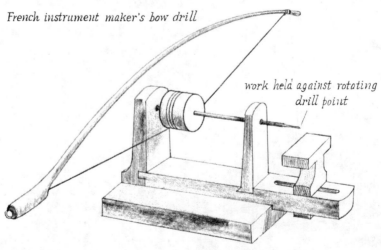

work held against rotating drill point

Crediting ancient cultures with inventive capacities no less advanced than our own, we could guess that the lathe appeared approximately at the time the wheel did, or when the principle of rotation was discovered. Early lathes were powered by a fixed bow that imparted a reciprocating action, though this does not appear to have been a handicap to good work. This type of drive persisted until well into the fourteenth century, when a way was devised to have the bow string wind around a drum independent of the work itself. The more advanced drive system of the great wheel was introduced about

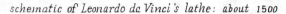

schematic of Leonardo da Vinci's lathe: about 1500

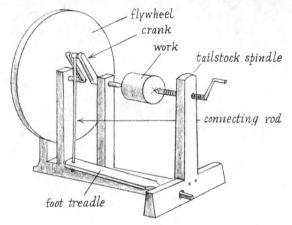

flywheel
crank
work
tailstock spindle
connecting rod
foot treadle

the same time that Leonardo da Vinci designed a foot treadle linkage attached to a crankshaft equipped with a flywheel.

If these machines strike us as crude, it's well to realize that the basic principles have not really changed. A modern electrically driven lathe may work to closer tolerances and at higher speed, but it is performing the very same work. There have been minor refinements over the bow lathe, but even these began appearing as early as 1480 when a cross slide was invented—a tool holder to replace human hands in the "automatic" turning of duplicated pieces. To paraphrase Robert Woodbury, "Continuous drive of the lathe also adapts easily to the use of power other than the craftsman's hands and feet: a dull apprentice boy, a horse gin, a waterwheel, a steam engine, or an electric motor."

[*Continued on page 116*]

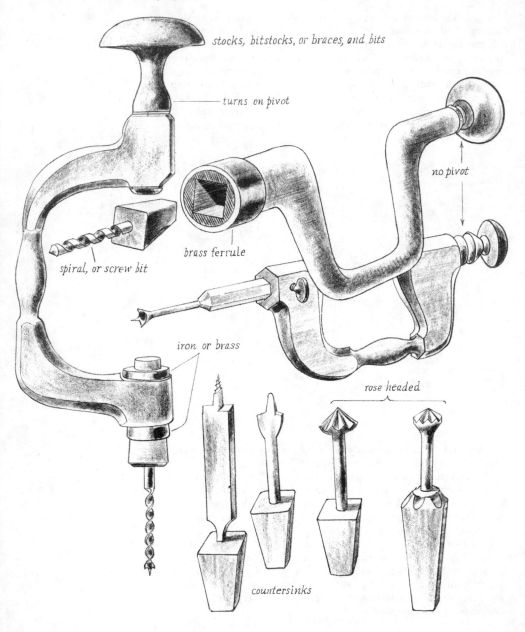

stocks, bitstocks, or braces, and bits

turns on pivot

no pivot

brass ferrule

spiral, or screw bit

iron or brass

rose headed

countersinks

one version of the "donkey's ear" used to clean up a sawed 45° miter

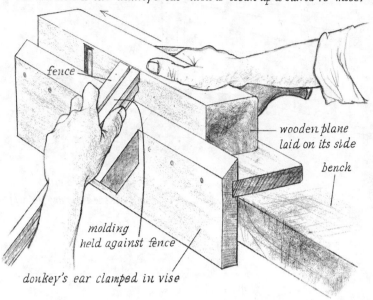

fence

wooden plane
laid on its side

bench

molding
held against fence

donkey's ear clamped in vise

jointer for joining edges of boards

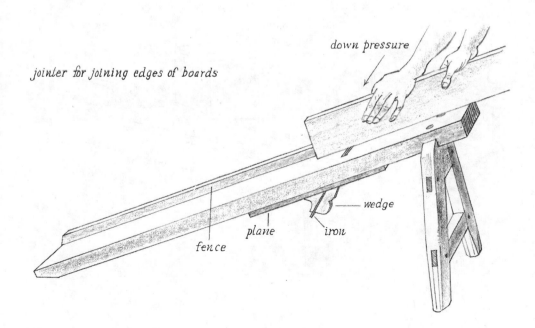

down pressure

wedge

plane   iron

fence

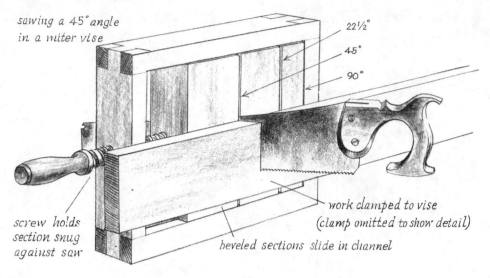

sawing a 45° angle
in a miter vise

22½°

45°

90°

screw holds
section snug
against saw

work clamped to vise
(clamp omitted to show detail)

beveled sections slide in channel

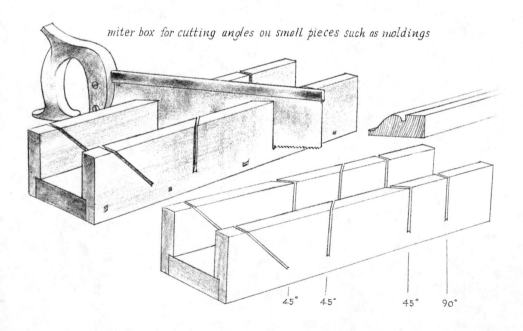

miter box for cutting angles on small pieces such as moldings

45°   45°   45°   90°

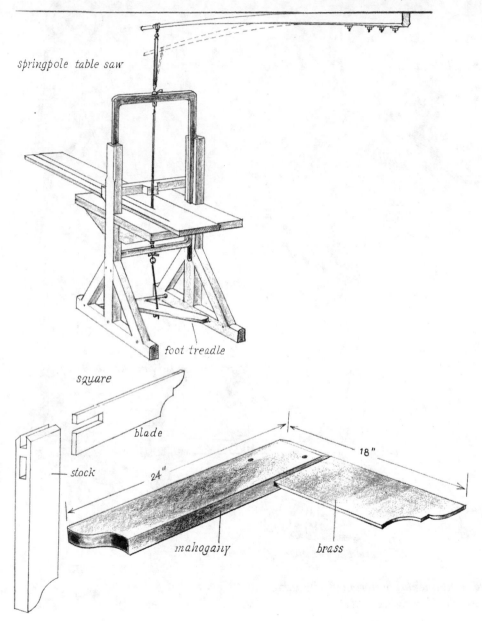

springpole table saw

foot treadle

square

blade

stock

24"

18"

mahogany

brass

shipwright's adze

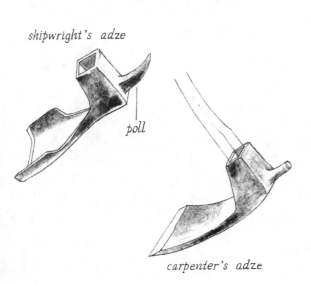

poll

carpenter's adze

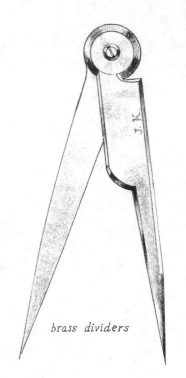

brass dividers

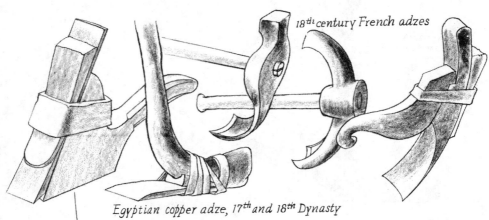

18th century French adzes

Egyptian copper adze, 17th and 18th Dynasty

*the fundamental function of this adze
is nearly the same as a plane*

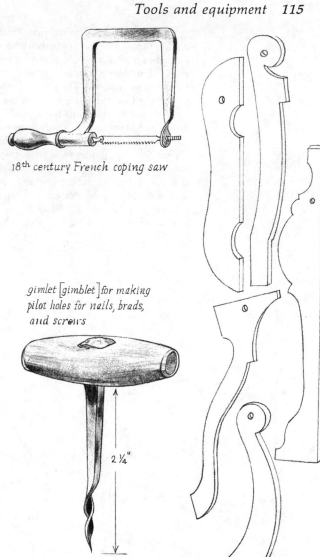

18th century French coping saw

flat pointed screws of the 18th century were started in a hole made by a prick punch

gimlet [gimblet] for making pilot holes for nails, brads, and screws

2 ¼"

wooden patterns

Wooden screws—the sort used in bench vises—were also hand-made. The device used to make these was called a *screwbox*. The term describes it well: a box in which a steel knife was held at the desired angle, fitted with a hole through which the piece of wood to be threaded was rotated. The piece of wood to be made into a screw was first turned on the lathe down to the correct diameter. It was then twisted and rotated into the screwbox, the cutting knife making a notch and starting the "thread" as the turned piece was advanced. The wooden worm immediately behind the knife caught the first thread thus cut, guiding and advancing the cutting of the screw at the correct pitch. In this kind of screwbox, all the wood was removed at one cut, unlike the tapered tap and die that cut gradually as the stock was advanced through a series of tapered knives.

Screws of half an inch diameter and larger were usually made with the wooden blank held in a vise, while the screwbox was "handed

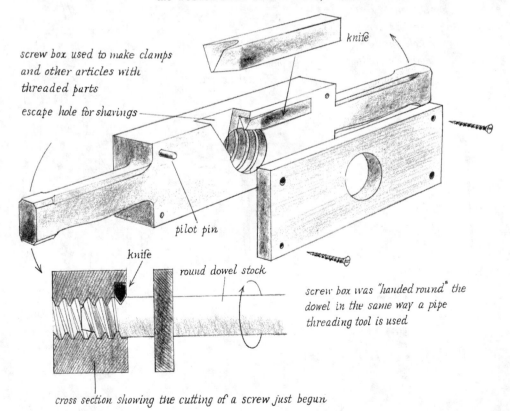

knife

screw box used to make clamps
and other articles with
threaded parts

escape hole for shavings

pilot pin

knife

round dowel stock

screw box was "handed round" the
dowel in the same way a pipe
threading tool is used

cross section showing the cutting of a screw just begun

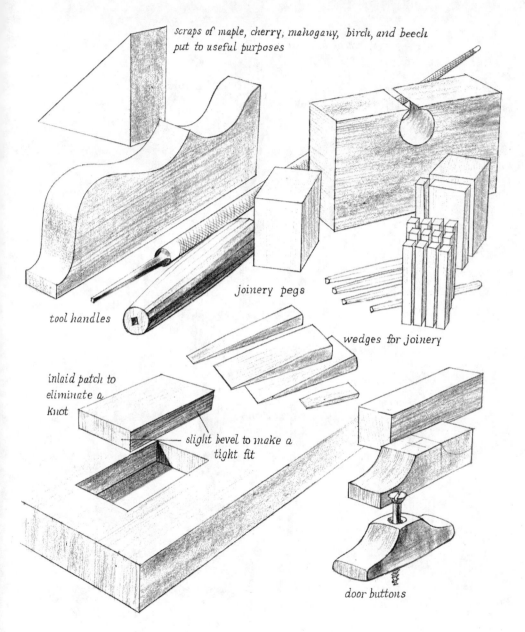

scraps of maple, cherry, mahogany, birch, and beech put to useful purposes

tool handles

joinery pegs

wedges for joinery

inlaid patch to eliminate a knot

slight bevel to make a tight fit

door buttons

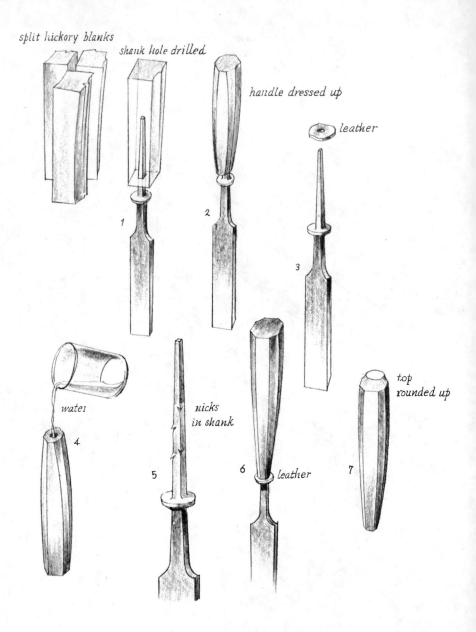

split hickory blanks

shank hole drilled

handle dressed up

leather

1

2

3

water

4

nicks
in shank

5

6

leather

7

top
rounded up

round'' just like a die stock. The screwbox was occasionally used in making screws of four-, six-, and even eight-inch diameters. These larger sizes were also made by hand with a saw, chisels, and rasps, after the fashion of the so-called spiral turning. Mechanical screw cutting was practiced a good many years ago, as far back as the 1500s when a foot lathe was introduced equipped with a traverse that advanced the cutting tool mechanically.

The application of all these tools to wood produced quantities of scraps of every possible kind of wood. Bushel baskets of this waste were probably consumed as kindling wood in the kitchen stove, but with what is known of the country furniture maker and his ingenuity, it's sensible to think he picked this scrap heap over and saved out the better and larger pieces for tool handles. There's something very satisfactory about using a tool fitted with a richly colored handle of cherry wood. M. T. Richardson flatly stated that octagonal handles are preferable, and provided a detailed and useful description of how to make good handles:

> *Select close, fine grained hickory; split out the blocks so as to insure straight grain . . . bore a hole with a small twist bit and rim out [ream] with a taper. . . Drive the block on the shank [of the steel tool] to within ⅛" of the shoulder; then dress up.*
>
> *Remove the block, having first marked [one side] to designate the face. Procure a thin piece of sole leather, punch a hole through it, dampen it and force it over the shank down to the shoulder. Fill shank hole [of the block] with water, allowing it to remain thereon five minutes. Then nick the corners of the shank . . . and drive on the handle.*
>
> *The leather will act as a cushion, to prevent rebounding, and the moisture in the hole will soften the wood so that the corners of the shank will cut their way without splitting; the nicks will assist to keep the handle on . . . when the leather and wood are dry. Finish the handle by removing the corners to make an octagon. Round up the top to a fullness of one-fourth of an inch. When the handle is completed, dip it in warm, raw linseed oil right down to the leather. Allow it to remain in the oil one night . . . burnish the entire surface with a bone or steel burnisher. . . A set made in this way will last as long as the chisels.*

A man with the patience to ''handle'' a whole set of chisels and gouges by this method had all the makings of a good furniture man, ready to undertake the great variety of woodworking methods that were a part of his trade.

EIGHT
Woodworking methods

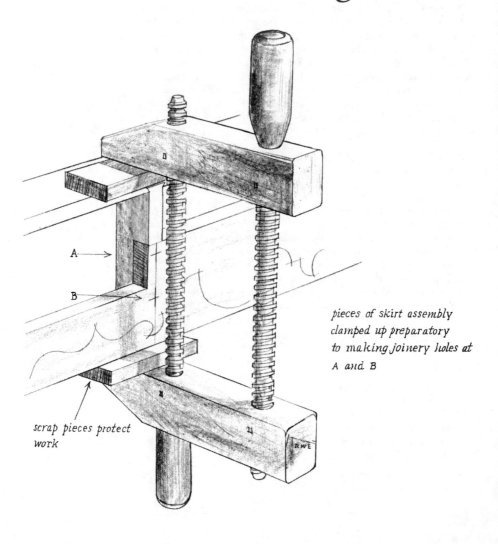

pieces of skirt assembly
clamped up preparatory
to making joinery holes at
A and B

scrap pieces protect
work

Some people have a practice of making a bushel of preparation to arrive at one gill of product.

—M. T. RICHARDSON

Indeed it does appear that an interminable amount of time and labor preceded the actual work at the bench. Seasoned lumber, a workshop, and a good set of tools were the furniture maker's indispensable necessities. Yet none of these alone, or all of them together for that matter, were equal in importance to skill—the experience and familiarity that transformed raw wood into useful and lasting pieces of furniture. The more ingenious and adroit craftsman would have produced good furniture even in a cramped workshop with the smallest number of tools. By the same token, neither the most spacious workshop nor the most elaborate set of imported tools were in themselves enough to guarantee a clumsy workman good results.

He may have worked according to traditional methods, but every furniture maker, since he was an individual with personal and sometimes peculiar ideas, evolved his own ways by intent, by accident, or by intuitive proclivity. Though all tools were much alike, it was the way he manipulated them that distinguished a fine craftsman from a mediocre one.

There are ways of killing a cat besides choking it with butter, says a popular phrase, and it is the same with any particular thing in the workshop—if it cannot be done in one way it can in nine cases out of ten be successfully accomplished in another.

—HANS J. S. CASSAL

The joints used by furniture makers were basic to all woodworking, but there was more than one way to make them at the bench. All dovetails were substantially the same in principle, and they all looked alike when done. Yet they could be successfully fashioned with a variety of saws, chisels, and work procedures. For example, one man may have cut his dovetails one by one, while another preferred cutting several at once. For one joiner the tenon saw was the best tool: for another a veneer saw and chisel. Whether in the making of a settle or a Windsor chair, accepted principles were followed, but the exact methods and sequence of achieving them varied in the hands of different furniture makers. In hollowing or scooping the seat of a chair, two different men could get pretty much the same result by two different methods: the one using an inshave, and the other a broad chisel and mallet.

The experienced cabinetmaker sensed the importance of the small details that to his critical eye made the difference between an

Dovetail illustrations, 128–137

Chairmaking illustrations 185–198

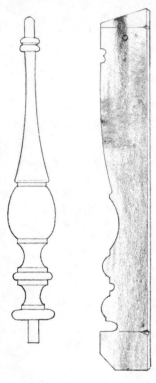

wooden pattern for a finial, useful for checking the progress of the turning— but not while the lathe is running

Dovetail illustrations, 134, 135

acceptable job and a superior piece of work. For instance, the better drop leaf tables usually had a flat recess shaved out of the leaf just where the wood met the hinge. This was not critical to the bare function of the hinge and table leaf, but it made a nicer job of it. The leaf could swing down and hug the sides of the frame without any interference from the hinges.

The countryman expressed his inventiveness in all these tasks, often discovering new shapes or new proportions, not infrequently by accident as his tools touched wood, as when the wood whirled on the lathe. For every time the skew bit into the wood a shape was instantly born, and there it stayed until or unless he chose to modify it or discard it.

And the clever man, when he saw an especially pleasing shape appear at the lathe, remarked its grace. Simply by stopping the lathe he might capture that shape by making a template, or pattern, there and then. Often what simply "happened" one day became a routine of his characteristic design, and he repeated it again and again.

A comparison of the skirts on a pine chest of drawers with those on a more elaborate piece such as the Dunlaps made will show a strong similarity of pattern. The first was not simply a cruder version of the more elegant style at all, for there appears to exist a universality of the workings of tools, and the shapes and curves that they most naturally follow. These designs and shapes were happening almost everywhere simultaneously—perhaps an evidence that tools and wood work best, even from a structural standpoint, along given logical lines. To cut a curve that is exotic or bizarre, both the tool and the craftsman's arms must be manipulated in an unnatural way; hence the finished product may also *look* bizarre, contrived, or awkward.

It's natural that the craftsman's eyes, hands, arms, and shoulders would have become so accustomed to cutting dovetails at one particular angle that the slightest deviation from this norm would have made itself known by how it "felt." In the same sense, a man can pick up a tool from the bench and know it's the right one or the wrong one just by the feel of its handle. This is not the same as saying the furniture maker didn't use all kinds of devices to insure accuracy—and often, uniformity. There was an advantage in using a template to mark out the pins of a dovetail, for example, especially where duplication was involved:

> There is a greater advantage in cutting two or more [pieces] together than there is if the pins are cut first and the dovetails marked off and cut separately. Each corner should be marked and numbered. Dovetails should not be cut broad in the front and very narrow at the back, as this weakens the joint, but should be only slightly tapered; these are the best and the strongest, and look well.

Having cut the dovetails, the next thing is to mark them off [on the board that is to be the drawer side], which is done by placing a corner as you intend it to come when finished; then insert the point of the dovetail saw into the cut, and draw it toward you [scribing, not sawing].

Some chop out the dovetails first, and clamp just the part for the pins, and then use a pounce-bag for marking. . . . Care should be taken to cut a shade outside the marks.

—RICHARD BITMEAD

When duplication of parts involved compound curves, as in making a set of cabriole legs, the waste pieces were left attached to the block of wood—they were not completely cut off. By this simple means most of the curved saw cuts were made without altering the rectangular shape of the original block of wood—making it easier to hold the work securely in the vise.

Cabriole leg illustrations, 153–156

It stands to reason that the furniture maker intended—and worked carefully—to make all four legs identical. There would be natural variation no matter what, and that only added charm to the finished piece. If in spite of everything a joint came out a bit off, the handcraftsman could compensate for this seeming inaccuracy by adjusting the next piece of wood to match.

Similar disciplined exactitude was called for in making mortise and tenon joints. If the tenon was not exactly parallel to the long way of the member it would throw the entire frame out of square; if the holes were not bored in precisely the right place, driving home the dowel pins could split the post before they drew the tenon up tight. A saw cut made a thirty-second of an inch too far one way or the other could spoil the joint. A sharp scratch awl or a penknife were considered the most accurate tools for marking out the joints. Traces of these marks can usually be seen clearly even on highly finished antiques, as there was seldom any attempt to obliterate them. Once marked off, the joint was cut with the aid of stop-blocks clamped to the work to guide the saw. The joiner used chisels to shave the surfaces down clean and to sharpen the corners of the mortise and a mullet to check the beveled edges of paneling for correct thickness.

Mortise and tenon illustrations, 150–157, 166–168, 170, 171

The lathe, although a unique tool, was inherently a dangerous instrument—high-speed rotation combined with razor-sharp hand tools. By its nature lathe work required considerable experience to produce good results: it wasn't an operation that could be dabbled with. Those who owned lathes, therefore, were likely to be engaged in some specialty such as chairmaking or the turning of chair rounds, bedposts, table legs, drawer pulls, and finials. Nevertheless, the average country workman, even though he did too little turned work to warrant the investment of a lathe, was quite capable of making

Lathework illustrations, 178–184

turnings in the old way, working them out of square stock with the drawknife, spokeshave, plane, rasp, and file.

Chair making is a branch generally confined to itself, as those who professedly work at it, seldom engage to make cabinet furniture. . . . In the chair branch it requires a particular turn in the handling of shapes, to make them agreeable and easy.

—THOMAS SHERATON, *CABINET DICTIONARY*, 1803

Windsor chair illustrations, 185–193

Among the wide variety of types of chairs, one of the most interesting was the Windsor chair, brought from England to America where it became very popular and where—judging from the innumerable variations of style—it truly came into its own. Originally a rough and ready common seat in farmhouse, tavern, general store, livery stable, and courthouse, its basic design was modified by country and city chairmakers alike into numerous useful and attractive variants, all of which nonetheless retained the fundamental construction details: well-curved arm and back bows, slender and graceful spindles, and legs tapered to an eye-pleasing proportion with no loss of strength. The native woods were admirably suited to its construction: thick, clear pine for the seat, easily saddled; back bow of hickory, white oak, or ash; and spindles and stretchers of hickory—slender and nicely tapered, yet sufficiently strong to bend and give with the weight of the occupant.

When the American chairmaker came to shape each individual stick of wood, he held to dimensions that were just large enough to maintain strength—and no larger. There was almost no excess stuff in these Windsors. And his skill at combining green and dry sticks in the same chair resulted in construction so tight that Windsors assembled in the 1700s are today still "firmly seated," and have required no reinforcing angle irons or tie rods. The country furniture maker could put together a chair that was inexpensive, light in weight, strong, yet pretty enough for any occasion.

Bentwork illustrations, 199–202

The construction of Windsors and many other kinds of chairs relied one way or another on *bentwork*. The heavier arm pieces could be sawed to the desired curvature without attempting to follow the natural grain of the wood, and this method was in very general use. However, a curved back rail that described a semicircle, and was made this way, would have to be joined, or pieced together to avoid having the grain run across the width of the rail. A much neater method involved steaming the wood to soften it and then bending it round, all in one piece. This made a stronger member because the inherent strength of the grain was utilized. The back bow and the spindles of course were bent, either from green wood or by one of the treatments using hot water or steam.

The art of bending consists in softening the wood fibers by steam or by boiling so they can be compressed into a smaller space than they occupy in their natural state; then, placing on the outer side of the wood to be bent a metal or other strap to take the strain, and bending the wood over a form to the required shape; this has the effect of compressing the inner side of the wood, and thus shortening [or upsetting] it sufficiently to accomodate to its new position.

—CARRIAGE MONTHLY

Once the wood has been treated with steam or by boiling, the bending must be done without delay, and the piece clamped or fixed in the mold as quickly as possible. Ordinarily the chairmaker had fifteen to twenty minutes in which to bend the wood before it began to "set up" rigid again. After bending, the wood will generally maintain the new shape unless it has undergone severe changes in moisture content. An increase in moisture content causes the wood to lose some curvature, whereas a decrease in moisture such as exposure to heat or further excessive drying tends to make the curvature more pronounced. Moreover, repeated change from more moisture to less and back again may cause the wood to return to its original shape.

Boiling wood in water produces a condition of great pliability, especially with hardwoods. If wood treated in this way is bent and allowed to dry it retains the bent shape rigidly, though it's believed that the strength will be somewhat impaired. This weakness was seldom critical for the chairmaker, however.

Steaming produced a similar condition of wood, and has been used since very early times.

The first rude attempts in this country were made in bending ox-bows [not yokes] in the early part of the last century [1700s]. The material, hickory strips split from tough hickory trees, was heated in hot ashes and sprinkled with water, and over these hot ashes green weeds or grass were thrown. The bark was used for the "strap," and the bending was done around a log.

—CARRIAGE MONTHLY

This method, too, required rapidity in handling the steamed wood, for heat alone produced a kind of "case hardening," a method that ancient tribes found useful in hardening and sharpening their wooden spear tips.

Green wood is perhaps more difficult to stabilize in its bent position because the wood retains most of its sap wetness and has not been treated the same as any other fresh cut timber, which is normally given a prolonged period of air drying. In the case of chair hoops and bows, however, the bent pieces are held firmly in position by the sockets in the seat, and by the several spindles of the back. In effect, the structure of the chair itself becomes the mold. Still, such a chair would not be considered finished enough to sit in until a more complete drying had taken place.

Another hazard in the way of bending green stock is that hydrostatic pressure (compression of the water-laden cells) may cause breakage if the wood is compressed by an amount greater than the volume of air space in the wood cells. The question of moisture content appears to be very important. Bending stock that has been dried to the point of 12 to 20 percent moisture content was thought to be the best. If wood is *too dry*, it must be given a much longer steaming or soaking. High pressure steaming of the type used today produces more plasticity but generally does not result in as successful bending as when the wood is treated at low pressure, or in existing atmospheric conditions. These would have been the conditions that the furniture maker had to work with, and presumably his simpler method created less separation of the layers of wood: the idea being to achieve enough plasticity but not too much.

The success of bending depends also on the radius of the bend. As the radius is made smaller the amount of upset, or compression, becomes greater than the amount of stretch; and the neutral line moves closer to the outside, or tension side of the wood. If this neutral line comes too close, the outer layers of wood tend to break. In recent times it was discovered that this tension between the layers of wood in a bent piece could be controlled to some extent by the application of *end pressure*, a technique that was almost certainly unknown to the average furniture maker in former times. The purpose of end pressure was to increase the amount of upset on the layers lying on the inside of the curved wood, and keep them within or under the breaking point of the layers along the outside (tension side). The art of controlling these limits in relation to the radius of a given curve has been highly developed, to such an extent that timbers as large in section as three by four inches can be steam-bent for the manufacture of boat frames.

The American chairmaker evidently took naturally to the bending of wood and the building of drying forms and steam boxes according to his own private notions, not necessarily aware of the scientific aspects of the process. At the same time—again since very early times—the makers of musical instruments have worked wood in this fashion, though we have not been left with any very copious literature or graphic explanation on the subject.

It is curious that in his tremendous treatise on cabinetmaking Roubo [Andre Jacob Roubo, L'Art du Menuisier, Paris, 1769–1774] never mentioned bending techniques. It should be noted that all of the tortuous curves of carriages, furniture, and building woodwork were sawn out. There are a few hints of the process of imparting the curve to a bentside [the curved side of a harpsichord]. In 1726 Blanchet had a "lead trough for soaking bentsides with the bending form."

The curious thing is that there is no mention of heat. Nowadays wood is exposed to hot water or, better, to steam for some hours and then clamped to the form. I have never experimented with simple soaking, but one would have to dry the bentside for a very long time after such a prolonged immersion.

—FRANK HUBBARD

It is possible to shape the bentside of a harpsichord without any preliminary treatment because the wood can be comparatively thin, and because the several knee braces along the inside of the case provide support against which the side panel can be bent on. "Oddly enough," Hubbard says, "I once had occasion to remove the bentside of an Italian harpsichord almost three-hundred years old, and within a day it had become almost straight. This suggests that it had not been soaked and bent on a form."

With all the pieces of the chair, table, cupboard, or bedstead put together, there was little more to be done except give the wood a final lick of finishing and add the hardware. Any remaining rough spots were touched up with a piece of glass or a scraper, and a final velvety luster given the wood with a handful of shavings scrubbed vigorously back and forth over the surfaces.

Wooden drawer pulls and knobs were classed as hardware, and these were easily and cheaply obtained. Though more costly, iron hinges, hasps, and locks were as available as nails, brads, and screws. And for a dearer price, the more elegant fittings of brass could be had in some of the larger cities. The relatively high cost of metal hardware may have accounted for the common practice of selling furniture *without* the hardware: it was then the buyer's privilege to select his own, pay for it, and have it attached.

Hardware illustrations, 203–205

The country craftsman used most of this woodworking technology as a matter of routine. The dovetail, the mortise and tenon joint, and panel construction were all part of his daily work. He could make a blockfront drawer with a neatly inletted lock, and when called upon embellish a piece with fluting or reeding. His skill was sometimes needed to make a shell-carved drawer front or a cornice for a highboy. If he had a lathe, he could turn out chair parts with as little concern as he made bedposts and finials. These and other basic methods are described on pages 128–205 with detailed illustrations and explanatory captions and labels.

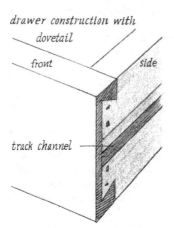

drawer construction with
dovetail

front   side

track channel

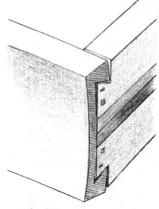

early dovetail with two pins
and a single wide tail—
vulnerable to warping

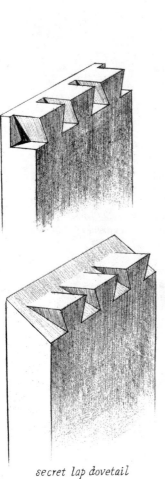

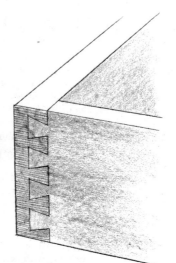

secret lap dovetail

five pin construction
probably no stronger than
three — and far more
laborious to make

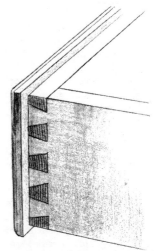

dovetail drawer front with
with rabbeted lip

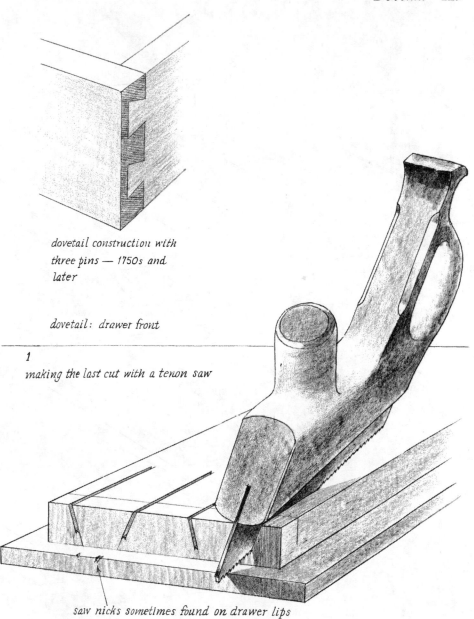

dovetail construction with three pins — 1750s and later

dovetail: drawer front

1

making the last cut with a tenon saw

saw nicks sometimes found on drawer lips

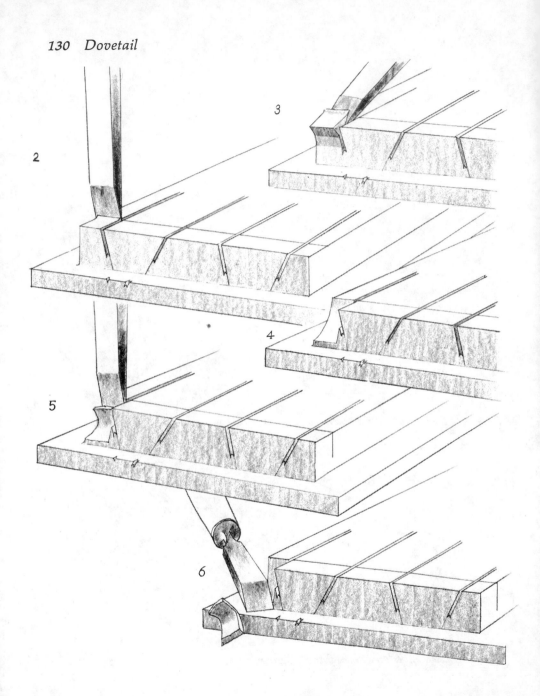

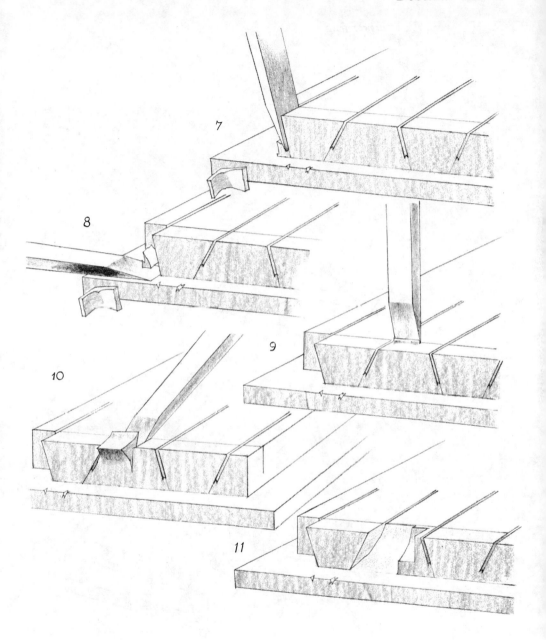

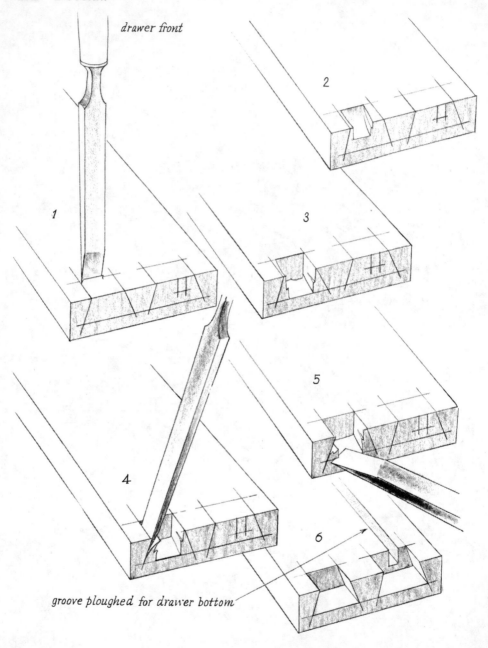

drawer front

1

2

3

4

5

6

groove ploughed for drawer bottom

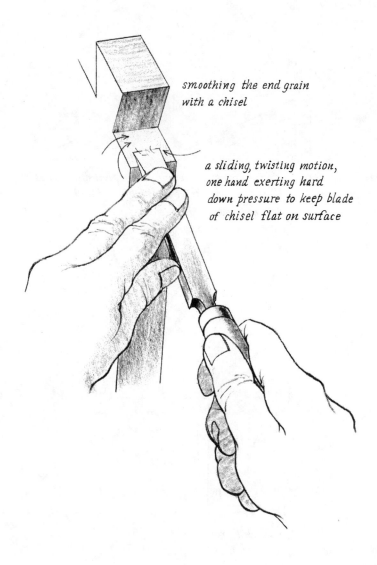

smoothing the end grain
with a chisel

a sliding, twisting motion,
one hand exerting hard
down pressure to keep blade
of chisel flat on surface

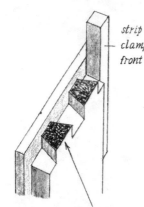

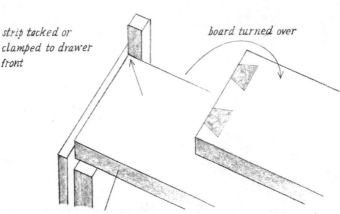

strip tacked or clamped to drawer front

board turned over

by the so-called "pounce" method, old gummy paint daubed on the ends of the pins transfers an accurate impression of their shape

board for side of drawer set on ends of pins — and registered against strip of wood — then tapped with hammer to take off the paint

when paint dries, dovetail cut and fitted

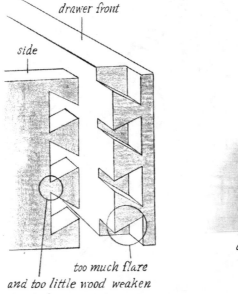

drawer front

side

too much flare and too little wood weaken dovetail construction

corners split off

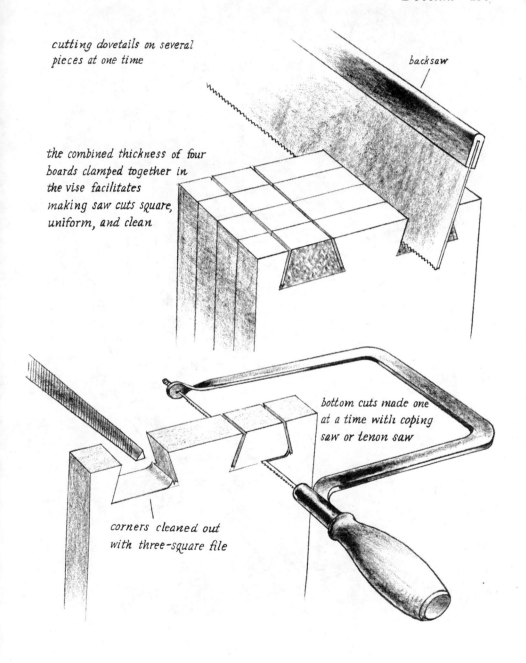

cutting dovetails on several pieces at one time

backsaw

the combined thickness of four boards clamped together in the vise facilitates making saw cuts square, uniform, and clean

bottom cuts made one at a time with coping saw or tenon saw

corners cleaned out with three-square file

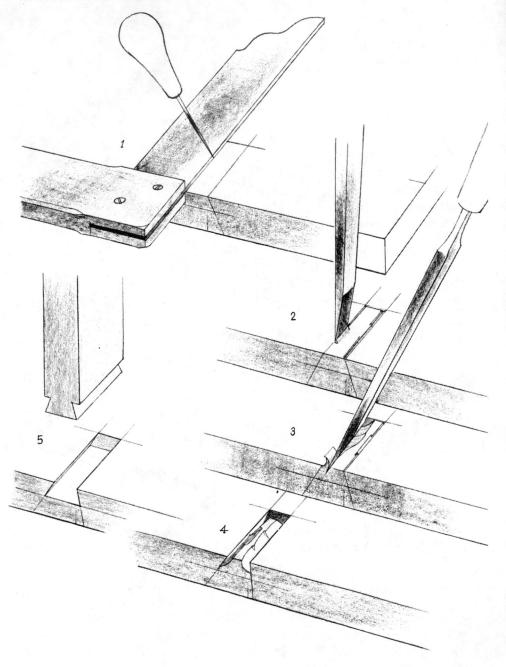

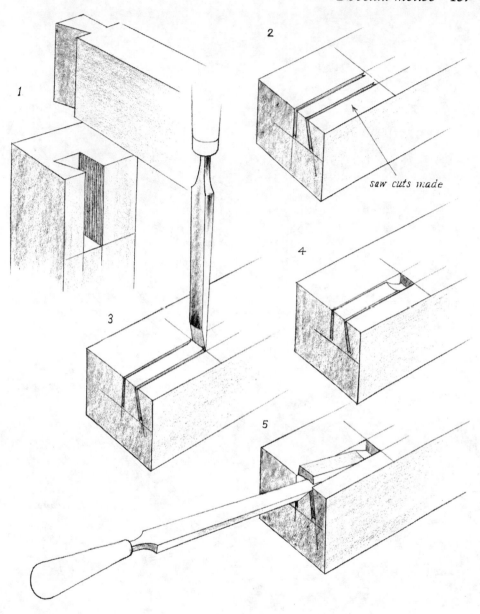

saw cuts made

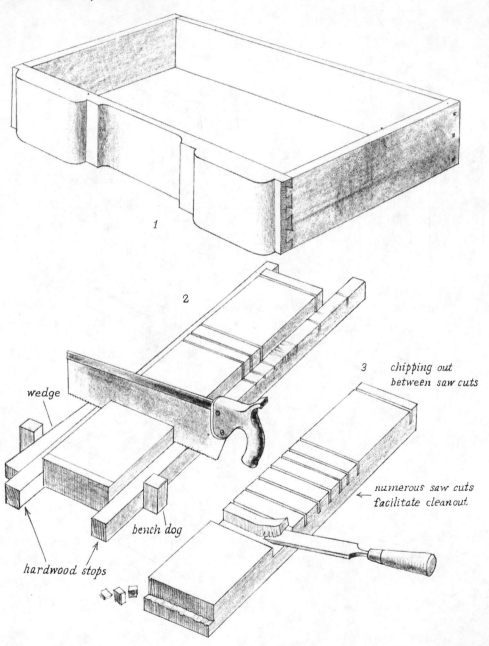

1

2

3   *chipping out
between saw cuts*

wedge

hardwood stops

bench dog

*numerous saw cuts
facilitate cleanout*

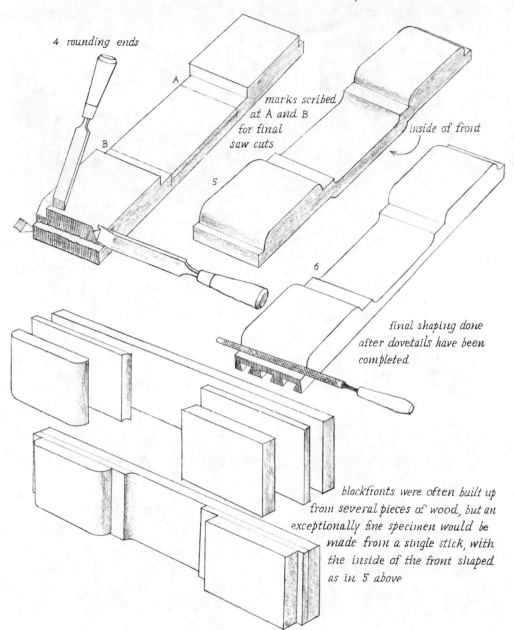

4 rounding ends

A

B

marks scribed
at A and B
for final
saw cuts

inside of front

5

6

final shaping done
after dovetails have been
completed

blockfronts were often built up
from several pieces of wood, but an
exceptionally fine specimen would be
made from a single stick, with
the inside of the front shaped
as in 5 above

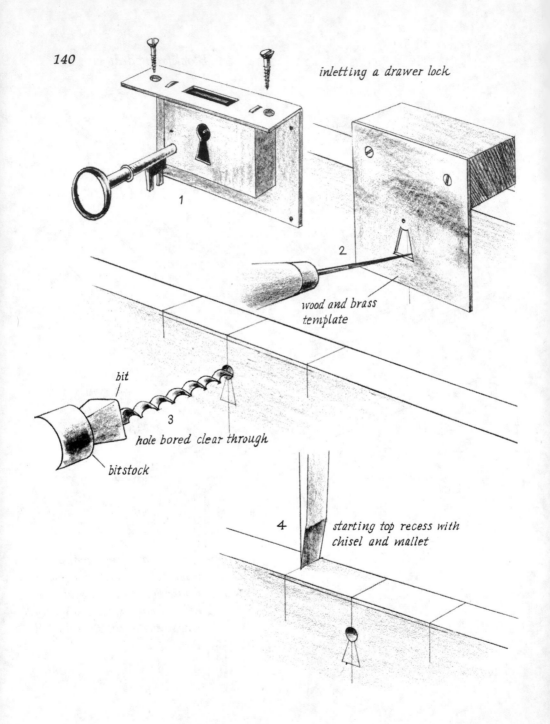

inletting a drawer lock

1

2

wood and brass
template

bit

3

hole bored clear through

bitstock

4   starting top recess with
chisel and mallet

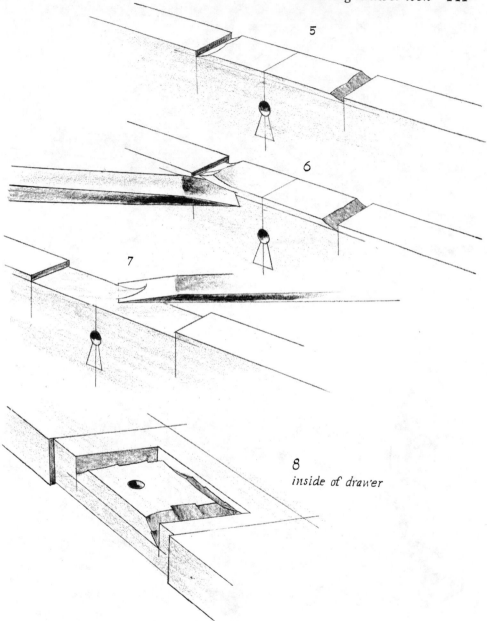

5

6

7

8
inside of drawer

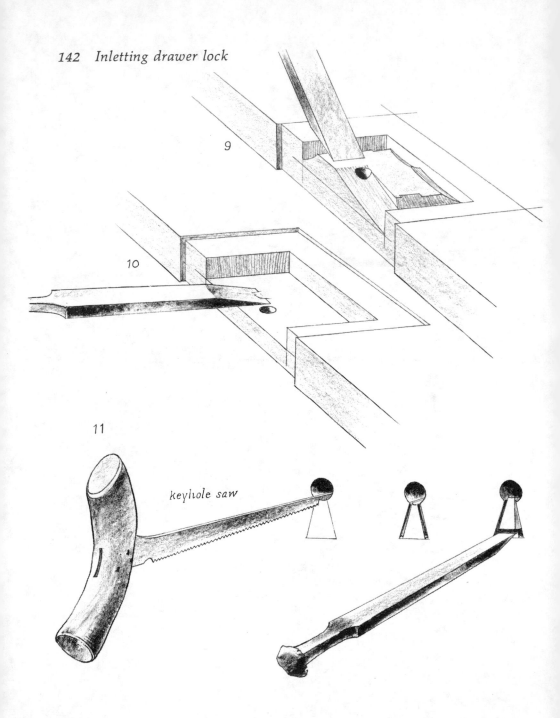

9

10

11

keyhole saw

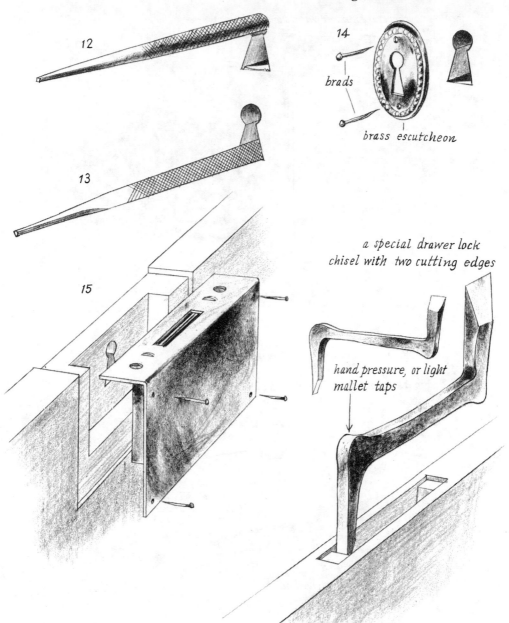

12

13

14

brads

brass escutcheon

15

a special drawer lock
chisel with two cutting edges

hand pressure, or light
mallet taps

secretary drawer with shell carving

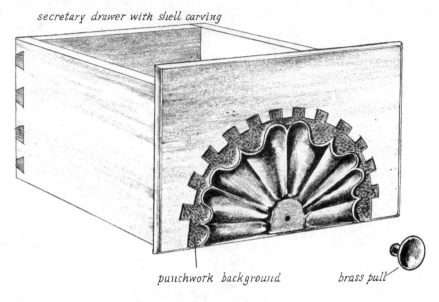

punchwork background   brass pull

marking out for first stage of carving

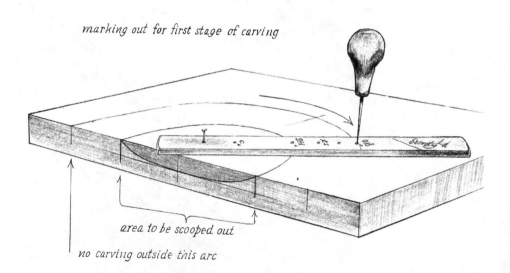

area to be scooped out

no carving outside this arc

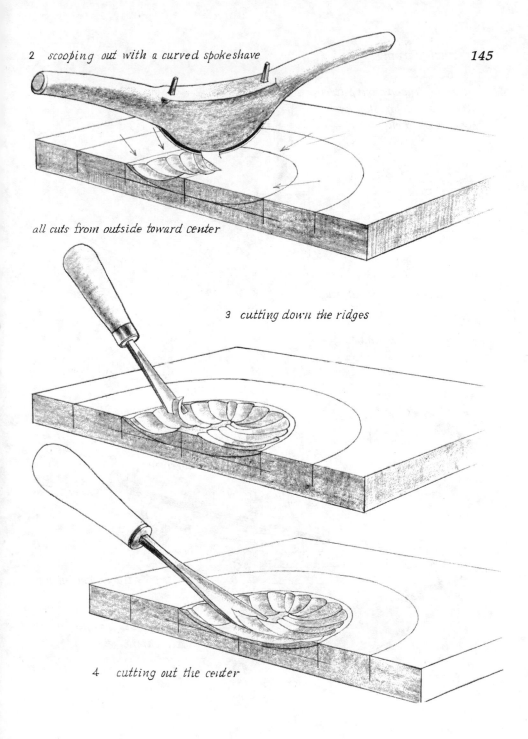

2 *scooping out with a curved spokeshave*

all cuts from outside toward center

3 *cutting down the ridges*

4 *cutting out the center*

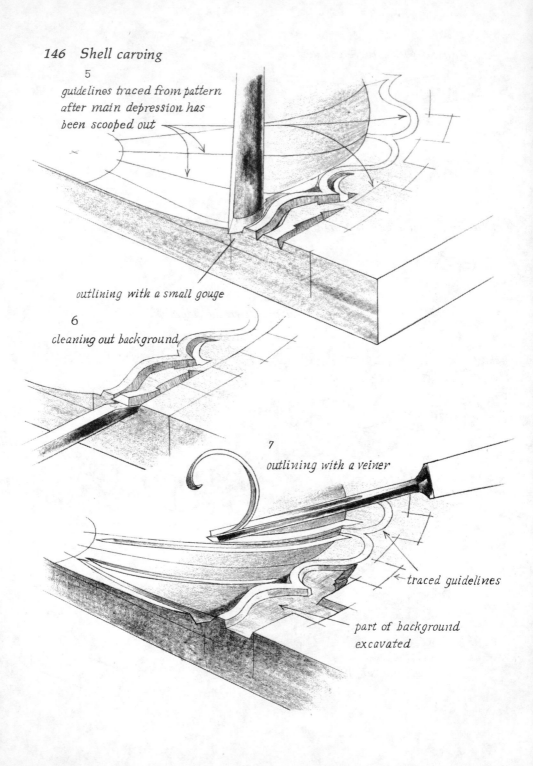

5

guidelines traced from pattern
after main depression has
been scooped out

outlining with a small gouge

6

cleaning out background

7

outlining with a veiner

← traced guidelines

part of background
excavated

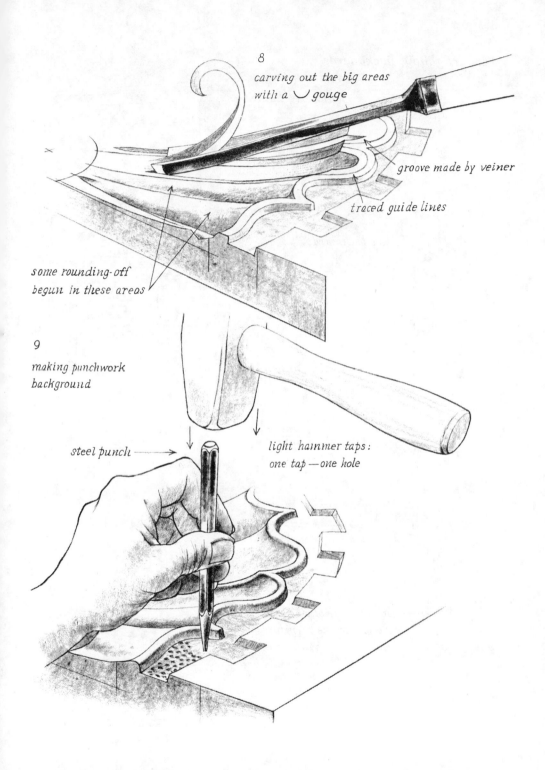

8

carving out the big areas
with a ⌣ gouge

groove made by veiner

traced guide lines

some rounding-off
begun in these areas

9

making punchwork
background

steel punch

light hammer taps:
one tap — one hole

hardware *attached*

pine *backboards*

*back legs were often made
straight so the furniture
would stand against the wall*

*backboard nailed
into rabbeted edge*

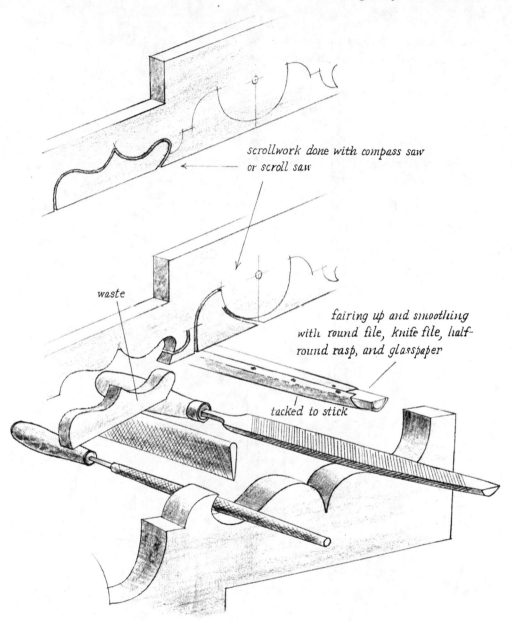

scrollwork done with compass saw
or scroll saw

waste

fairing up and smoothing
with round file, knife file, half-
round rasp, and glasspaper

tacked to stick

the mechanics of the mortise and tenon joint as
shown in assembling a table leg and stretcher

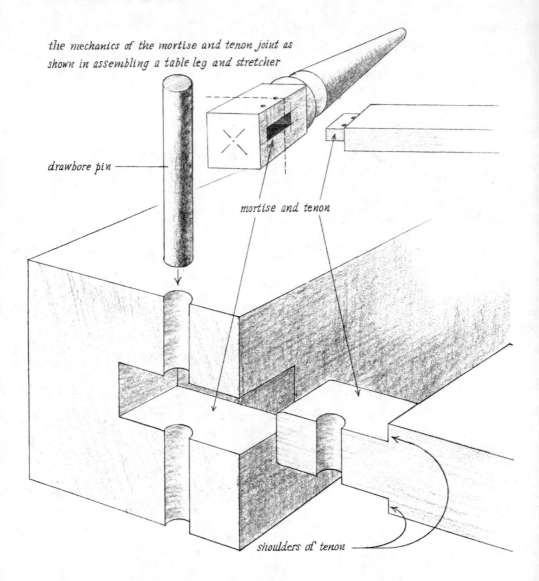

drawbore pin

mortise and tenon

shoulders of tenon

drawbore pin driven in part way,
but not engaged with tenon

joint driven together
"mallet tight"

the pinhole in tenon is intentionally bored closer to the
outside edge of the joint: as the pin is hammered home,
it draws the joint up tight, by means of this leverage

in a well-made joint, this crack
should be no bigger than a
needle scratch

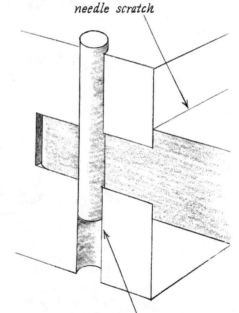

depth of mortise is made greater than length
of tenon — a pocket for any chips or sawdust
that otherwise could keep joint from closing

pins were not always full length —
especially when out of sight

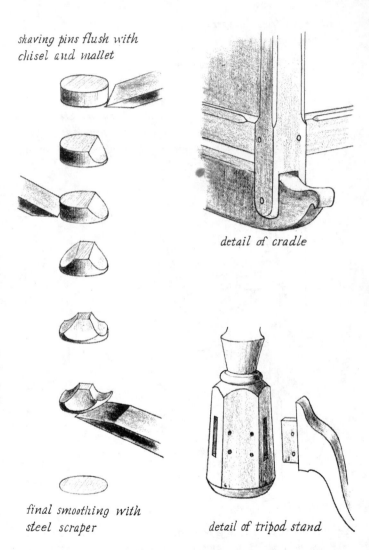

shaving pins flush with
chisel and mallet

detail of cradle

final smoothing with
steel scraper

detail of tripod stand

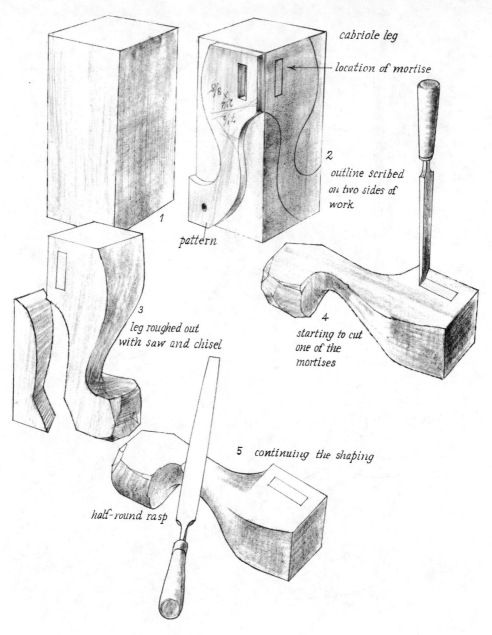

cabriole leg

location of mortise

2
outline scribed
on two sides of
work

pattern

1

3
leg roughed out
with saw and chisel

4
starting to cut
one of the
mortises

5 continuing the shaping

half-round rasp

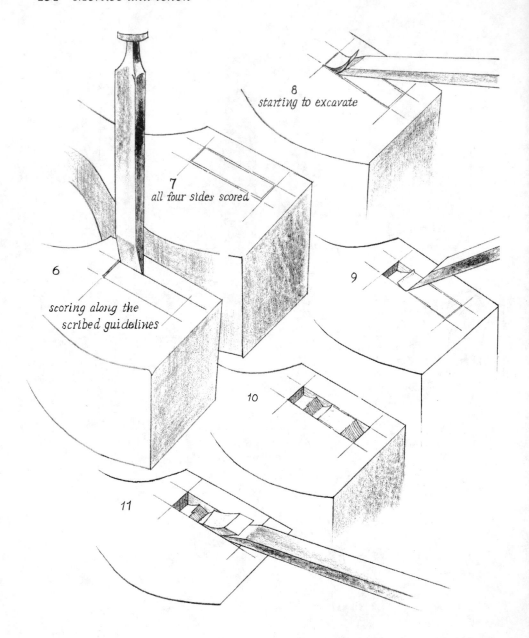

6   scoring along the scribed guidelines

7   all four sides scored

8   starting to excavate

9

10

11

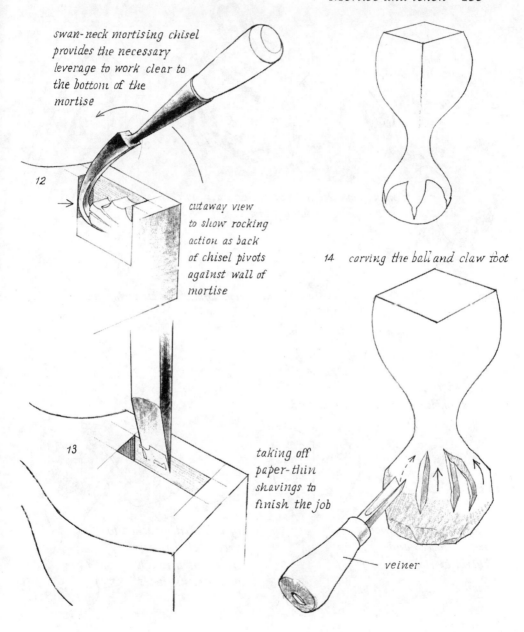

swan-neck mortising chisel
provides the necessary
leverage to work clear to
the bottom of the
mortise

12

cutaway view
to show rocking
action as back
of chisel pivots
against wall of
mortise

14   carving the ball and claw foot

13

taking off
paper-thin
shavings to
finish the job

veiner

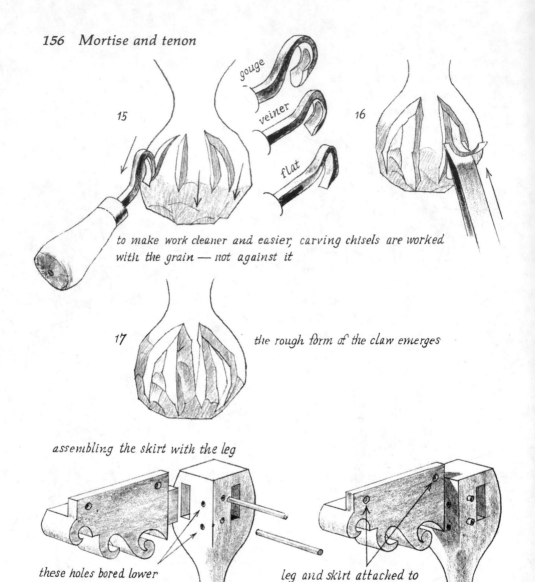

gouge

veiner

flat

15

16

to make work cleaner and easier, carving chisels are worked
with the grain — not against it

17

the rough form of the claw emerges

assembling the skirt with the leg

these holes bored lower
pegs will pass under those
shown at right

leg and skirt attached to
carcass of furniture by
screws put through
countersunk holes

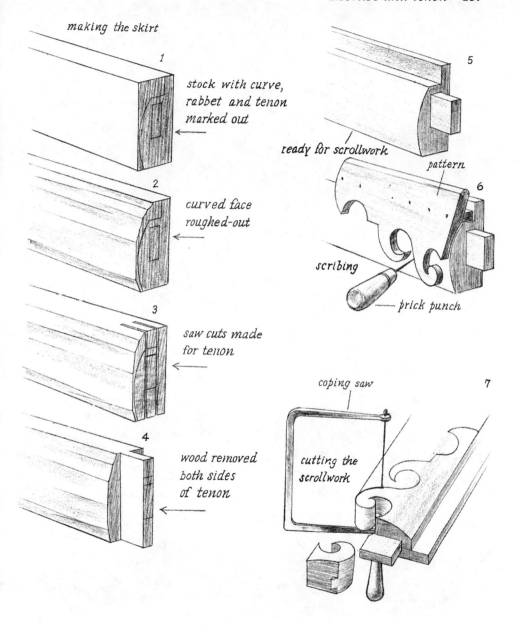

making the skirt

1

stock with curve, rabbet and tenon marked out

2

curved face roughed-out

3

saw cuts made for tenon

4

wood removed both sides of tenon

5

ready for scrollwork

pattern

6

scribing

prick punch

coping saw

7

cutting the scrollwork

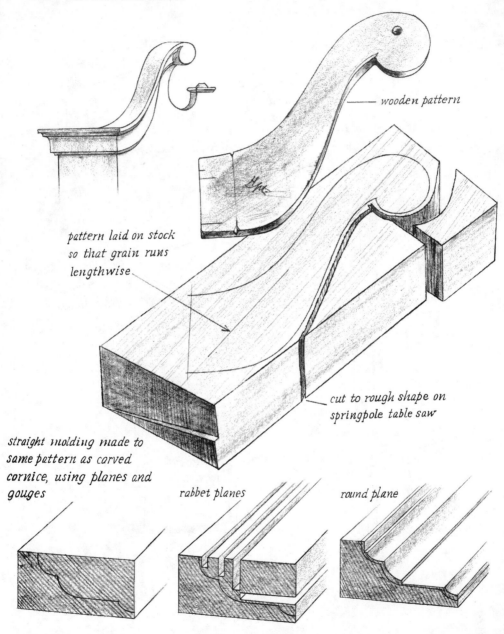

wooden pattern

pattern laid on stock
so that grain runs
lengthwise

cut to rough shape on
springpole table saw

straight molding made to
same pattern as carved
cornice, using planes and
gouges

rabbet planes

round plane

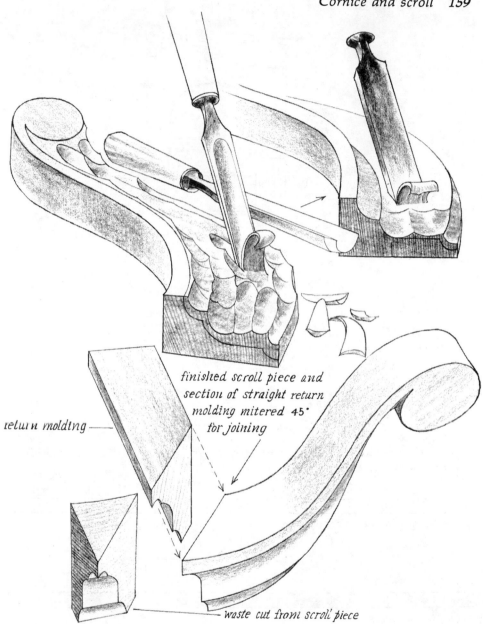

finished scroll piece and
section of straight return
molding mitered 45°
for joining

return molding

waste cut from scroll piece

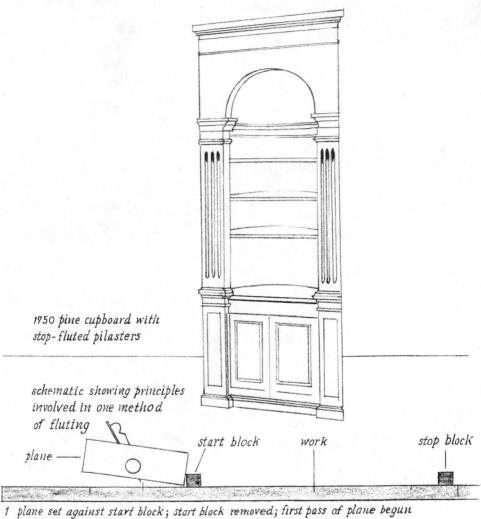

1750 pine cupboard with
stop-fluted pilasters

schematic showing principles
involved in one method
of fluting

plane ———

start block   work   stop block

1 plane set against start block; start block removed; first pass of plane begun

2 planing continues

3   *plane strikes stop block*

4   *plane lifted off — ready for next pass as in diagram   1*

5   *stop flutes touched up with gouge*   *last inch or so*

the board, or work, is cut off after all flutes are cut

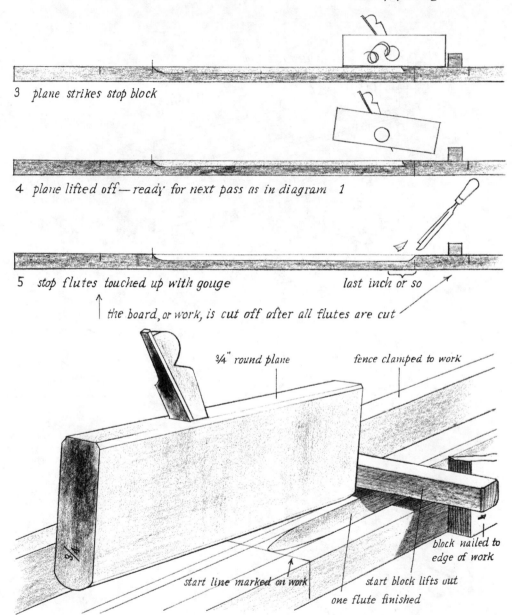

¾" round plane   *fence clamped to work*

block nailed to edge of work

start line marked on work   *start block lifts out*

one flute finished

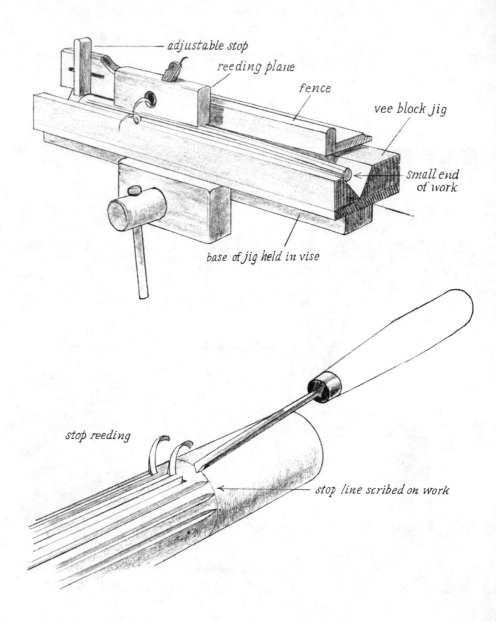

adjustable stop

reeding plane

fence

vee block jig

small end of work

base of jig held in vise

stop reeding

stop line scribed on work

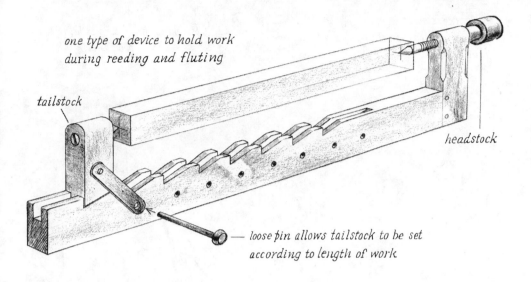

one type of device to hold work
during reeding and fluting

tailstock

headstock

loose pin allows tailstock to be set
according to length of work

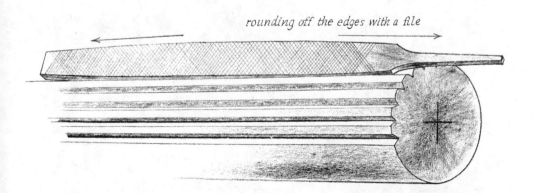

rounding off the edges with a file

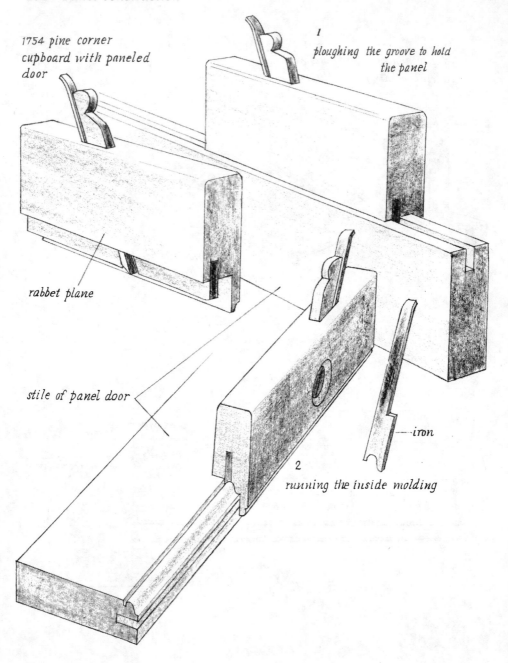

1754 pine corner cupboard with paneled door

ploughing the groove to hold the panel

1

rabbet plane

stile of panel door

iron

2

running the inside molding

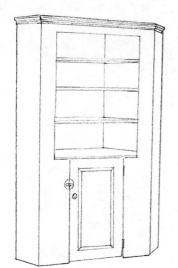

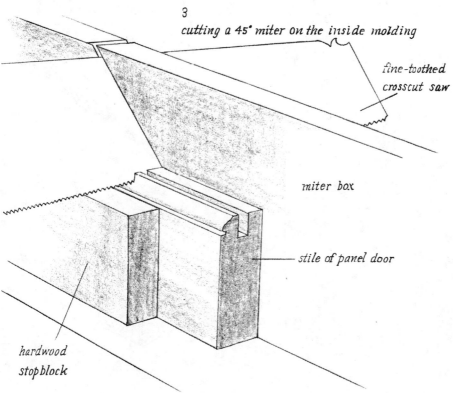

3

cutting a 45° miter on the inside molding

fine-toothed crosscut saw

miter box

stile of panel door

hardwood stop block

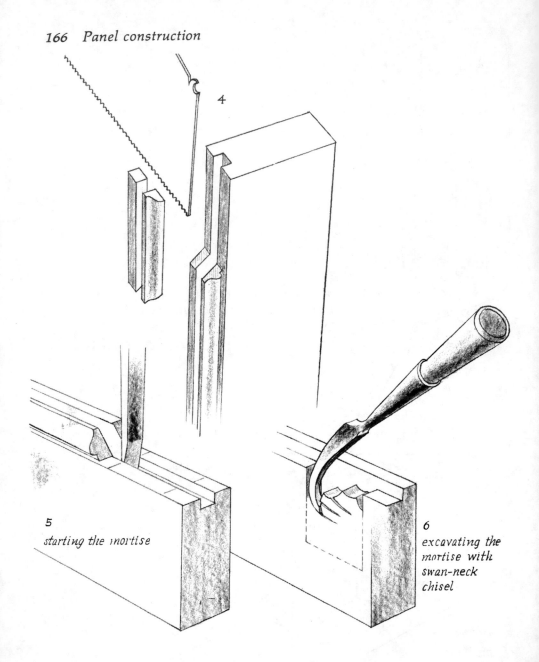

4

5
starting the mortise

6
excavating the mortise with swan-neck chisel

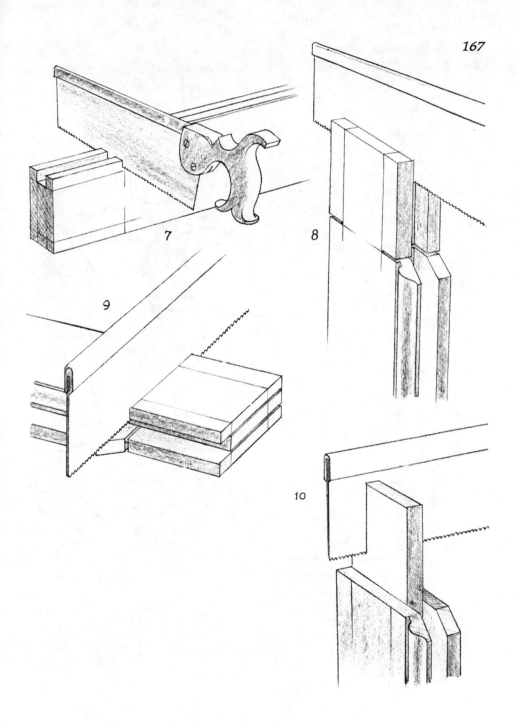

7

8

9

10

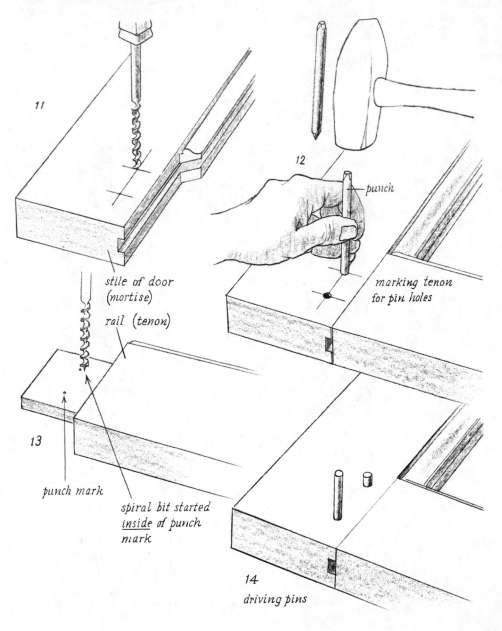

11

stile of door
(mortise)

rail (tenon)

13

punch mark

spiral bit started
inside of punch
mark

12

punch

marking tenon
for pin holes

14
driving pins

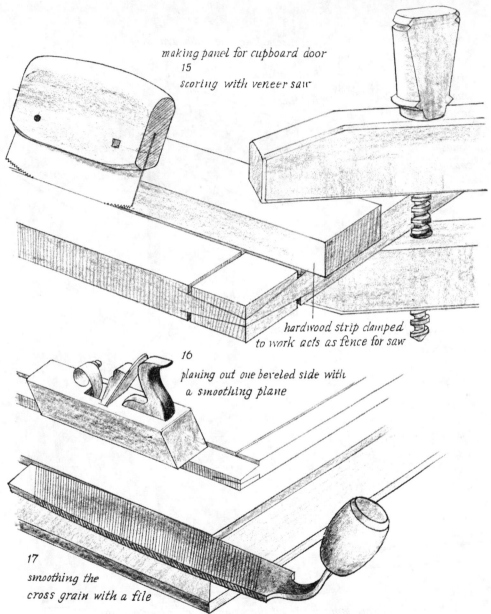

making panel for cupboard door
15
scoring with veneer saw

hardwood strip clamped
to work acts as fence for saw

16
planing out one beveled side with
a smoothing plane

17
smoothing the
cross grain with a file

18

assembling the cupboard door

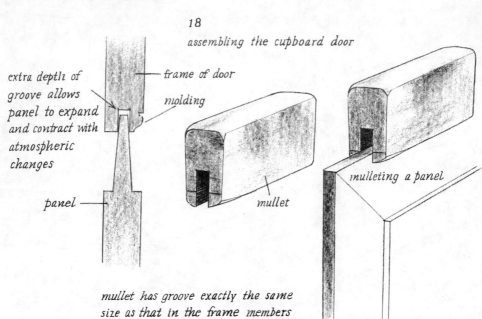

frame of door

extra depth of
groove allows
panel to expand
and contract with
atmospheric
changes

molding

panel

mullet

mulleting a panel

mullet has groove exactly the same
size as that in the frame members
and is used to get the beveled edges of panels the
correct thickness

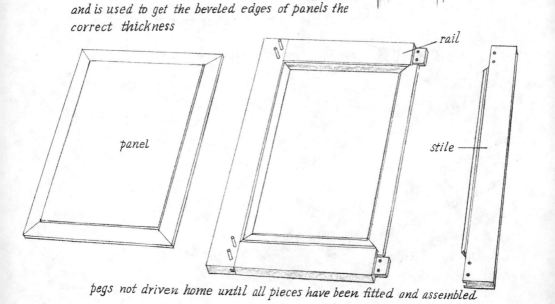

rail

panel

stile

pegs not driven home until all pieces have been fitted and assembled

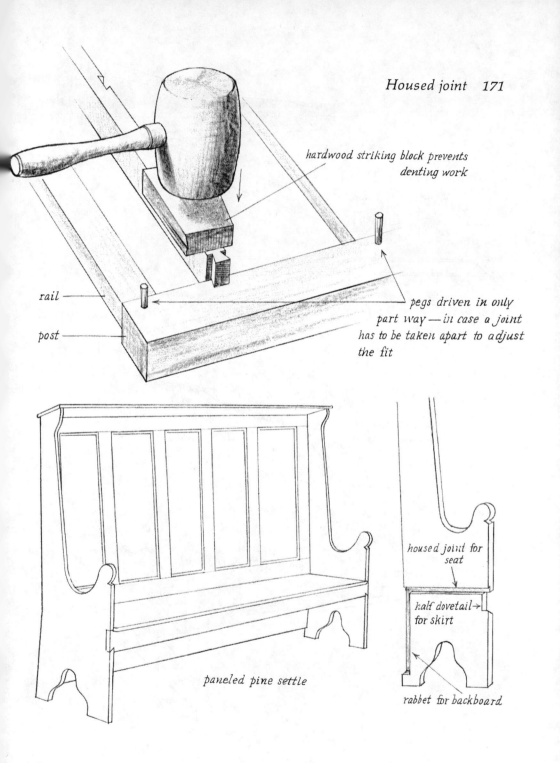

hardwood striking block prevents
denting work

pegs driven in only
part way — in case a joint
has to be taken apart to adjust
the fit

rail

post

paneled pine settle

housed joint for
seat

half dovetail →
for skirt

rabbet for backboard

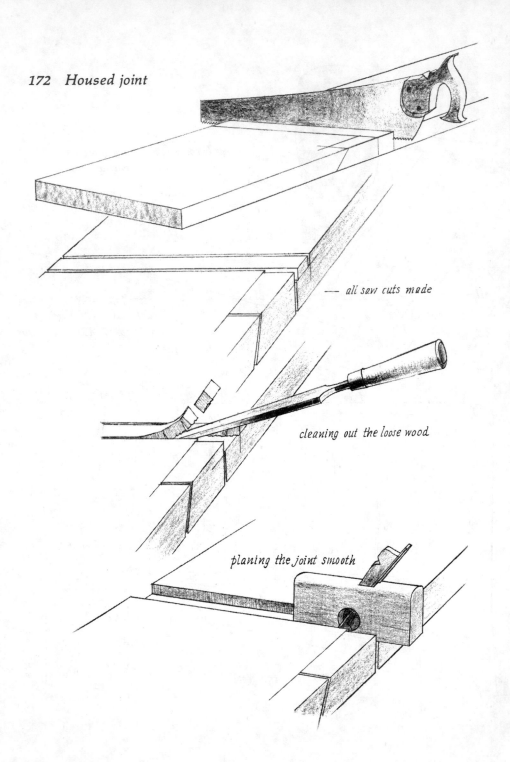

all saw cuts made

cleaning out the loose wood

planing the joint smooth

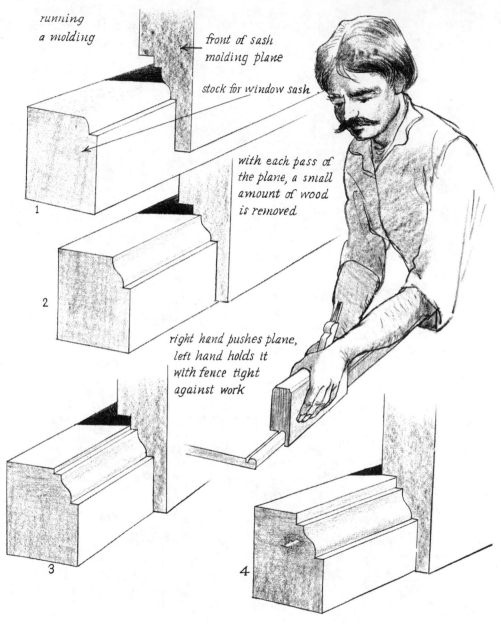

*running
a molding*

*front of sash
molding plane*

stock for window sash

*with each pass of
the plane, a small
amount of wood
is removed*

*right hand pushes plane,
left hand holds it
with fence tight
against work*

1

2

3

4

making muntins for window sash

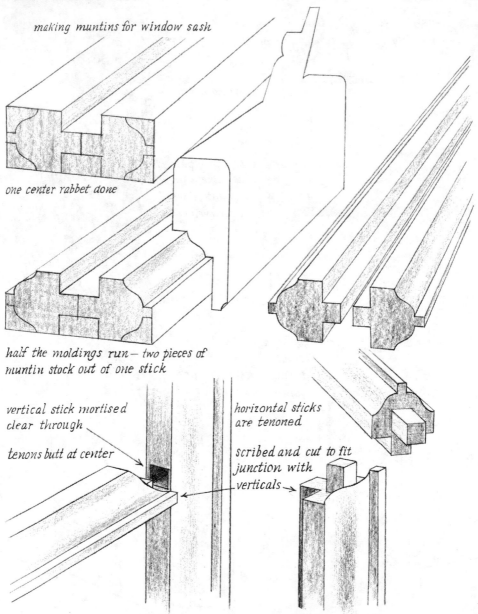

one center rabbet done

*half the moldings run — two pieces of
muntin stock out of one stick*

*vertical stick mortised
clear through*

*horizontal sticks
are tenoned*

tenons butt at center

*scribed and cut to fit
junction with
verticals*

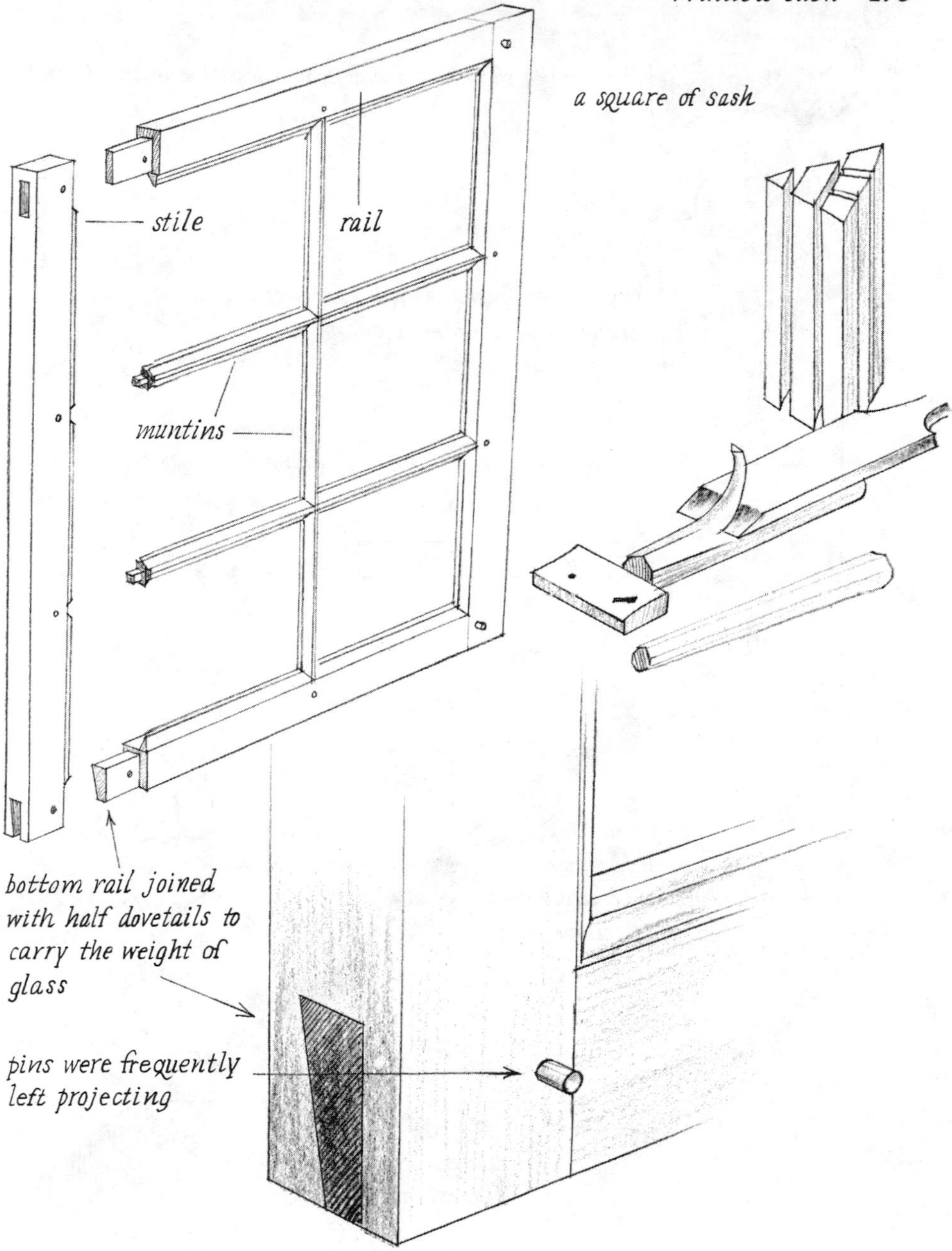

a square of sash

— *stile*

rail

muntins —

*bottom rail joined
with half dovetails to
carry the weight of
glass*

*pins were frequently
left projecting*

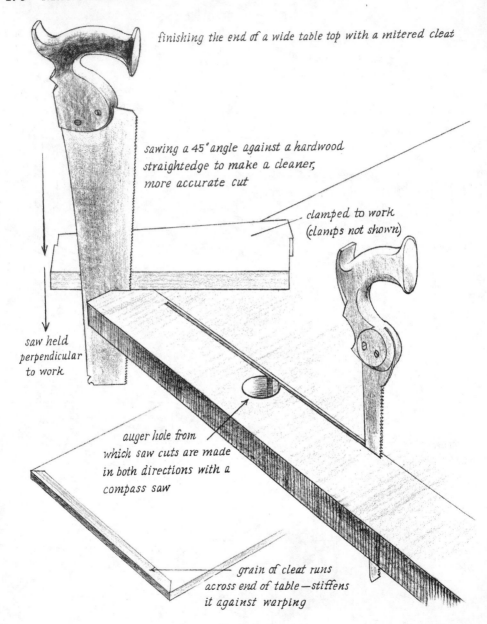

finishing the end of a wide table top with a mitered cleat

sawing a 45° angle against a hardwood
straightedge to make a cleaner,
more accurate cut

clamped to work
(clamps not shown)

saw held
perpendicular
to work

auger hole from
which saw cuts are made
in both directions with a
compass saw

grain of cleat runs
across end of table—stiffens
it against warping

truing up end grain edge of table top with a rasp

table top

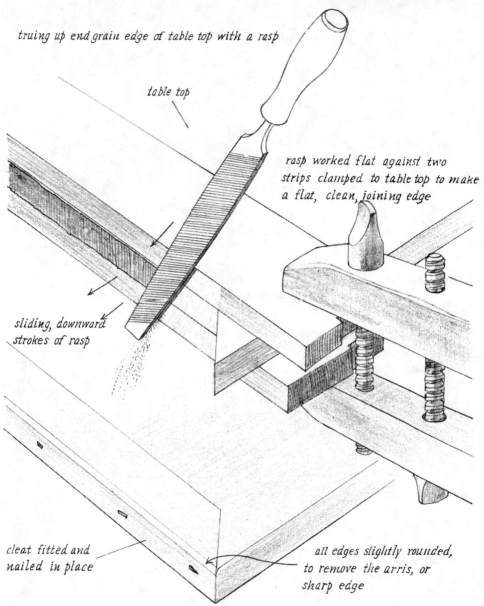

rasp worked flat against two
strips clamped to table top to make
a flat, clean, joining edge

sliding, downward
strokes of rasp

cleat fitted and
nailed in place

all edges slightly rounded,
to remove the arris, or
sharp edge

clock case finial of wood

ball and spike turned with
a dowel base to fit socket
in the cupola base

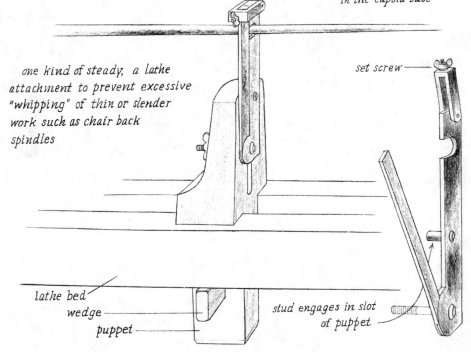

one kind of steady, a lathe
attachment to prevent excessive
"whipping" of thin or slender
work such as chair back
spindles

set screw

lathe bed

wedge

puppet

stud engages in slot
of puppet

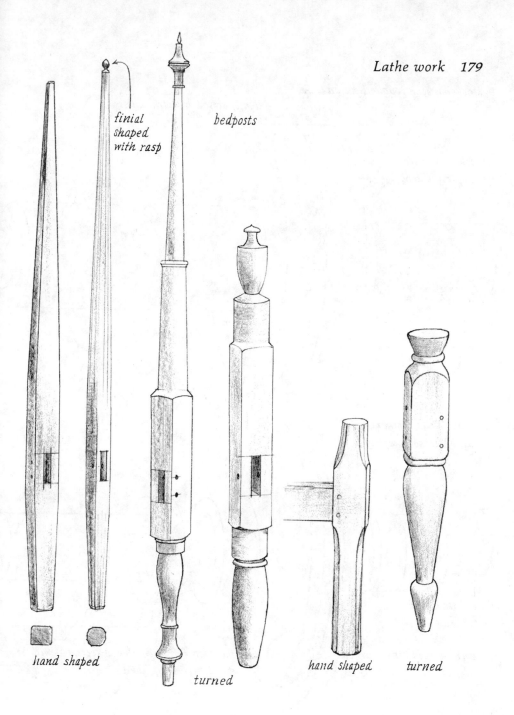

finial
shaped
with rasp

bedposts

hand shaped

turned

hand shaped

turned

1 stock has been roughed-out on lathe

— lightly scored to mark center

depthened in with parting tool

rotation of lathe —

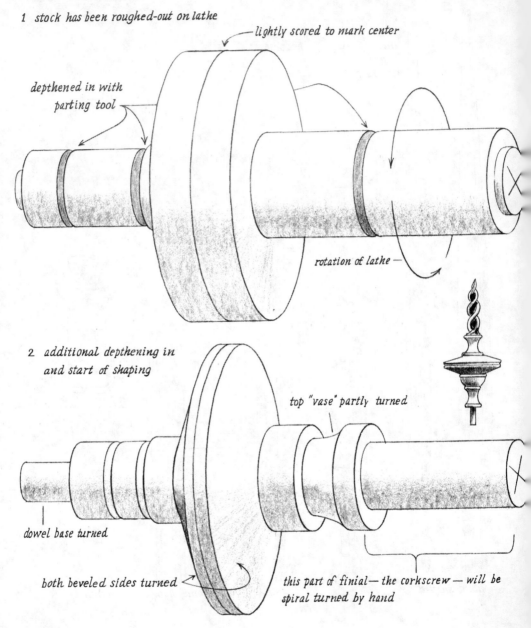

2 additional depthening in and start of shaping

top "vase" partly turned

dowel base turned

both beveled sides turned

this part of finial — the corkscrew — will be spiral turned by hand

3

finished except to round edges

lightly scored to mark edge of ring

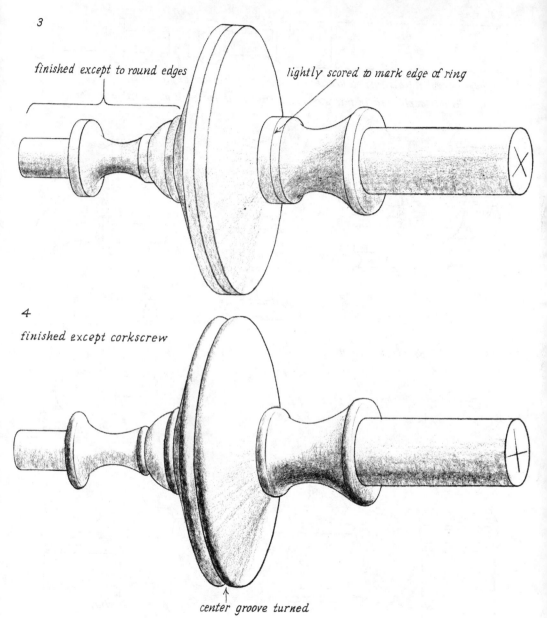

4

finished except corkscrew

center groove turned

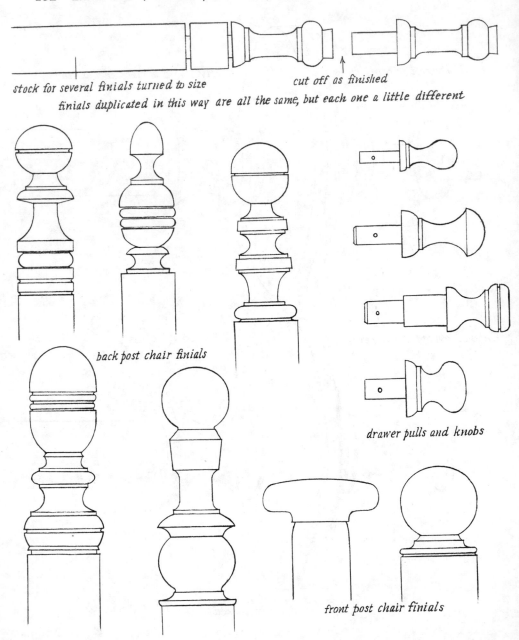

stock for several finials turned to size   *cut off as finished*

finials duplicated in this way are all the same, but each one a little different

back post chair finials

drawer pulls and knobs

front post chair finials

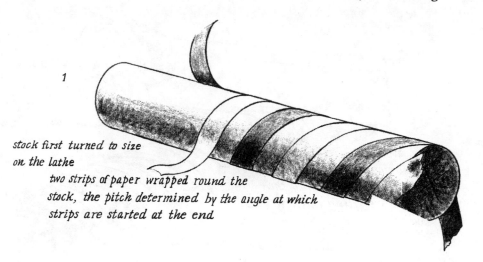

1

stock first turned to size
on the lathe

   two strips of paper wrapped round the
stock, the pitch determined by the angle at which
strips are started at the end

lines traced onto wood along
edges of both strips of paper, and a
heavier, center line plotted spirally from one
end of the stick to the other

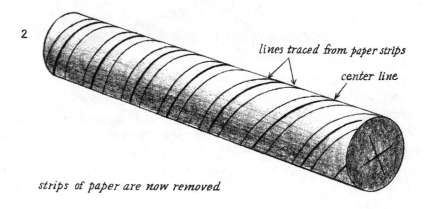

2

lines traced from paper strips

center line

strips of paper are now removed

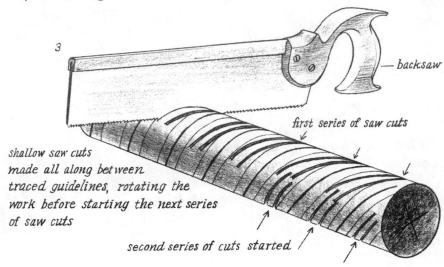

3

— *backsaw*

first series of saw cuts

shallow saw cuts
made all along between
traced guidelines, rotating the
work before starting the next series
of saw cuts

second series of cuts started

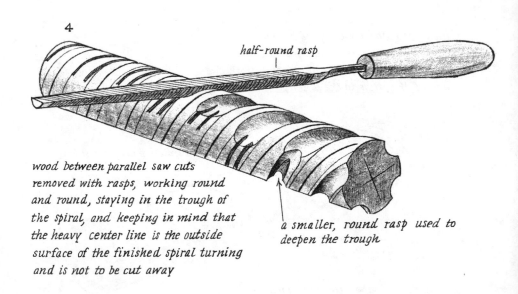

4

half-round rasp

wood between parallel saw cuts
removed with rasps, working round
and round, staying in the trough of
the spiral, and keeping in mind that
the heavy center line is the outside
surface of the finished spiral turning
and is not to be cut away

a smaller, round rasp used to
deepen the trough

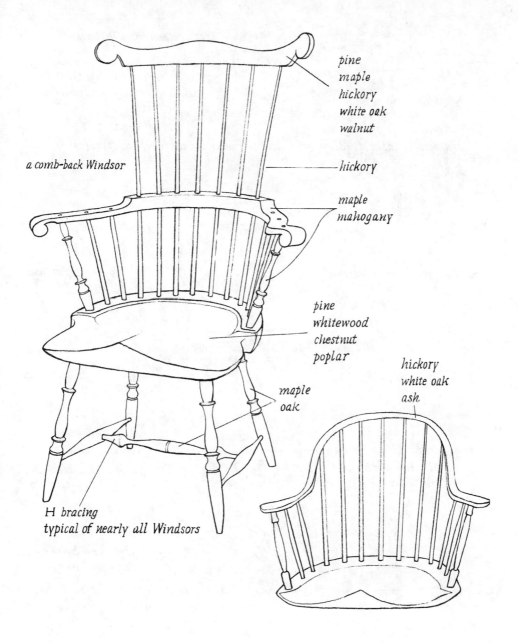

pine
maple
hickory
white oak
walnut

a comb-back Windsor

hickory

maple
mahogany

pine
whitewood
chestnut
poplar

hickory
white oak
ash.

maple
oak

H bracing
typical of nearly all Windsors

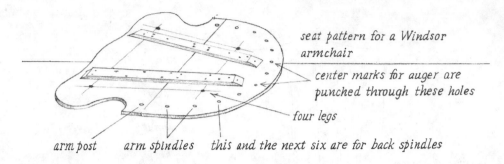

seat pattern for a Windsor
armchair

center marks for auger are
punched through these holes

four legs

arm post   arm spindles   this and the next six are for back spindles

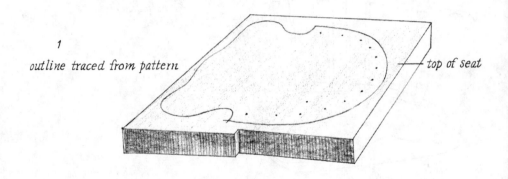

1

outline traced from pattern   top of seat

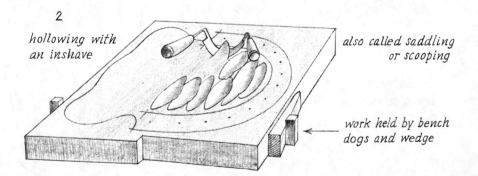

2

hollowing with
an inshave

also called saddling
or scooping

work held by bench
dogs and wedge

3

front contour has been sawed out
so that shaping of the ears can
be done with the drawknife —
when shaping of the seat is finished,
back contour will be sawed out

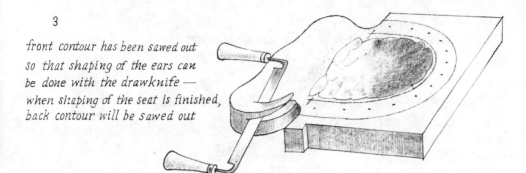

4

shaping of seat finished, holes bored, waste wood removed, and channeling done

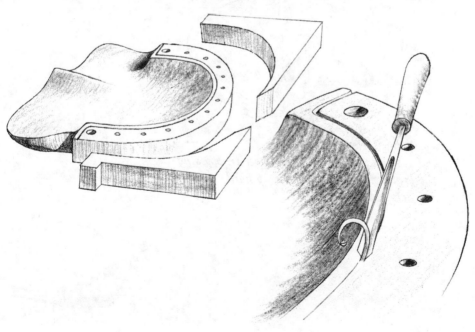

5

assembling legs, stretcher, and seat bottom side up

these four pieces put together as a unit and then attached to seat

this unit attached last

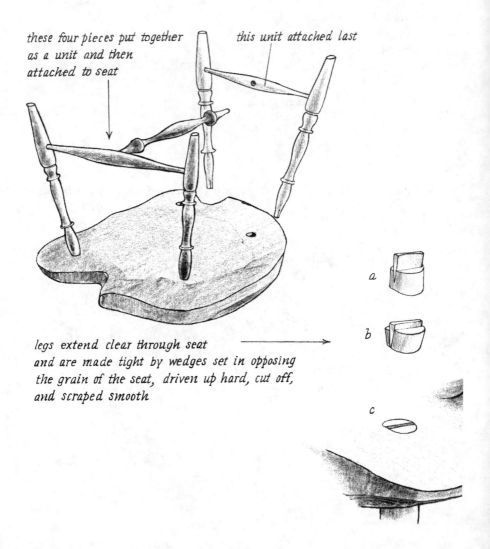

legs extend clear through seat and are made tight by wedges set in opposing the grain of the seat, driven up hard, cut off, and scraped smooth

a

b

c

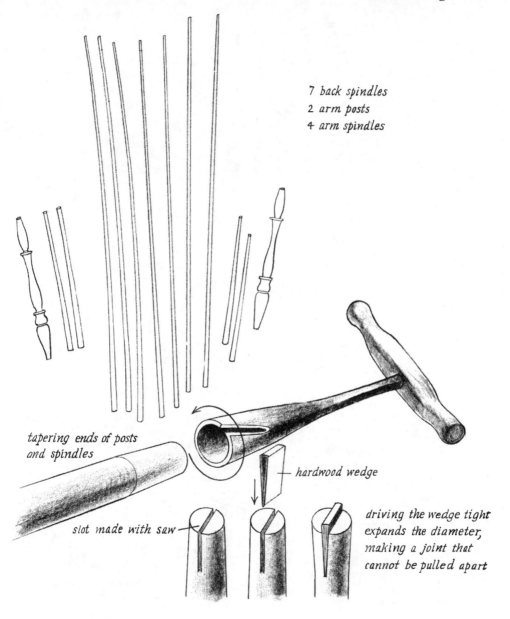

7 back spindles
2 arm posts
4 arm spindles

tapering ends of posts
and spindles

hardwood wedge

slot made with saw

driving the wedge tight
expands the diameter,
making a joint that
cannot be pulled apart

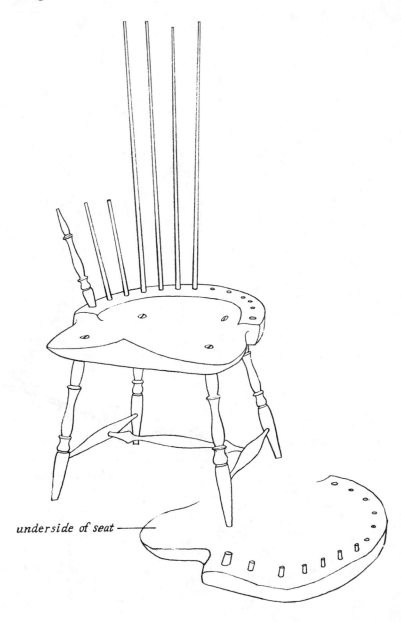

underside of seat

*the spindles will spread
and fan out when the
comb is put on — the
final operation*

*working the arms down
over the back spindles*

*spindles and arm posts
must all be "worried"
into their respective sockets
pretty much at the
same time*

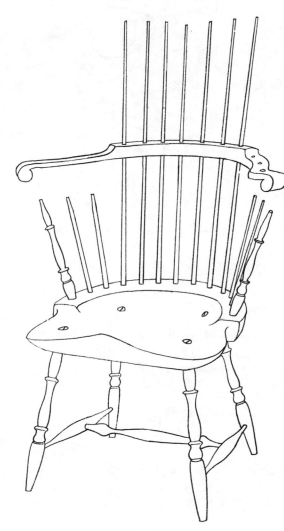

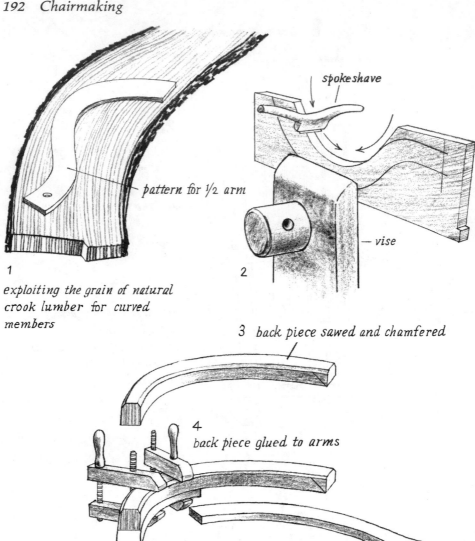

pattern for ½ arm

1

exploiting the grain of natural
crook lumber for curved
members

spokeshave

2

— vise

3 back piece sawed and chamfered

4
back piece glued to arms

holes for spindles bored _after_ gluing

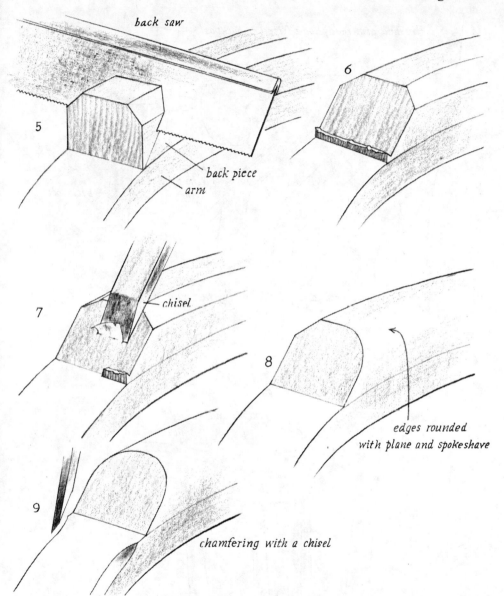

back saw

5

back piece

arm

6

7

chisel

8

edges rounded
with plane and spokeshave

9

chamfering with a chisel

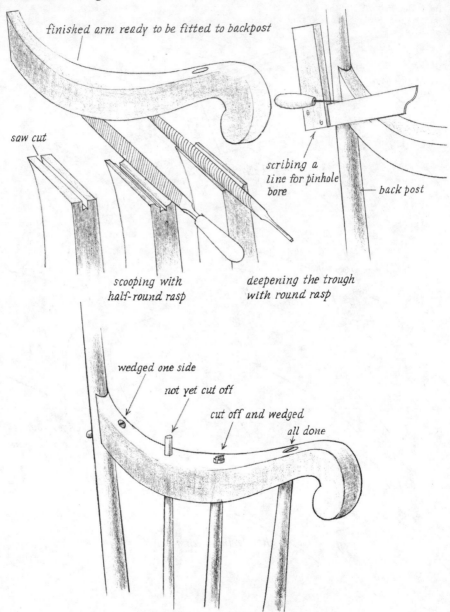

finished arm ready to be fitted to backpost

saw cut

scribing a
line for pinhole
bore

back post

scooping with
half-round rasp

deepening the trough
with round rasp

wedged one side

not yet cut off

cut off and wedged

all done

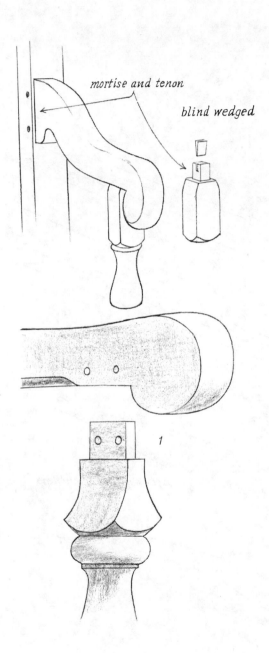

mortise and tenon

blind wedged

1

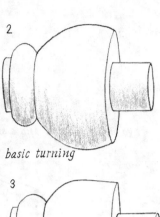

2

basic turning

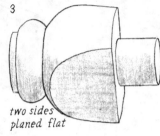

3

two sides planed flat

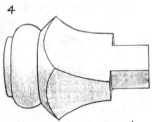

4

opposing sides scooped

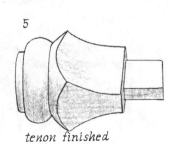

5

tenon finished

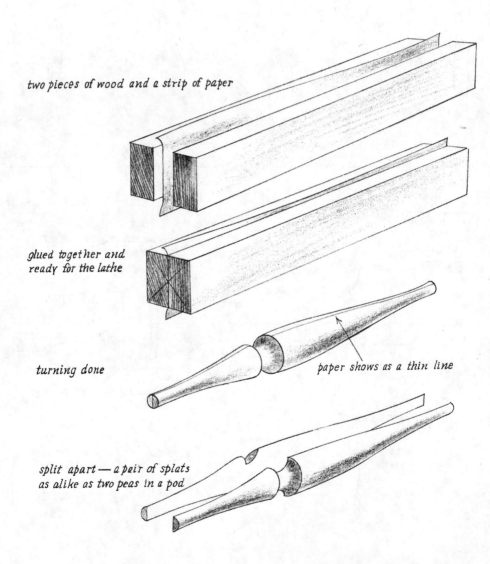

two pieces of wood and a strip of paper

glued together and
ready for the lathe

turning done

paper shows as a thin line

split apart — a pair of splats
as alike as two peas in a pod

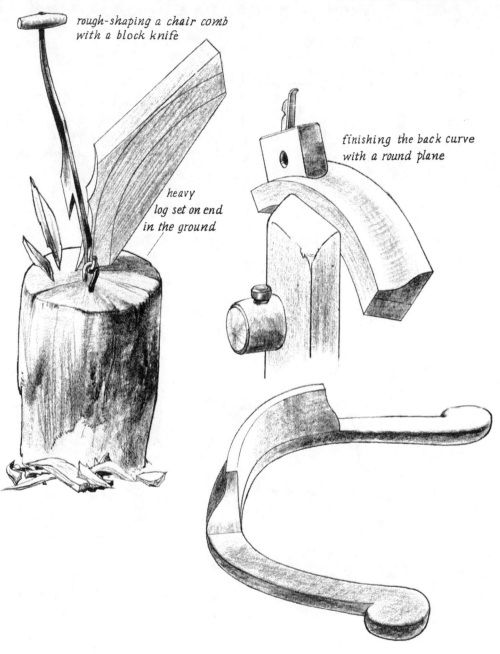

rough-shaping a chair comb
with a block knife

finishing the back curve
with a round plane

heavy
log set on end
in the ground

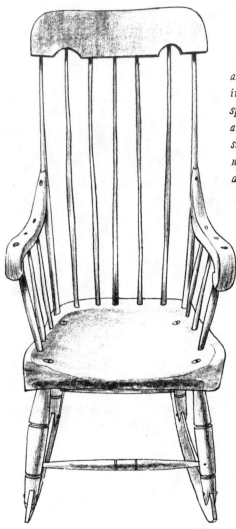

*a country rocker with
irregular, whittled back
spindles of hickory and
a general lack of cabinetmaking
sophistication that is
nevertheless comfortable
and well put together*

arms steamed and bent

carved knuckles

one type of small steam box for bentwork

*loading door— closed
during steaming*

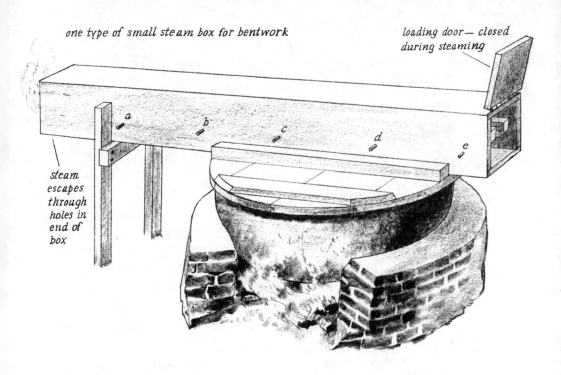

*steam
escapes
through
holes in
end of
box*

*steam generated in iron kettle enters box through apertures in box;
circulates around pieces suspended on iron bars a, b, c, d, e, and
escapes through vent holes in far end of box*

*steam boxes of this same general type
are still in use today in ship and boat yards
where wooden vessels are built*

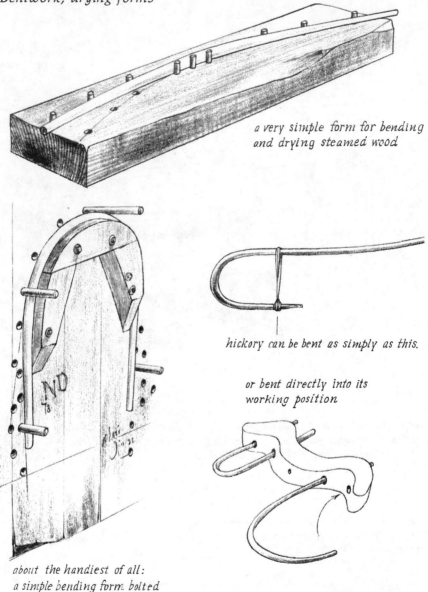

a very simple form for bending and drying steamed wood

hickory can be bent as simply as this.

or bent directly into its working position

about the handiest of all: a simple bending form bolted to the shop wall — and plenty of holes to spare!

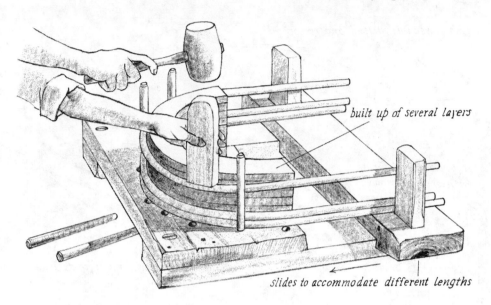

built up of several layers

slides to accommodate different lengths

heavy form for preparing several pieces at the same time

simplified drawing of a 17ᵗʰ century Italian harpsichord, showing main structural elements of the frame

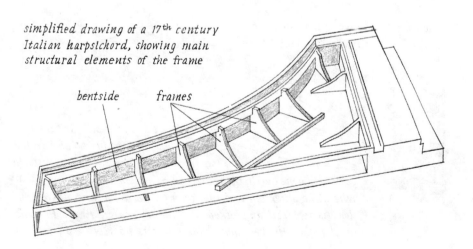

bentside   *frames*

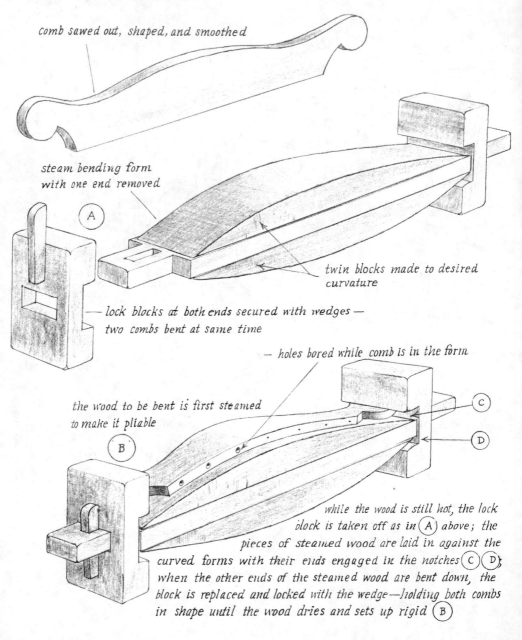

comb sawed out, shaped, and smoothed

steam bending form
with one end removed

Ⓐ

twin blocks made to desired
curvature

— lock blocks at both ends secured with wedges —
two combs bent at same time

— holes bored while comb is in the form

the wood to be bent is first steamed
to make it pliable

Ⓑ

Ⓒ

Ⓓ

while the wood is still hot, the lock
block is taken off as in Ⓐ above; the
pieces of steamed wood are laid in against the
curved forms with their ends engaged in the notches Ⓒ Ⓓ;
when the other ends of the steamed wood are bent down, the
block is replaced and locked with the wedge—holding both combs
in shape until the wood dries and sets up rigid Ⓑ

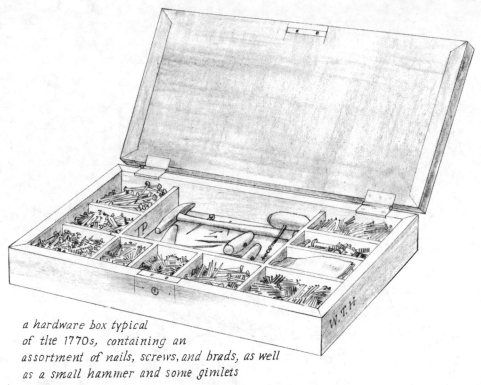

*a hardware box typical
of the 1770s, containing an
assortment of nails, screws, and brads, as well
as a small hammer and some gimlets*

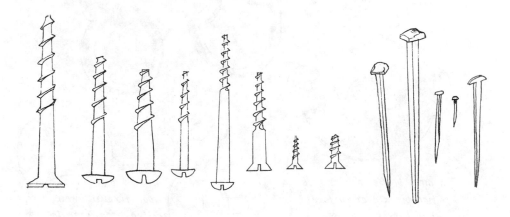

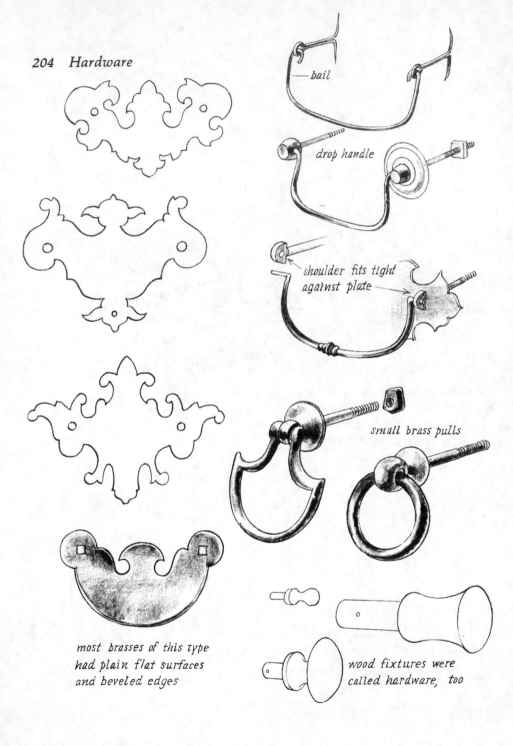

bail

drop handle

shoulder fits tight
against plate

small brass pulls

most brasses of this type
had plain flat surfaces
and beveled edges

wood fixtures were
called hardware, too

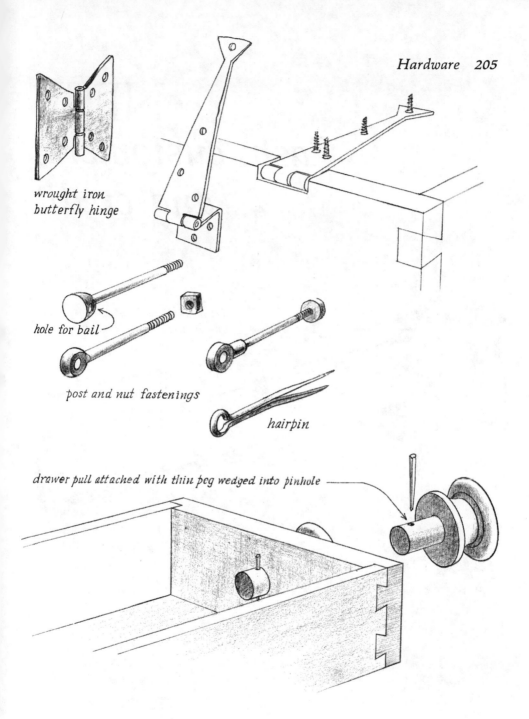

wrought iron
butterfly hinge

hole for bail

post and nut fastenings

hairpin

drawer pull attached with thin peg wedged into pinhole

NINE
Cash, customers, and credit

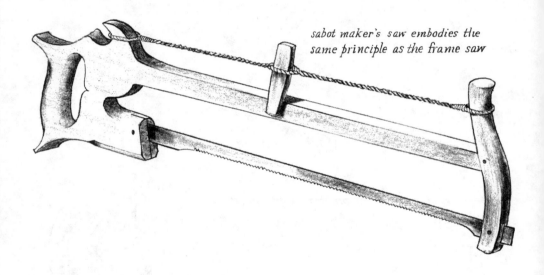

*sabot maker's saw embodies the
same principle as the frame saw*

Most country furniture was made to order, whether by rural husbandmen, full-time cabinetmakers, or itinerant journeymen. Although numerous deeds, wills, and other legal documents show that completely finished pieces of furniture were left behind, it is probable that they were undelivered orders and not part of a built-up inventory.

The country furniture maker had a mere handful of customers—his own family, the close neighbors, and perhaps the villagers in the next town. But as the urgency of life in the colonies eased a bit, permitting more serious concentration on trade as such, the furniture maker found his clientele increasing. Bedford was one of the New Hampshire towns in the Dunlap territory. There were 93 frame houses in all; each one housing an average of 8 people, which accounted for a theoretical market of 744 potential users of furniture. Even if some of these families made their own furniture—and perhaps some did—there remained a good number of customers, which was greatly increased by counting the population in nearby towns. For example, in the five major towns where the Dunlaps worked, there were a total of over 5,000 people:

New Hampshire Towns	1790*
Antrim	528
Bedford	744
Goffstown	1,275
Henniker	1,127
Salisbury	1,372
	5,046

In East Hampton, New York, at the time the Dominys were working there, a head-count occupation analysis of the entire village showed a total population of 2,000, of which 549 were engaged in agriculture, 116 in manufacturing and the trades, 106 in some kind of maritime occupation, 8 in commerce, 7 in the professions and engineering, and 3 were pensioners from the Revolutionary War or some other military action. A good many of these people were surely Dominy customers, yet this local population alone was not sufficient to provide support for the several family craftsmen. The Dominys were 112 miles from New York City—isolated on the eastern end of Long Island, but they were enterprising enough to have enlarged their market and overcome this geographic handicap. Their furniture and clocks, as well as their clock-repairing services, found ready acceptance in Connecticut across Long Island Sound, and farther down the Island on both the north and south shores. They had

*See "Sawdust and shavings" 13: Furniture Made by Dunlap Family.

customers in the Connecticut towns of Haddam, Hartford, Lyme, New Haven, and Stonington; and in Moriches, Patchogue, Quogue, and Smithtown on Long Island. A circle drawn around these villages encompassed a fairly impressive sales territory.

At least until the advent of the steamboat, Dominy furniture could be had cheaper right in East Hampton than the same article shipped from New York by wagon or schooner. The size of their market was sufficiently large without New York; and they made good use of sail to deliver furniture to reasonably close destinations. The time came, however—and the steamboat appears to have hastened its arrival—when a furniture business that was as isolated as theirs could no longer compete with mainland craftsmen. This development may have been the principal cause for the decline in their trade.

The Dominys were a versatile lot, and that may have saved them from an even earlier decline. All of them—father, sons, and grandsons—were actively engaged not only as furniture makers but also as clockmakers, house builders, millwrights, turners, tool-makers, gunsmiths, surveyors, and farmers.* Naturally, not all of these trades were pursued simultaneously, though anyone of the family was capable of turning his hand to any of them. In addition to producing some 890 pieces of finished woodwork—and there were probably many more not recorded—the Dominys also made periodic circuits of the countryside, peddling and repairing clocks and watches, working from house to house in typical huckster fashion. To make these junkets as productive as possible, they published commercial notices in the local newspapers two or three months in advance, giving their expected itinerary. By this means they could deliver completed orders, pick up new ones along the advertised route, and at the same time repair a clock, glue a dresser drawer back together, or replace some missing chair rungs out of a small stock they carried along, before moving on to the next village.

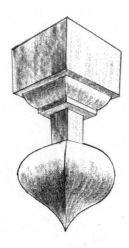

carved pendil from the Parson Capen house, Topsfield, Massachusetts, 1683 — an example of 17ᵗʰ century versatility

The clockmaking branch of their enterprise accounted for a considerable income, even though in the sixty years they worked only about ninety clocks have been tallied to their credit. A good clock took a long time to build—counting the works and the wooden case—and demanded a great many time-consuming operations. Their clocks brought prices ranging from $180 to more than $1,000, and were reputedly excellent timekeepers. Probably because of their many-faceted industry the Dominys may have devoted less time to farming than some other cabinetmakers. They rented out land that they themselves could not cultivate, generally the fields farthest from the house, accepting a share of the crops in lieu of cash rental. The so-called home lot adjacent to the dwelling was reserved to

*See "Sawdust and shavings" 14:   Diversity of Shop Work, Dominy Craftsmen.

produce what they could grow and harvest without diverting too much time from the workshops. And, as conditions required, various Dominy men supplemented the family income by hiring themselves out to work. From these various sources a fairly substantial annual revenue could be pieced together, over and above the bounty of the garden and some bartered commodities.*

Much of his business the country furniture maker transacted right in the shop. But he also relied on mail orders, shipping it when done by whatever means was practical: horse and wagon, schooner, and later by railroad. One Dominy customer, who evidently had a project under way, wrote Felix from Quogue, New York:

> *I will be down on Saturday—If you think you can make me the said Gunbox in the course of next week will you try to get out some oak stuff ready for it—It will require to be about 3' 6"—in the clear [clear lumber without knots]—as to the breadth I am not certain—Also if your father has any good stuff for shafts or you can get any from the Harbor, will you ask him to get out a pair 7' 6" long in readiness to put them together when I return—I am aware that nothing more can be done til he has the waggon but my arrangements are such that I wish them painted and dried during the week—and every little helps.*

As with the Dominys' situation, geography affected the work of furniture makers in several ways: the number and variety of pieces they built, the kinds of wood at hand, and the prices they could ask. The larger and more prosperous the town, the greater the demand for furniture and the better the chance for a good price. The fancier styles produced by city cabinetmakers seem to have influenced the country workman very little. His way of life left him with virtually no leisure in which to study, and his contact with city ways was almost nonexistent. The occasional appearance of an itinerant peddler with a piece or two of "city-made" furniture may have been the only influence from the outside. And even so, there's nothing to say that the country furniture maker paid much attention to it.

Roads were generally bad, quite often in summer but nearly always in winter, as Timothy Dwight noted in another of his journal entries for 1810:

> *The next day we crossed the [Connecticut] river to Hadley; and on Friday the 22nd, we rode through Hatfield, Whately, Deerfield, Greenfield, Bernardston, and Gill, to Northfield: thirty-four miles. About two-thirds of the roads are good; of the remaining third, seven miles are a heavy sand, and the rest stony and rough.*

*See "Sawdust and shavings" 15: Typical Goods and Services.

Dwight wrote that many of the small bridge crossings were as rough as corduroy, gave a jolting ride, were unsafe, and when they broke through, went for months on end before repairs were made. Conditions like these persisted in New England for a great part of the year—hard-packed bumps in summer, impassably deep snows in the winter, and another long stretch of treachery while the mud season came and went. So general were the hazards of overland travel that funeral parties often could not reach either the church or the cemetery until spring—which gave rise to the proliferation of family burying lots right on the farm. So tedious was negotiation of these highways that communications between Virginia and London were faster than between New York and Boston.

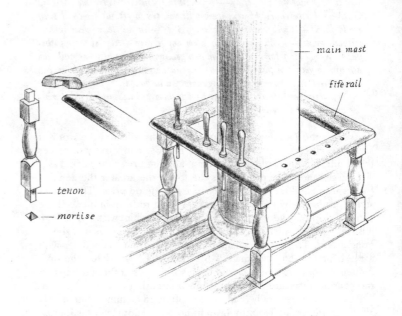

In the case of Portsmouth, New Hampshire, geography helped develop the market for furniture and other woodwork. The largest town in the state, it was a major seaport populated with scores of men connected with the maritime industries—shipbuilders, ship owners, outfitters, captains, tradesmen, and manufacturers of everything from nails to sails. They all needed furniture or the services of a good cabinetmaker who was equal to the quality work that these well-to-do people wanted and were prepared to buy. There was a tremendous amount of work in building a wooden ship, and every

sheet horse on a sailing vessel

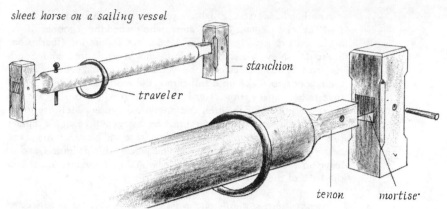

stanchion

traveler

tenon   *mortise·*

bit of it required skilled woodworkers. Even after the hull had been launched, the cabinetmakers went aboard to finish her off inside with handsome paneling, turned railings, and special fittings for the officers' quarters. Ashore it was no different: the liberal bank rolls of the seaport erected some of the stateliest homes in the country, and commissioned the carving of ships' figureheads and garden statues whose quality and taste rivaled the art of sculptors.*

Local trade in furniture increased steadily, and so did the export business. In one year more than five hundred chairs were shipped from New England to the West Indies, along with one hundred desks or so, several dozen tables, and nine cases of drawers—a volume of goods said to be comparable to the output of Philadelphia. The Salem, Massachusetts, firm of E. & J. Sanderson, of which Jacob Sanderson was a partner, exported furniture to Charleston, Baltimore, Savannah, the West Indies, and much farther away to South America and Africa.** The expansion of exports generally also meant an increase in imports. Ships did not return home empty, least of all to New England owners. There was an energetic trade in imported timber from several countries—a trade that started as early in American history as the 1670s. In *The Colonial Background of the American Revolution* Charles M. Andrews refers indirectly to this early shipping:

> *Thus before the end of the seventeenth century the sphere of English occupation in the New World encompassed more than twenty settlements, which extended from New England to Barbadoes.*

*See "Sawdust and shavings" 19:   Extracts from Invoice of 1807; 21:   Prices for Furniture and Carving.

**See "Sawdust and shavings" 18:   Partial Bill of Lading, Schooner *Ruth*.

Another Sanderson, Elijah, in partnership with Benjamin Swan, Joel Tay, and Captain John Waters, who owned the schooner *Molly*, made and exported furniture to Alexandria, Baltimore, Charleston, Savannah, New Orleans, the East and West Indies, and South America. It was the custom for several furniture makers to combine their goods to make up a full cargo, the work of recognized men sharing hold space with lesser known makers whose quality was not always as good. Elijah often commissioned Samuel McIntire to do carving, so it was not unnatural that he instructed the ship's captain to sell his stuff first: it was superior furniture and he meant to get the better price. Elijah usually branded his pieces with his initials, and to leave no doubt as to the terms of sale, would *write* the instructions on the back of the invoice:

> *Sometimes there is a difference in the goodness of the work and stock and when the whole is sold together at a particular rate . . . it is a disadvantage . . . therefore I wish you to sell mine by itself.*
> —MABEL MUNSON SWAN

But there were dozens of other furniture makers who profited from the brisk export trade too: John Cahoon and Silas Cook of Newport, Francis Pulcifer of Salem, and Job Clark of Newport, who made furniture that Cahoon shipped. In four years, Cahoon paid Clark something like £1,380—mainly for desks of cedar. Perhaps the biggest exporter—if long distance overland hauling qualifies—was Lambert Hitchcock, who by the year 1826 was operating a three-story brick furniture factory that employed one hundred men, women, and children; and who sent his chairs into very nearly every part of the country inhabited by white men.

And finally, the furniture maker, cabinetmaker, or joiner—call him what you will—held one other customer in high esteem: the church. Some richer, some poorer, they were mostly all built of solid wood, from the sills to the steeple spire, with delicate window sash, beautiful banisters, paneled pew boxes, doors, and graceful pulpits.

There were some furniture makers who had hired help, either in the shop itself or in the fields they worked, both of which had the effect of increasing the hours at the bench. Many of these hands were boys, simply paid by the day, or in some cases contracted for as apprentices. There were standard forms for these indenture contracts, frequently rewritten or changed to suit the individual situation, for the terms were not rigidly set.* Special conditions were added by writing them in, as in some of the agreements drawn up by Major John Dunlap. The stipulations he sometimes included went

*See "Sawdust and shavings" 20: Typical Form of Indenture Contract.

beyond the formal ones, perhaps because he himself worked continually with problems of arithmetic, trigonometry, and geometry; and, it would appear, he made provisions that would benefit the apprentice when it came time for him to strike out on his own, with the "obligation satisfied." For example, the concluding sentences of Dunlap's contract with one William Houston of Bedford, New Hampshire, stipulated that "at the End and Expiration of the Aforesaid time the Aforesaid John Dunlap is to Dismiss the said William from his service and help him to make the Wooden part of a set of tools fit for the trade."

Promising help could sometimes be found through word-of-mouth recommendations carried on the effective village grapevine. But newspapers were also used extensively, many of the advertisements combining with impartiality their wants for lumber with those for live help, and emphasizing the generous wages to be paid, though these were seldom mentioned:

Wanted by said Wadsworth as Apprentices to the above business, one or two likely Boys, 13 or 14 years old—Also to purchase, a quantity of square edged Whitewood Plank, from 18 to 20 inches wide.

Wanted from 18 to 15 Journeymen Cabinet and Chair-Makers to go to Charleston, South Carolina where they will receive generous encouragement for further particulars, apply to Capt. Joseph Baker, on Board the Sloop Romeo, *laying at the Coffee House Slip.*

Wanted Immediately a Journeyman Cabinet-Maker to whom good wages will be given. Enquire of John Valley, Tolland.

If all the parties got together for the drawing of a contract, everything was in order. But if the unforeseen happened and a dispute necessitated a cancellation of agreement, then the indenture could be voided simply by tearing off the part of the document that carried the signatures.

Newspaper advertisements were also widely used to hawk the cabinetmaker's wares, specified in rather spare terms, though not failing to mention quality, durability, and in some instances to give guarantees of one kind or another:

For Sale by Jacob Forster of Charleston 1400 field and high Maple bedposts, all turned of the best wood and in the newest mode for less than the turning will cost.

Cherry furniture. William Flagg Most respectfully informs his Friends and the Public in general, that he has taken a Shop, two doors North of Mr. Elisha Babcock's Printing Office—where he makes all kinds of Mahogany or Cherry Furniture—such as sideboards, selection of straight

Fronts, Easy chairs, Sofas, Secritaries, Bureaus, Oval Breakfast, all made in the neatest N. York fashions.

He will warrant his Work for 7 years, the ill usage of carless [careless] Servants only excepted.

They intend (if properly encouraged) to furnish every description of cabinetwork, elegant and common to fancy on agreeable terms. They make Heart-back Cherry Chairs from 7 to 9 dollars each; Windsor ditto from 8s to 15s each.

Pungs and sleighs; of any model on short notice. All kind of stuff fit for Cabinet or Shop work, received in payment.

In an advertisement that Lawrence Daniel ran in a Providence newspaper, he asserted:

He carries on the chair-making Business . . . in the newest and best Fashions, neat, elegant and strong, beautifully painted . . . warranted of good seasoned Material, so firmly put to-gether as not to deceive the Purchasers by an untimely coming to pieces.

Isaac Fowle and Edmund Raymond advertised that they had begun business in the shop formerly operated by the "late Mr. Skillin, where they intend to carry on House and Ship ornamental carving in its various branches."

And Thomas Ash advertised in a 1774 issue of the *New York Gazatteer* that at his place of business:

At the corner below St. Paul's Church in the Broad-Way, makes and sells all kinds of Windsor chairs . . . he has now by him, and intends keeping always a large quantity, so that merchants, masters of vessels, and others may be supplied upon the shortest notice. N.B. Shop goods will be taken in pay.

If a New York cabinetmaker could accept barter terms and announce the fact in the newspaper, then the inhabitants of rural towns and villages had been practicing the art for many years. Barter was a way of life, the most practical means of exchanging goods and services, particularly before, during, and just after the Revolution when currency was of unpredictable value. Farmers who took their produce to market were sometimes paid in cash, but generally the swapping system prevailed: so many cheeses for so many hides, a given weight in pork for a fair trade in sugar, tea, spices, and dry goods. If you had what the other fellow wanted, then both could be judged satisfied. Still, there were times when this method weighed out of balance:

> *We took oats, peas, butter, two cloth, flannel cloth &c. Why I have taken three and a half tons of butter in a single summer and autumn at ten cents a pound. It was hard getting anything out of it at that price. We used to get a big profit on our goods and that helped out. For two or three years after Ralph Jewett and I went into trade together, we sold $20,000 a year of dry goods. . . We built what is called the Loring Store the year that the railroad was built; and it cost $1,600. The first year we paid for the store, supported two families, and in addition to this a net profit of $2,600 . . . We bought prints in Boston at ten cents a yard and sold for a shilling. . . The people then had no expensive habits.*
>
> —CATHERINE FENNELLY: FROM JOURNAL OF LUCIUS LORING, STOREKEEPER, BROOKFIELD, MAINE, 1820

Of special interest to the furniture maker, lumber of all kinds was one of the most negotiable currencies at hand. The canny trader dickering with the customer had a good bargaining lever on his opponent to demand nothing but the best clear lumber—perhaps even greater than if he had been dealing in cash.

Country barter was not always consummated on the spot: the terms of the trade were set down in the ledger, to be collected or settled up at a later date, for example at harvest time if crops were part of the bargain. This required a fine faith and trust, which in the absence of evidence to the contrary seems to have worked well, and to everyone's benefit. In a small village where every inhabitant was known to every other, it had to be a mean character indeed who would try to back down on a barter agreement. As a consequence, tradesmen and cabinetmakers carried accounts of this sort for months on end. They would have found it difficult to give any accurate reckoning of their value at a moment's notice.*

A furniture maker might accept payment in the form of potatoes, and not collect until they were dug in the fall. Those same potatoes served him as payment to the sawmill for some "mapol bords," which when made up into a chest of drawers eventually might earn the furniture maker twenty days' labor from the man who bought the chest. This system generated the means of producing a tremendous amount of work. Counted as income, these goods, services, crops, and a dash of cash represented a very comfortable living.

A good source of steady income derived from the making of window sash, an item that showed up constantly in furniture makers' records. Windows were commonly made in two sections: the upper one fixed stationary in the window frame, with only the lower

*See "Sawdust and shavings" 16: Extracts from Account Book of John Dunlap.

section movable. Windows with both sections movable—the "double-hung" windows with sash weights—were a much later development. Each of these half sections was referred to as a "square of sash," entered in many account books as "Squars of Sash." Early windows made in the days when glass was thin and fragile had twelve pieces of glass in each section, an arrangement known as "twelve over twelve" sash. As the strength of glass was improved, sash was made eight over eight, six over six, and sometimes as twelve over six. Making sash took some time, as the work required numerous mortise and tenon joints and careful rabbeting of the muntins to receive the glass. Making the sash and setting the glass were generally considered two separate chores; and often the sash was delivered to the customer *without* glass. The entries in the account book for such a transaction would look something like this:

to *fifty Seven Squars of Sash*	£8	16	0
to *three pound of putte*	1	16	0
to *15 Squars of Sash and Seting*	3	6	8
to *Setting 52 Squars of Glass*	2	18	0

Attempts to make significant comparisons of the cost of various pieces of furniture are more than just difficult—they are frustrating, even when starting from the going rate for wages, which by the way were regulated by a kind of price control. Keeping track of the debits and credits was not the simplest work the furniture maker performed, when his only guide was the certainty that the monetary situation was thoroughly confused. Just how confusing can be seen in this quotation from *The Dunlaps & Their Furniture*:

There was rapid inflation between 1777 and 1781. Initially a paper dollar was equal to one silver dollar, but later it took one hundred and twenty paper "Continental dollars" to purchase a silver one.

From 1760 to 1775, one pound "old tenor" was equal to one shilling "lawful" (LM). In 1775, Congress issued a total of eight million dollars in "Continental money," which it promised to pay in "Spanish milled dollars" or the equivalent in gold or silver. This was assigned to the states for redemption, but New Hampshire had more paper money than it could redeem, and eventually this became worthless. With effect from January 1, 1795, legal money was to be in dollars, one United States dollar equal to six shillings "lawful."

Nevertheless, life went on. The more successful furniture makers were substantial, upper middle class people whose real estate holdings and personal property valuations were slightly above the average. In spite of this, there was the customary shaking of heads over the oppression of the times:

> *Hard times—High rents and high prices for everything we eat and wear are themes of universal complaint. Bacon, beef, veal, lamb, poultry, eggs, butter and all the little et ceteras of the table, are double former prices. . . Cut down every useless expense and useless indulgence: get up an hour sooner in the morning, and go to bed an hour later at night; work in a little additional elbow grease during the day, and if blessed with health, the poorest among us may soon bid defiance . . . to debts, duns and difficulties in the bargain.*
>
> —PHOENIX, SEPTEMBER 23, 1836

These "high prices" may strike us today as comical until the true value of the old dollar is taken into account:

1 bushel salt	*$1.12*
1 cake soap	*.05*
1 bushel corn	*1.00*
1 barrel cider	*1.25*
1 pound dried apples	*.06*
1 dozen eggs	*.10*
1 bushel potatoes	*.30*

Furniture makers, like everyone else, prospered or failed, accumulated wealth or a parcel of debts, raised families, were subject to taxation, and when the time came—died. Perhaps then and only then, with his will probated and his estate settled, could a true and accurate appraisal be made of his actual worth. For example, Christian Selzer left an estate of $30,000; John Jackson Jarves, a cabinetmaker and chairmaker, left his wife and children the sum of $25,000, and in addition, six buildings; in Boston, the estate of John Cogswell was valued at $4,218.65; and a bequest large enough to found Bacon Academy was paid out of the estate of Pierpont Bacon, a trained house joiner who, at the age of twenty-one "betook himself to Colchester on foot with his tools on his back," and prospered in his trade.

TEN
Sawdust and shavings

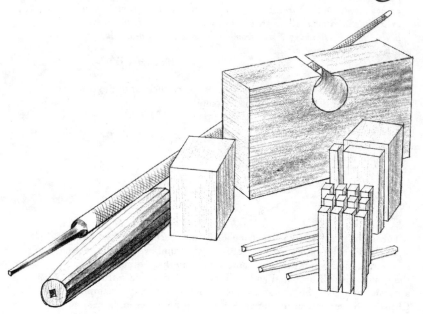

1

CRAFTSMEN OF SUFFIELD, CONNECTICUT c. 1700

Carpenters	28
Furniture makers	13
Joiners	12
Chairmakers	5
Dish turners	5
Housewrights	5
Wheelwrights	2
Woodworkers	2
Carriage makers	1

2

PART-TIME OCCUPATIONS OF FURNITURE MAKERS

Cabinetmaker	Millwright
Carpenter	Piano case maker
Carver	Pound keeper
Case maker (clocks)	Sawyer
Chairmaker	Selectman
Coffin maker	Shipbuilder
Constable	Tavern keeper
Drum maker	Tax collector
Fence viewer	Teamster
Gunsmith	Town clerk
Housewright	Turner
Joiner	Undertaker
Justice of the peace	Upholsterer

3

TALLY OF CABINETMAKERS IN NEW ENGLAND, NEW YORK CITY, & PHILADELPHIA c. 1730

Boston	295	Massachusetts	940
Salem, Mass.	173	Rhode Island	201
Newport, R.I.	104	Connecticut	143
Charlestown, Mass.	97	New York City	96
Providence	96	Philadelphia	82
New York City	96	New Hampshire	33
Newburyport, Mass.	85	Vermont	7
Philadelphia	82	Maine	1
Manchester, Mass.	70		1,503
Hartford, Conn.	38		
Ipswich, Mass.	35		
Suffield, Conn.	26		
Portsmouth, N.H.	10		

4

SPECIFICATIONS FOR CONSTRUCTING A WINDMILL
FROM CHARLES F. HUMMEL, *With Hammer in Hand: The Dominy Craftsmen of East Hampton, New York**

Sir, I received yours of the 9th Inst. which informs me, that if your timber will answer, you have concluded to put two run of Stones in your Mill—I believe it will do well. 2nd   If you frame girders across for your bridge beams to lie upon 8 feet and 4 Inches from top of stone beams to top of said girders, the lower storey will answer as agreed upon; but if you conclude to have the bridge beams lie on those girths which support the upper floor perhaps the lower storey had better be as much as 10 feet high—3rd   The top had better be enlarged as much as the bottom or the arms will come too near— 4th   The stone beams may be 2 Feet 10 inches apart, & the posts under them stand flush with the inside of the beams & 5 Feet between them the other way—5th   The post in center of Mill may be from 18 to 24 inches [thick] and long enough to rise 4 Feet 8 Inch above the stone beam—6th   The plank rim to be in 6 pieces—7th Cogg Wheel to be 8 Feet diameter & Spur wheel 5 Feet 3 I[nches] with 52 Coggs each $3^{1}/_{4}$ by $1^{3}/_{4}$ and 12 inches long—Cants of spur wheel 17 Inches wide & 4 thick—Faceing of D 7 inches wide and 3 thick—the width of arms 9 In & $4^{1}/_{2}$ thick—The wallower 3 Feet 10 Inches, plank diameter—2 Inches thick, 25 Rounds—14 Inches between shoulders & 3 Inches diameter—Rim that holds the coggs for turning mill top—5 Inches thick and 9 or 10 I[nches] wide— Stocks 34 Feet or 35 Feet long, 8 Inches thick and 10 Inches deep at center, ends proportioned so as to suit the points when hewed 8 Inches one end & $4^{1}/_{2}$ Inches the other—thickness of stock $3^{1}/_{2}$ Inches or 4 Inches at end.

Size of Burr Stones 4' -4" diam. and the rock stones 4'-8 or 9" diam. and the runner 17 or 18" through the eye.

N.B.   The Post in center may be Crotch on one of the sleepers and a large stone placed under the end.

*Baltimore, Genealogical Publishing Co., 1965

5

EARLY FURNITURE MAKERS, 1634–1696
ADAPTED FROM CHARLES H. POPE, *Pioneers of Maine and New Hampshire*

BRANSON, George, *Dover, New Hampshire*: Killed by his bull. Inquest July 2, 1637

CATE, James, *Portsmouth*, carpenter: Had a bill against the town February 4, 1660

CHADBOURNE, William, carpenter: Made agreement March 4, 1634, in company with James Wall and John Goddard, to come to Piscataqua and settle on lands of John Mason. Built a house on his part of the land and gave it to his son-in-law Thomas Spencer.

COLE, William, carpenter, *Boston*: Had allotment of 2 acres February 20, 1637 at Mt. Wollaston. Removed to Exeter, N. H. 1639. His wife Eunice accused of witchcraft; tried, convicted, sentenced to receive corporal punishment and life imprisonment. 1662 she petitioned to be set at liberty after suffering so much imprisonment, pleading the needs of her husband, 88 years of age, and the ruin of their small property which she had helped collect during 20 years. Her petition granted on condition of her departing from the jurisdiction; but she could not avail herself of the decision because she could not pay arrears or give bonds, and she remained in prison several years longer.

DAVIS, Robert, carpenter: A servant of Henry Taylor of Portsmouth. Was ordered 1651 to bring into court a certificate that his wife was dead; ordered 1652 to go to his wife in England by the first ship. Sold land October 4, 1660. Sold house and land at Sagamore Creek August 31, 1667.

ELLINGHAM, William, carpenter, millwright, proprietor:* Had lands granted by the town; built a sawmill. Bought land on Agamenticus River and erected mills there.

EMERY, Anthony, carpenter, *Romsey, England*: Came in the *James* April 1635. Settled at Newbury, Massachusetts 1637. Proprietor. Licensed to sell wine in 1643. Selectman in 1648.

GODDARD, John, carpenter, *Dover, New Hampshire*: Resided at or near Bloody Point; was one of those who petitioned about 1642 to be included within the limits of Dover. Brought suit against Francis Williams and Thomas Wonerton for false imprisonment in 1642; recovered 2 shillings and 6. Wife Welthen; sons John, Benjamin; sons-in-law: John Gilman, Arthur Benwick, James Thomas. [*See* Chadbourne, above]

HANCOCKE, John, carpenter: Contracted with Committee of Ports-

*A person with a legal title to property.

mouth to build a new meeting house 40 feet square and 16 feet high, a flat roof and a substantial turett [cupola] with a gallery about it &c and to repair the old meeting house and fit it up for a house for the minister.

JOY, Richard, carpenter: In the employ of Winter at Richmond Island, worked on a ship that was launched June 14, 1641.

KING, Thomas, carpenter: In service of Nicholas Langworthy of Stonehouse, England. Came to Richmond Island and worked for Winter in 1634.

LOCKE, John, carpenter, *Portsmouth*: Had a grant of house lot in 1656. Married 1652 Elizabeth Berry. Had by her eleven children. He was killed by Indians August 26, 1696.

MONTAGUE, Griffin, carpenter, *Muddy River, Boston*, 1635: Sold the time of his apprentice John Bundy to William Brewster of Plymouth March 6, 1636. Removed to Exeter. August 1659 contracted to furnish 150 pounds of Geese and duck feathers to David Leudecus, edgeling of Dover.

ROYAL, William, cooper and timber cleaver.

WILLIAMS, Francis, gentleman: "A prudent man of better quality than the rest," was chosen governor of the lower Piscataqua in 1633. Brought over his wife and nine other members of his family about 1636. Rec'd grant of 900 acres of land from Gorges, recorded August 1644.

6

COMPARISON OF HARDNESS*
ADAPTED FROM SAMUEL J. RECORD, *The Mechanical Properties of Wood*

	END SURFACE	RADIAL SURFACE	TANGENTIAL SURFACE	AVERAGE
Honey locust	1,862	1,860	1,832	1,851
White oak	1,183	1,163	1,147	1,164
White ash	1,121	1,000	1,017	1,046
Beech	1,012	897	918	942
Sugar maple	992	918	901	937
White elm	536	456	497	496

*Tested by the load required, in pounds, to imbed a 0.444″ steel ball to half its diameter.

7

COMPARISON OF CLEAVAGE STRENGTH,
PSI *(pounds per square inch)*
ADAPTED FROM SAMUEL J. RECORD, *The Mechanical
Properties of Wood*

	WHEN SURFACE FAILURE IS RADIAL	WHEN SURFACE FAILURE IS TANGENTIAL
Honey locust	552	610
White oak	382	457
White ash	333	346
Beech	339	527
Sugar maple	376	513
White elm	210	270
White pine	144	160

8

COMPARISON OF MOISTURE AND SHRINKAGE
ADAPTED FROM SAMUEL J. RECORD, *The Mechanical
Properties of Wood*

	SPECIFIC GRAVITY*	MOISTURE CONTENT %	SHRINKAGE IN VOLUME FROM GREEN TO OVEN-DRY STATE %
Honey locust	.695	53	8.6
White oak	.599	66	14.3
White ash	.533	42	12.1
Beech	.556	61	16.5
Sugar Maple	.562	56	14.3
White elm	.430	66	—
White pine	.363	74	7.8

*Relative density

9

INVENTORY OF BENJAMIN CHENEY
East Hartford, Connecticut

one Inch orger [auger]
half inch orger
¹/₃ ditto
hand saw
Shave
frow
Small broad ax
groving plow
harving plow
2 rabbit plaines
3 oges
quarter Round orger
half orger
Gouge
5 chisels
foot wheel
old ax
holing ax
broad chisels
narrow chisels
mortising chisels
1 jointer
1 set mach plains [match planes—tongue and groove]
Iron square

10

INVENTORY OF LEWIS MILLER, CARPENTER
York, Pennsylvania 1796

auger	gouges
drawknife	grindstone
handsaw	maul
compass saw	hatchet
gimlet	hammer
brace	jointer plane
chisels	glue pot

11

INVENTORY OF NICHOLAS DISBROWE
Hartford, Connecticut

Plan stacke and Iorns
Seven chessells
passer bitts & gimblets
parsell of small tools
& two payer of compasses
& five hand saws
two fros
payer of plyers
two rasps
file and a saw
two parser stake
a shave
two hammers & fower axes
two bettells & fower wedges
bitt and five augers
two tropes
two payer of joynts [hinges] & a payer
of hooks and Ringes
an adys
warming pan
two smoothing Iorns
grin stone

12

INVENTORY OF CHARLES GILLAM
Old Saybrook, Connecticut

ADAPTED FROM ETHEL HALL BJERKOE, *The Cabinetmakers of America*

frame saw
fine back saw
a new saw
a hand saw
iron frame saw
a small saw
5 pair of moulding plains
2 square rabits [planes]
2 pr. match plains
a screw plain
joynter
pareing chisel
2 carpenter's chisels
3 gouges
3 hammers
2 hold fasts
one ½ inch angle
a tap borer
2 Cornish [cornice] gouge
mortising chisel
small anvil
3 bench hooks
4 squares
one brace
3 bits for same
a glue pot
7 turning chisels
2 benches
lignum vitae dust
parcel of collours
boxes
brushes and gums
glue 109 lbs
oaker [ochre pigment]
a levell
umber [pigment]

13

FURNITURE MADE BY THE DUNLAP FAMILY
New Hampshire

	John 1746–1792	Samuel 1752–1830	James 1787–1875
Bedsteads	12	49	34
Cradles	5	3	
Bureaus		8	
Chairs	469	344	136
Clock cases	2	1	
Coffins	6	11	
Chests	18	5	2
Cases of drawers	43	64	12
Desks	14	9	
Candle stands	5	16	9
Rakes	172	28	7
Sleighs		2	
Tables	72	95	28
Totals	818	635	228

14

DIVERSITY OF SHOP WORK, THE DOMINY CRAFTSMEN
East Hampton, New York c. 1765–1810

Cradleing ¹/₂ acre of oats & Banding
1 day and Isaac on Garden fence
2 days & Isaac makeing doors &c
an Axletree and whorl to a wheal
a Yoke for a Cow
mend gun lock
29 lb of Venison at 2¹/₂
¹/₂ fox skin
makeing a Plough
a Desk
6 Chairs
a Table
mend table
Stocking a lock [gun]
5 days of my self and Jereme at 8ˢ both
makeing Window frame & 20 sq of Sash
setting glass and pulling in ye frame &c
makeing a pair of Smiths Bellows
mending Loom blocks
a Shuttle
2 spoles and 1 head
a Pair of flyars
Stocking a gun &c
trimming fine Saw
mending a fork handle
repairing Chest of Drawers
fit sashes Seting 12 lights in putty
mend Wool Wheal
shuttle
mend Swift
a Band on Gun stock
band on gun cuting sight loop & trim stock
[sale of] 3 lb of Brass @ 0 - 1 - 0
whet saw
mend bellows
Nat ¹/₂ day on Corn
¹/₂ day & little better Rakeing Hay
a Tea Pot Handle
puting furniture [hardware] on a Desk
a Trundle bedstead

mending Tea Table
Abraham Mulford's Mill To 3^{1}/$_3$ days work
   on Sills & Braces &c at 7/ [shillings]
makeing 24 sqr^s of sashes at 4^d
measuring land at Akabonck
surveying land at longhill
mending shovel Handle
mending a Silver Spoon
makeing a Great Harrow
a Coffin for his Corps [Samuel Parsons]
a large Square Table
a Chest with 2 Draws you found Brass &c
1 doz Handles put on Knives & Forks^a 3^d
an other Doz Handles put on Knives &c
mending Pistol lock
Hardening your Gun-Hammer
Trimming Dovetail Saw
Mending 4 Rakes
Nat near 1^{1}/$_2$ days on Sled at 3/6
Pasteuring 1 Cow from 15th of May to 23 of August inclusive
   14 weeks 2 days at 0 - 1 - 3 per week/omitting odd days &c
mend 3 chairs
1 Ax-Helve
Eel Spear Pole
hang Grindstone & frame
makeing Chest your boards (0 - 12 - 0)
Chest for Peter   (1 - 4 - 0)
Clean & Sharpen Surg^s Ins^t
makeing a Coffen for your Father, part your stuff

15

TYPICAL GOODS AND SERVICE PURCHASED BY DOMINYS

FROM CHARLES F. HUMMEL, *With Hammer in Hand: The Dominy Craftsmen of East Hampton, New York*

a pair of large Compasses
15 Handles @ 8ᵈ & 5 Scutcheons @ 4ᵈ
1 Plane iron
½ lb of Powder & 1 lb of Shot
4 joints of hinges & screws
a tenont saw
Watch Springs
1 load of wood and Carting poles from the Barn
Carting Dung
a horse to go to Amaganset
3 Draw locks at 1ˢ
8½ lb of Cheese at 6ᵈ
Forgeing Drills &c
1 Day work of team Carting wood
Makeing a pair of leather Breeches
a Hand saw
2 Lb of Red Lead
1½ [days] scowering & makeing Sope
Carting 600 foot of Bord from Sag Harbʳ
the use of lot joining my home Corn
a Cag of paint
248 lb of Beef at 3ᵈ
Sundry articles that you broᵗ for me viz
1 doz 4 Keyᵈ Till locks
1 groce of Screws
3 dozen Brass Knobs (Large) at 2/6
Sawing 49 Feet of Cherry Plank

16

EXTRACTS FROM ACCOUNT BOOK OF MAJOR JOHN DUNLAP
FOR THE YEAR 1774

			£	s	d
Jen 22	to one Round Table		21	0	0
	to Six fore Backt Chairs		18	0	0
	to five Days Work		12	10	0
	to Six Banester Backt Chairs		24	0	0
	to one Round Table		27	0	0
Jen 26	McNeal Dr				
	to one Case of Drawers		63	0	0
	to one Tea table		7	0	0
	to Six Chair Fraims		12	0	0
Feb 3	to two Hundred and Sixty fore feet of Cherretry Boards				
Feb 21	to Eight Chair Fraims		12	0	0
Feb 24	Thomas Shirla Dr to three chair fraims for John Butterfield		4	10	0
	to 6 Banefter Back Chairs		24	0	0
	to 6 Common Chairs		13	10	0
	to Making half a Cart Body		4	0	0
	to Making one Case of Drawers		66	0	0
Mar 1	Asa Patte Dr one Tea table		10	0	0
	to one Candle Stand		6	0	0
Mar 4	to three Banester Backt Chairs		12	0	0
	to one Cheretry Tea Table		10	0	0
	to one Grin Stone		12	0	0
Mar 5	three plane oirns		1	16	0
	one Moyter Gouge [miter gauge]		0	10	0
	one pair of Compefes		0	8	0
	one Hamer		1	4	0
Mar 23	one Case of Drawers		66	0	0
	one Desk		48	0	0
	Six Banester Back Chairs		24	0	0
	Six fore Back Chairs		18	0	0
	to Mending two Raks		1	2	0
	to three New Raks		3	4	0
Mar 31	Credet John Clogston to 280 feet of thin Marchantible Boards		3	15	0
May 2	James Marrs Dr				
	to putte 5 pound		3	0	0
	John 6 Days Samuel 6 Days the Boy 5½				
	John 5 Days Saml 5 Days the Boy 5 Days				
	Saml one Day the Boy one Day John half a Day				
	The Whole Comes to		73	5	0

May	6	Seteled With Samuel Dunlap and thair			
		is Due to him in old Tenor	262	11	0
May	16	to 8 feet of mapol Boards	2	5	0
		to 40 feet of Refuge pine Boards	0	9	0
		Credet Daniel Mcfarland			
		one pair of oxen halling Boards	1	0	0
		to Boy & fore oxen after Boards	3	0	0
Jun	16	to one Window	6	0	0
Jul	2	Robert McGregore Dr			
		28 Squars of Sash	4	4	0
		12 Chairs	36	0	0
		6 Chair fraims	9	0	0
		36 Squars of Sash for Thomes Karr	5	8	0
		96 Squars of Sash for Mr McCurdy	14	8	0
Jul	5	to Setting Glafs	0	12	0
Jul	7	to one Bedsteed	6	0	0
		to 97 Squars of Sash panted & glafs set	25	17	0
		to Making Seven Window fraims	7	0	0
		to half a Day putting in Window fraims	1	5	0
		to one Chest of Drawers	25	10	0
Jul	22	Credet to Robert McGregore			
		Shop Goods	37	13	0
		Six Hundred and one Quorter of mapol Boards	30	13	0
		one chisel	0	18	0
		Led	0	7	0
		one Ax	6	0	0
Aug	1	Credet Mr Kelley Boston old Te[nor]			
		to 12 Small Gimblets	0	12	0
		to 2 Chisels one Gouge / one Saw set 5 each	1	0	0
		to one Book of Arthmetick	1	10	0
		to 12 Brases and 6 Skuchens [Escutcheons]	2	1	0
		to one thousand of Brads			
Aug	27	to one point & half of Lintfeed oyl	1	2	0
Sep	28	Credet to Moses Little			
		to 400 of Joice	6	0	0
		to 266 feet Mapol Boards	9	3	0
		to 382 feet of Joice	7	12	0
Oct	7	Bought of Jean Kennedy two Saws for fifteen			
		Shillings Lawfull and paid thirteen Shillings			
		and Six pence for them			
Oct	21	to one pound of Shingle Nails	0	18	0

Nov 2	William McDougal Dr			
	to three plainftocks [plane stocks]	4	15	0
	to twlve Squars of Sash panted	2	8	0
	to one Day of Laying a flooer	2	10	0
	to Bottoming five Black Chairs	5	0	0
	to puting on a table Leaf & making a Drawer	3	0	0
	to Making a Coffen	3	0	0
Nov 23	William Rodgers Dr			
	to one Day & half Work	3	15	0
	to five Days - JD	12	10	0
	to five Days S.R.	5	0	0
	to half a Box of Glafs	30	0	0
Dec 2	to two Hundred of Brads	1	0	0
Dec 6	agreed with Alex gillcrest for one years			
	fire wood from this Date for	48	0	0
	to 2 oxen after harth Stons	1	10	0
	to three Hundred and forty one feet of plank	14	8	0
	to one Days Making Chairs	2	0	0
Dec 24	this Day Seteled With Samuel Dunlap			
	and thair is Due to him	66	7	0

May 19   1784
Time Lost
half a Day geting Shoes Mended at Wm Kenedys
Working at Deering Nine Days Lost
half a Day Choping at W Gillmors June 3
two Days getting Married June 8 & 9
to pastering a horse frome the 12 of June
to half a Day Shoing the hors

PREPARATION OF GLUE
FROM JOHN PHIN, *Hints and Practical Information for Cabinetmakers*

Glue is prepared from waste pieces of skin, horn, hoofs, and other animal offal. These are steeped, washed, boiled, strained, melted, reboiled and cast into square cakes, which are then dried. The strongest kind of glue is made from the hides of oxen; that from the bones and sinews is weaker. The older the animal the stronger the glue. . .

To prepare glue for use it should be broken up into small pieces, and soaked in as much cold water as will cover it, for about twelve hours. It should then be melted in a double glue pot, covered to keep the glue from dirt. Care must be taken to keep the outer vessel full of water, so that the glue shall not burn, or be brought to a temperature higher than that of boiling water. The glue is allowed to simmer for two or three hours, then gradually melted, so much hot water being added as will make it liquid enough, just to run off a brush in a continuous stream, without breaking into drops. When the glue is done with [i.e. for the day] some boiling water should be added to make it very thin before it is put away. Freshly-made glue is stronger than that which has been repeatedly melted. Too large a quantity should not therefore be made at a time.

The addition of a little bichromate of potash will render glue impervious to moisture after exposing to the light, and a small quantity of methylated spirits [ethyl alcohol, or denatured alcohol] will greatly improve its keeping qualities.

The cohesion of a piece of solid glue, or the force required to separate one square inch, is four thousand pounds. The strength of common glue for coarse work is increased by the addition of a little powdered chalk. The hotter the glue the greater its cohesion; therefore in all large and long joints the glue should be applied immediately after boiling.

To prevent glue cracking: glue frequently cracks because of the dryness of the air in rooms warmed by stoves. The addition of chloride of calcium to glue will prevent this disagreeable property of cracking. Chloride of calcium is such a deliquescent salt that it attracts enough moisture to prevent glue from cracking. Glue thus prepared will adhere to glass, metal, etc., and can be used for putting on labels without danger of their dropping off.

Glue to resist moisture.—To two quarts of skimmed milk add a half a pound of the best glue; melt them together, taking care they do not boil over, and you will have a very strong glue, which will resist damp or moisture.

PARTIAL BILL OF LADING, SCHOONER *RUTH*
DECEMBER 13, 1788
ADAPTED FROM MABEL MUNSON SWAN, *Samuel McIntire, Carver, and the Sandersons: Early Salem Cabinet Makers*

4	clocks with mahogany Cases @ 20	80:	0:	0
1	Mehogany Desk & book case	24		
2	Black Walnut Desks & Book Cases	30		
4	" " 4 ft tables @60/	24		
2	Burch " " @ 36	3:	12:	0
3	Black Walnut Swelled Desks	22:	10:	0
4	Maple Desks	14:	8:	0
276	Squares sash 10 by 14 lights	12:	1:	6
18	Burch Chairs	10:	16:	0
7	Plain cherrytree desks	31:	10:	0
6	Mahogany bedsteads compleat	36:	0:	0
17	window frames	10:	4:	0
36	common chairs 3/6	6:	6:	0

The schooner *Ruth* proceeded to Charleston, South Carolina, where five weeks later she disposed of . . . articles of furniture at auction, and brought back, in addition to many pounds sterling, 53 logs of cedar, as her supercargo had been ordered.

19

EXTRACTS FROM INVOICE, 1807

		£	s	d
Mr Jacob Sanderson to Sam¹ McIntire Dr:				
Augt 11th	To Reeding & Carving 4 legs for work table	3	0	0
27th	to Carving & fluting 18 chairs @ 6/ each	18	0	0
Sept 29th	to Carving 12 Arms 4/6	0	75	0
Oct 21st	to Carving 12 leaves for window Cornaic @ 1/6	3	0	0

20

TYPICAL FORM OF INDENTURE CONTRACT, 1785
FROM CHARLES S. PARSONS, *The Dunlaps and Their Furniture*

This Indenture Witnesseth that David Stone Son of Josiah Stone late
of Temple Deceas'd in County of Hillsborough & State of New
Hampshire, hath (by ye leave and consent of his Guardian John
Cragin Jr. of ye County & State afors'd yeoman) put himself and by
these presents doth voluntarily put himself an apprentice to John
Delap of Bedford in·ye aforesd County & State, House & Shop
Joyner to learn his art Trade or Mystery & after ye manner of an
apprentice to Serve him ye Term of five years from ye fifteenth day
of April 1785 & no Longer, during all which times In ye Said
apprentice his Said Master Shall faithfully Serve, his Secrets keep,
his Lawfull Commands every where gladly obey. He shall do no
Damage to his Sd Master, nor See it done by others, without letting,
or giving notice thereof to his Sd Master. He Shall not waste his
Masters Goods, nor lend them unlawfully to others. He Shall not
Commit fornication nor Contract Matrimony within ye Sd Term. At
Cards, dice or any unlawfull game he Shall not play. His own goods,
or the goods of others during ye Sd Term, without license of his Sd
Master, he Shall neither by nor Sell. He shall not absent him Self day
nor night from his Sd Masters Service without his leave, nor haunt
Ale Houses, Taverns, or play Houses: but in all things behave
himself as a faithfull Apprentice ought to do, during ye Sd Term And
ye Sd Master Shall use the utmost of his endeavours to teach or
Cause to be taught & instructed the Sd Apprentice in ye Trade &
Mistery he now profeseth, Occupieth or followith, and procure or
provide for ye sd Apprentice Suffitient Meat Drink Apparel Washing
& lodging, Doctoring & nursing if needed, fitting for an Apprentice
during ye Sd Term, and also Teach or Cause to be taught ye sd
Apprentice, to read, write, & Cypher if Capable of learning And ye
Sd Master at ye end of Sd Term, Shall Dismiss ye Sd Apprentice
with two good Suits of Apparel Sutable for an Apprentice, the one
for Lords days & ye other for Common days. In Witness wherof
they have interchangeably Set ther Hands & Seal this 15 day of April
Domini 1785
Sign'd Sealed & Delivered
in presents of us.

William Houston   *John Dunlap (seal)*
Matthew Aikens   *David Stone (seal)*
                                                     John Cragin

PRICES FOR FURNITURE AND CARVING, 1742–1803

	£	s	d
Christopher Townsend, Newport, R.I.			
1742 By one Walnut coffin for my child	3	0	0
1746 By one Desk and Book Case	65	0	0
Richard Robinson, Boston			
1747 a square table	7	0	0
Job Clark			
1754 Seeder Desks	12	0	0
Phillips Potter *and others*, Providence, R.I.			
1757 An agreement signed by Potter and other cabinetmakers, listed furniture prices:			
Mahogany high Cases of draws at	100	0	0
Walnut do with tear of draws	75	0	0
Black walnut High Case of draws	85	0	0
Eliakim Smith, Hadley, Mass.			
1760 Case of Dras for Rebecca (prices in Old Tenor)	40	0	0
Case of draws	26	0	0
A Desk upon French feet	13	0	0
John Townsend, Newport			
1764 1 maple chair	40	0	0
8 mahogany chairs @ 40	320	0	0
1 large tea board	14	10	0
Eleazer Trevett, Newport			
1766 2 Maple Desks	180	0	0
Joseph Powell, New York			
1768 two Book Cases and a large Table for the use of the General Assembly	11	43	0
George Weeden, Newport			
1768 cabin table for ship *Cleopatra*	32	0	0
cabin table for Brigantine *Britania*	25	0	0
ditto for brigantine *Neptune*	28	0	0
Benjamin Tayer [Tayre], Newport			
1 cabin table for Ship *Benjamin*	35	10	0
William Davis, Newport			
1772 1 red cedar desk	144	0	0

John *and* Simeon Skillin, Boston
1778 So the records go, John carved a figure-head for the ship *Confederacy*, built at Norwich, Connecticut. One bill is for two figureheads, £31 15 0, with a 10% discount for prompt payment. Two other

bills list charges for carving a Grand
Turk Head 11 ft long, £16; and for
Carv'd work done for a chest of drawers
£6 15 0. The Skillin skill was applied
to other work as well:

To a figure of a Hermit for a Garden	7	10	0
To a Figure of a Shepherdess	6	0	0
To a Figure of Plenty	7	10	0
To a Figure of a Gardener	7	10	0

Samuel McIntire, Salem, Mass.

1796	a Case of Drawers	1	19	0
	carving a Freeze Roses	1	4	0

Oliver & Ebenezer Plumb

1797	Heart-back Cherry Chairs	7-9 dollars each
	Windsor ditto	8s-15s each

Ebenezer Tracy, Lisbon, Conn.

1802	2 Shop Chairs	0	17	0
	3 Green Painted Chairs	1	2	6
	Painting 2 chairs	0	4	0

Job Edward Townsend, Newport

1803	To a Cherry Stand	0	13	0
	To a Low post Bedstedd	12	4	0

Glossary

ANNULET: a narrow, flat or rounded molding forming a ring around a cylindrical member

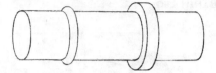

APRON

ARROW-BACK

ARCH-BACK

ASTRAGAL: a small convex molding raised on a flat surface

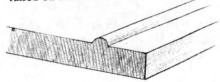

BACKBOARD

BANDING: a strip of inlay, usually of contrasting color, made around the edges of a drawer front or table top

BANDY LEG

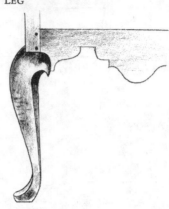

BANISTER-BACK

BAIL

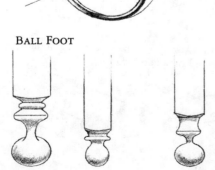

BALL FOOT

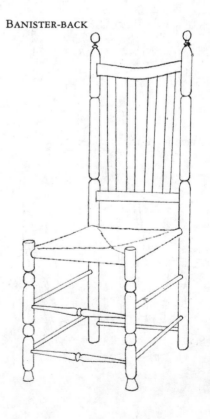

BATTEN

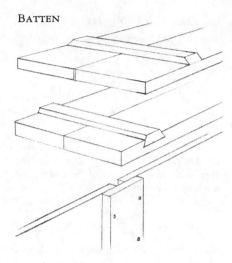

BEAD, BEADING: a narrow, usually half-round molding, either run as a continuous strip or carved in the form of a row of beadlike knobs.

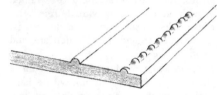

BEAD AND BUTT MOLDING

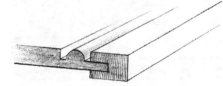

BENCH STOP

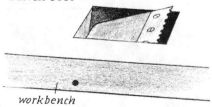

workbench

BEVEL: an edge surface planed or cut at an angle to the main surfaces

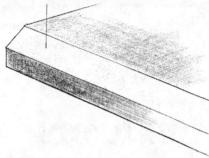

BIRD'S-EYE: a pattern resulting from sawing through areas in a log where a fungus growth, or undeveloped buds, have produced knotlike markings resembling birds' eyes. In lumbering vernacular: a small spot with the wood fibers clustered around a center in the shape of an ellipse—especially in sugar maple.

BITSTOCK, BIT BRACE, BRACE, STOCK: various terms all meaning a boring tool with offset crank handle, and a chuck to hold drills or bits

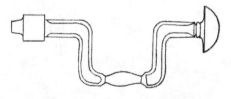

BLIND-NAIL, BLIND-NAILING: a method of nailing joined boards to conceal the nail heads

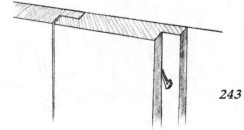

243

BOASTING (also *bosting*): "The first thing to be done in carving is to draw your pattern on the wood; this is called *boasting*."
—JOHN PHIN

In stonecutting and sculpture: the rough preliminary shaping with chisel or gouge.

BOBBIN TURNING

BOSTON ROCKER: late modification of the Windsor chair, with seat curved up in back to meet the spindles

BOW-BACK

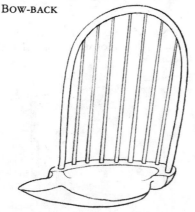

BROKEN-ARCH PEDIMENT

BULLNOSE: a plane with the iron set even with the front end of the frame, for working into corners

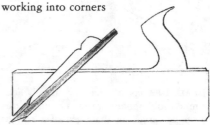

BURL: the twisted, erratic, close-grained growth in certain individual trees. Because of its density, used for mallet heads; as veneer, valued for its delicate and exotic figure

BURNISHING: method of producing a sheen on wood by rubbing with a hard tool such as wood, bone, or glass; alternatively: scrubbing with a handful of wood shavings

CABLE MOLDING

CABRIOLE LEG

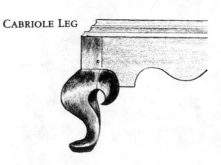

244

CANAL MOLDING

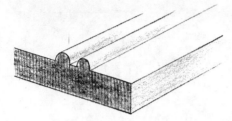

CANT: an oblique or slanting surface

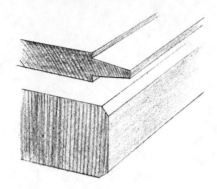

CAPTAIN'S CHAIR: a low-back Windsor having an attached comb

CARCASS, CARCASE: the joined framework or skeleton of furniture that supports top, drawers, and other members; furniture so constructed

CHAMFER, CHAMFERING: also called a *splay*

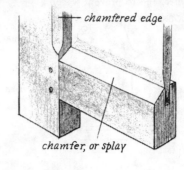

chamfered edge

chamfer, or splay

CHAMFER STOP

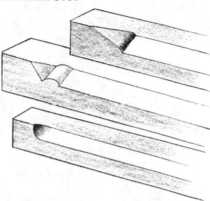

CHEST-ON-FRAME: a chest of drawers that fits into the rabbeted top rim of a lower chest with feet

CHICKEN COOP CHAIR: colloquial term for a stick chair, or Windsor

CLAW AND BALL

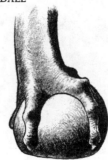

245

CLEAT: a strip of wood fastened across one or more boards to hold them together, and to prevent warping

CLOCK CASE

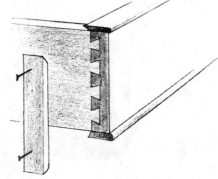

bonnet

hood

body

base

COCKSHEAD HINGE

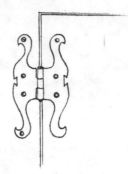

COMB

COMB-BACK

COCKBEAD, COCKBEADING: a rounded, raised molding, either run-in or applied with glue and brads

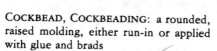

CORNICE, CORNAIC

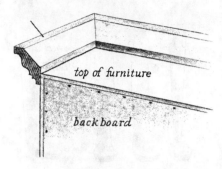

top of furniture

backboard

DEADPIN

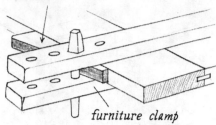

furniture clamp

DEAL: an archaic term variously applied to planks of pine or fir, to lumber of the same kind from Norway, or to any one of several soft woods

CREST, CRESTING

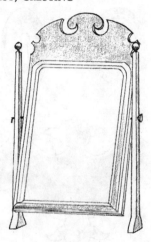

DOUBLE-BEARING ARM

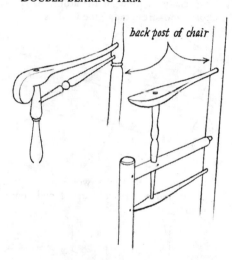

back post of chair

CROTCHWOOD (lumber): wood from the area in a tree where two major limbs fork from the main trunk, often showing erratic swerves in the grain; used mostly as veneer wood

CURLY FIGURE: pattern revealed by sawing across wavy grain, exposing fibers running in crooked lines forming alternate light and dark streaks; apparently caused by contortions in the wood at the base of large limbs

DOUBLE-QUIRK BEAD

247

DOVETAIL

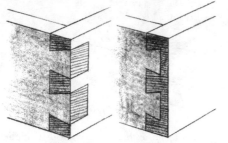

through dovetail *stop dovetail*

DUTCH FOOT

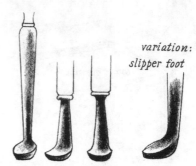

variation:
slipper foot

DOWEL: turned wooden rods from which are cut short *dowel* pieces used, especially in modern furniture, to reinforce and strengthen glued joints

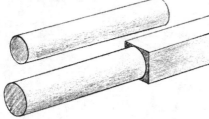

DRAWBORE PIN: the wooden pin that draws and secures a mortise and tenon joint

ESCUTCHEON

FALL-FRONT

248 DROP LEAF: a type of table in which the leaves, or *flaps* are hinged to fold down against the frame; also the swinging gates that support the leaves

FAN-BACK

FINIAL: the turned or carved terminal top end of a post, bedpost, chair, or other furniture; made either as part of the member, or attached with a dowel pin

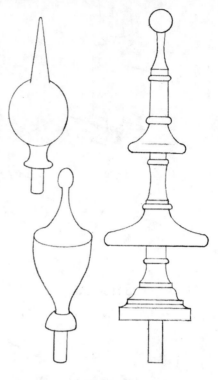

FEATHER CROTCH: figure resulting from sawing boards from the crotch of a tree, showing a delicate, feathery pattern

FIDDLE-BACK: pattern that appears in quarter-sawed lumber, in which the crests of successive undulations of grain are cut through—an effect often seen in some mahogany, maple, and sycamore

FIGURE: various patterns that result from sawing wood with twisted, wrinkled, or otherwise distorted grain:
bird's-eye
burl, burly
crotchwood
curly, curled
feather crotch
fiddle-back
ripple
wavy

FILLISTER

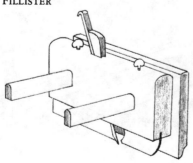

FLAP

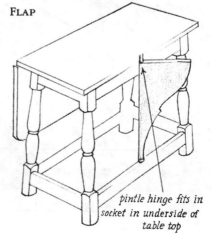

pintle hinge fits in socket in underside of table top

249

Flap Hinge

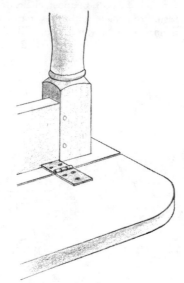

Fox-tail Wedging

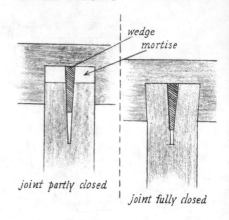

wedge
mortise

joint partly closed

joint fully closed

Fox-wedge

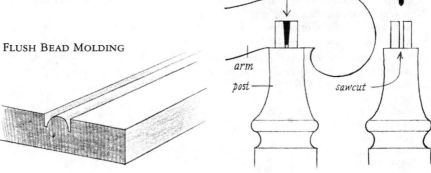

arm

post

sawcut

Flush Bead Molding

Fox-wedges

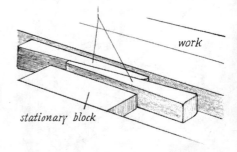

work

stationary block

Fluting, Flute

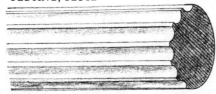

FRAME SAW

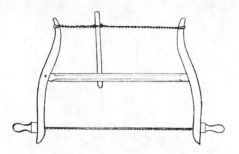

FRETWORK: ornamental carving, often pierced through to make a latticework

GALLERY

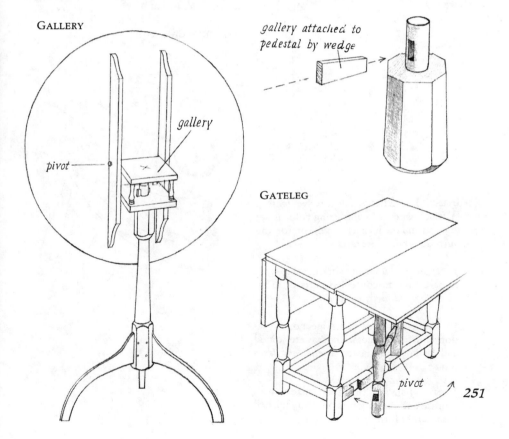

gallery attached to pedestal by wedge

gallery

pivot

GATELEG

pivot

GROOVE: a channel, slot, or *rabbet* used in joinery; the plane to cut a groove

GUNSTOCK STILE

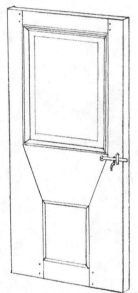

panel door made with gunstock stiles

JOINT OF HINGES

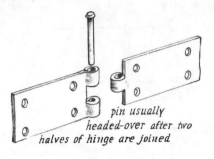

pin usually headed-over after two halves of hinge are joined

KERF: a slit or notch made by a saw; the width of a saw cut

KNUCKLE CARVING

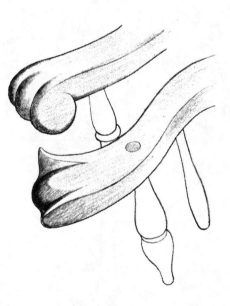

INLAY, INLAYING: a decorative feature in which wood of contrasting color is set into, or *inlaid* in a channel cut for the purpose; akin to *marquetry*

JERRYWORK: inferior workmanship used to save time in concealed parts of furniture; *slipshod work; jerrybuilt*

JOINERY: the trade of a joiner; construction built up of members that are joined and fastened, as in the *mortise and tenon* joint

252

JOINT, JOINED: furniture made with mortise and tenon joints, as distinguished from *turned* furniture

LADDER-BACK

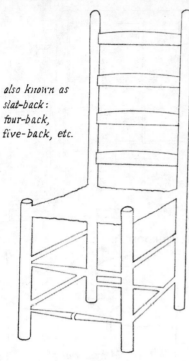

also known as
slat-back:
four-back,
five-back, etc.

LUNETTE: a semicircular carved feature often worked into the bonnet, or top of a chest or clock case

MARQUETRY: an intricate style of inlay in which woods of different colors are fitted and glued into recessed areas to create a design

MATCH PLANE(S)

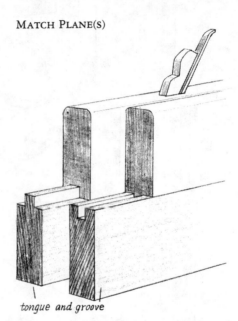

tongue and groove

LISTEL: similar to *annulet*

LOOP-BACK

MORTISE: a boxlike rectangular cavity cut into a piece of wood to receive a tenon cut on the end of another; in a looser sense: a rectangular hole cut clear through, to receive a tenon pierced by a slot into which a wedge is fitted (*See* tusk-tenon)

253

Mortise and Tenon

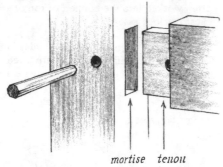

mortise tenon

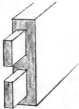 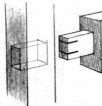

double tenon   *through and wedged*

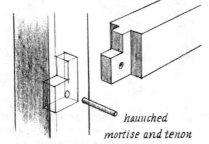

*haunched
mortise and tenon*

Mullet: a wooden, grooved block for trying the thickness of beveled panel edges and drawer bottoms; *mulleting*

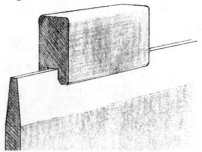

254

Muntin

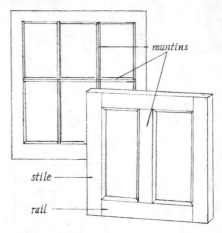

muntins

stile ——

rail ——

Mushroom Finial

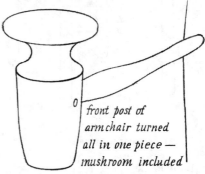

*front post of
armchair turned
all in one piece —
mushroom included*

Necking: any small molding or ring turned on the upper part of a post, pillar, or pilaster; or as part of a finial

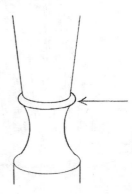

OGEE: a reverse curve as applied to the contour of a molding or cornice

OGEE BRACKET

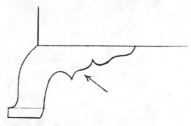

ONION FOOT: a squat, flattened, and bulbous version of the *ball foot*

OVOLO MOLDING

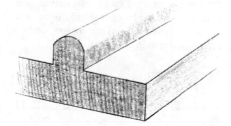

PATINA: surface texture and color resulting from age, wear, polishing, rubbing, or waxing

PEDIMENT

PENDANT (also *pendil*) a carved or turned hanging ornament

PIERCED SPLAT

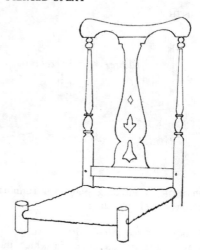

PIGEONHOLE

PINTLE HINGE

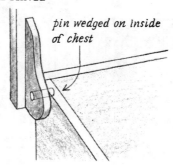

pin wedged on inside of chest

255

PLAIN SAWED: lumber cut from a log in successive slices without rotating the log on the carriage, as opposed to *quarter sawed*

PLINTH

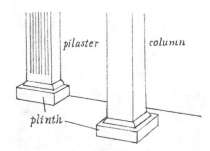

PLOUGH: a molding plane for running grooves, as in paneling

PLUCK-UP: the pitted surface caused by planing against the grain, in which the fibers are torn loose by the plane and stood on end

PUNCHWORK: background stippling in carved work, done with a punch and mallet

QUARTERED: lumber cut from a log along the radial lines as opposed to *plain sawed*

QUIRK BEAD, QUIRK

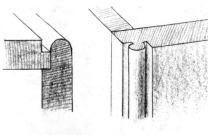

RABBET, REBATE

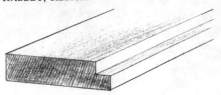

RAIL: horizontal member in the basic structure of furniture, usually referring to the top rail

RAKE: the angle at which the cutting iron of a tool is set

REEDING

RESERVE: the raised central part of a panel on which initials, name, or date are often carved

RIFT SAW, RIFT-SAWED: a circular saw with six-spoke blades into which cutting knives are fixed; used for *rifting* timber into boards; akin to *riving, riven*

RING-TURNED

RIPPLE: thin rays in evenly spaced rows running across the grain in plain-sawed lumber; individually they are indistinct, but because of their layered arrangement, appear as horizontal striations or *ripples*

RIVEN, RIVE, RIVING: boards made by splitting from a log with a froe and beetle (maul or mallet)

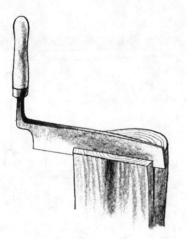

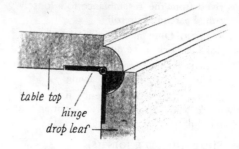

table top

hinge

drop leaf

ROD-BACK: a chair of the Windsor type in which the arm is *joined* to the back spindles, rather than being one continuous piece

RUN MOLDING: molding that is worked directly into the wood, as distinguished from molding made up separately and applied with glue and brads. *Run your moldings with smooth, steady passes of the plane.* The term *shot molding* means the same thing (*See* shooting board)

SADDLE, SADDLING: scooping of a chair seat to fit the human posterior. Allied terms: *scoop, scooping, hollowing*

SASH PLANE: any of several planes with irons shaped to cut the various run moldings in sash making

SAUSAGE AND BALL TURNING

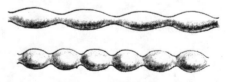

SCRATCH CARVING: a design produced by the shallow incised lines of a simple tool such as a scratch awl

SCRATCH MOLDING: a fine edge molding made with a scratch awl and a straightedge, and cleaned up with a file

ROLLED ARM

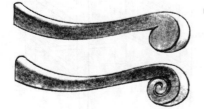

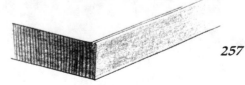

257

SCROLL: a spiral or winding shape, derived from the resemblance to a loosely rolled parchment scroll

SETTING OFF: marking off the dimensions of work to be done on the lathe

SETTING OUT: marking on wood the guidelines for cutting or sawing

SHOOTING BOARD: a bench jig to hold work while running, or "shooting" a molding

SHOT AND GLUE JOINT(S)

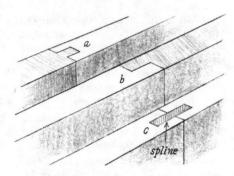

a: tongue and groove

b: half lap   *c: spline*

SHOULDER PIECE

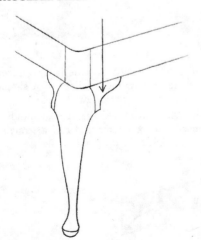

SKIRT

SLAT: a narrow horizontal member, as in a chair back, cut from thin wood and often steamed and bent; then joined to the posts with mortise and tenon joinery

SLAT-BACK: chair construction with two or more horizontal slats joined to the posts; similar to *ladder-back,* but generally with fewer slats

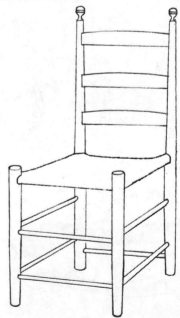

SNIPE HINGE(S)

SPINDLE: a slender, rounded, vertical member either hand-shaped or turned on a lathe; as the *back spindles* of a chair

SQUARE TURNING

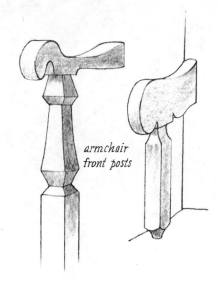

armchair front posts

SPLAT

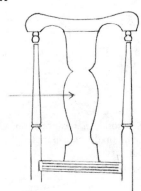

SPLAY: Synonym of *chamfer*

SPLIT SPINDLE: a turned piece with one side flat—made by turning on the lathe two identical pieces of wood glued together with a piece of paper between; when separated, there are two *splits*

STAPLE HINGE(S), LOOP HINGE(S): *See also* snipe hinge

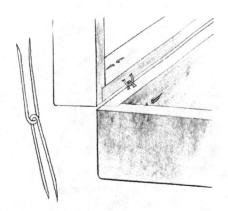

STILE: vertical structural members in furniture, to which horizontal members are joined

STOCK, OR BLOCK KNIFE

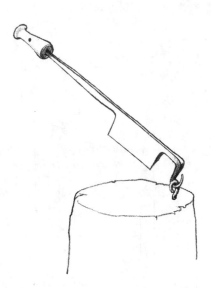

STOP FLUTING

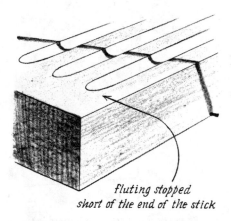

*fluting stopped
short of the end of the stick*

STRAPWORK: crisscross carving resembling woven straps, often with the areas between the crossings pierced clear through; also called *latticework*

STRETCHER

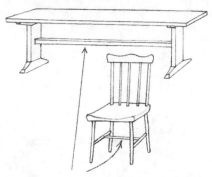

STUFF: wood to be worked up and made into furniture: boards, lumber, stock, bolts, etc.

TENON: Also colloquially: *tenant, tendon*

TESTER: a solid, flat canopy on a four-posted bed, made as a paneled "roof," often with carving

THREAD ESCUTCHEON

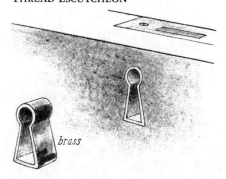

brass

THUMBNAIL MOLDING: a narrow bead-like edge molding, shallow and resembling the line made by a thumbnail; on older furniture, made with a scratch awl and file

THUMB PLANE

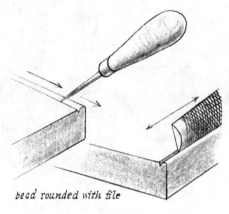

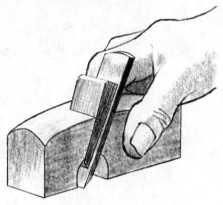

bead rounded with file

TOTE: *All the difference is in the Tote or Handle, which every Workman maketh according to his own Fancy.*

THUMB MOLD

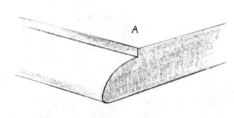

A

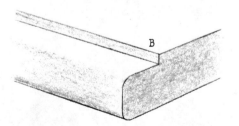

B

TURNIP FOOT

261

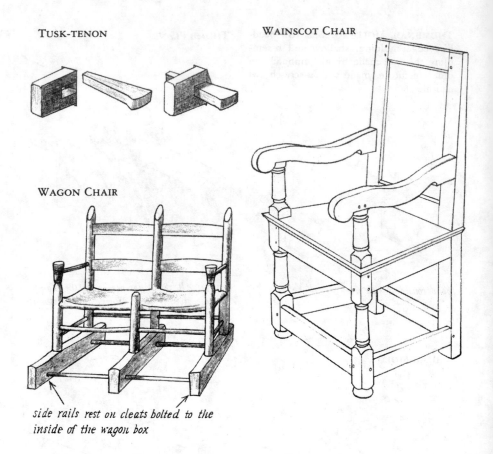

TUSK-TENON

WAINSCOT CHAIR

WAGON CHAIR

*side rails rest on cleats bolted to the
inside of the wagon box*

262

WANE, WANY

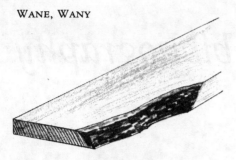

WAVY GRAIN: pattern in wood cut from the limb area of a tree where compression occurs as the trunk and branches expand and are distorted through seasonal growth. The pressure creates "wrinkles" in the grain, which when sawn through may resemble some familiar object, as in the *fiddle-back* figure

WINDING: twisting or racking of a joined piece of furniture such as a door; out of true, especially a corner-to-corner diagonal warp

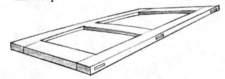

A select bibliography

ANDREWS, CHARLES M., *The Colonial Background of the American Revolution*. New Haven: Yale University Press, 1958.

ANDREWS, EDWARD DEMING AND FAITH, *Religion in Wood*. Bloomington: Indiana University Press, 1966.

———, *Shaker Furniture*. New York: Dover Publications, 1950.

BISSELL, CHARLES S., *Antique Furniture in Suffield, Connecticut*. The Connecticut Historical Society and the Suffield Historical Society, 1956.

BITMEAD, RICHARD, *The Cabinetmaker's Guide*. New York: D. Appleton & Company, 1913.

BJERKOE, ETHEL HALL, *The Cabinetmakers of America*. New York: Doubleday & Company, 1957.

BURGESS, JAMES W., *A Practical Treatise on Coach-Building*. London: Crosby Lockwood & Company, 1881.

"Carriage Wood Bending," *Carriage Monthly*, Vol 40, April, 1904.

CASSAL, HANS J. S., *Workshop Makeshifts*. London: L. Upcott Gill, 1898.

DAHL, ALFRED A., AND WILSON, J. DOUGLAS, *Cabinetmaking ana Millwork*. Chicago: American Technical Society, 1953.

DOLAN, J. R., *The Yankee Peddlers of Early America*. New York: Bramhall House, 1964.

DOW, GEORGE FRANCIS, *Arts and Crafts in New England, 1704–1775*. Topsfield: The Wayside Press, 1927.

DWIGHT, TIMOTHY, *Travels in New England and New York*. London: William Baynes & Son, 1823.

FASTNEDGE, RALPH, Ed., *Shearer Furniture Designs: London Book of Prices, 1788*. London: A. Tirant, 1962.

FENNELLY, CATHERINE, *Life in an Old New England Country Village*. New York: Thomas Y. Crowell Company, 1969.

Forest Products Laboratory, *Wood Handbook No. 72*. Washington: United States Department of Agriculture, 1955.

GARDINER, JOHN LYON, *Notes and Observations on the Town of East Hampton, N.Y.* New York: The New York Historical Society.

GLOAG, JOHN, *The Chair: Its Origins, Design and Social History*. South Brunswick and New York: A. S. Barnes & Company, 1964.

GREENHALGH, RICHARD, Ed., *Joinery and Carpentry*, 2 Vols. London: Sir Isaac Pitman & Sons Ltd., 1929.

HEDGES, HENRY PARSONS, *Address and History of East Hampton, N.Y.* Sag Harbor: Corrector Office, 1850.

HINCKLEY, F. LEWIS, *Directory of the Historic Cabinet Woods*. New York: Crown Publishers, Inc., 1960.

HOLTZAPFFEL, JOHN JACOB, *Turning and Mechanical Manipulations*, 4 Vols. London: Holtzapffel & Company, 1881.

HUBBARD, FRANK, *Three Centuries of Harpsichord Making.* Cambridge: Harvard University Press, 1965.

HUMMEL, CHARLES F., *With Hammer in Hand: The Dominy Craftsmen of East Hampton, New York.* Charlottesville: University Press of Virginia, 1968.

JONES, BERNARD E., *Wood Turning Made Easy.* London: Cassell & Company Ltd., 1925.

JONES, P. D'A., AND SIMONS, E. N., *Story of the Saw.* London: Speare & Jackson Ltd., 1961.

KETTELL, RUSSELL HAWES, *The Pine Furniture of Early New England,* 2 Vols. Garden City, N.Y.: Doubleday Doran & Company, 1929.

LOCKWOOD, LUKE VINCENT, *Furniture Collector's Glossary.* New York: Walpole Society, 1913.

MERCER, HENRY CHAPMAN, *Ancient Carpenters' Tools.* Doylestown: The Bucks County Historical Society, 1929.

MORGAN, EDMUND S., *The Puritan Dilemma: The Story of John Winthrop.* Boston: Little, Brown & Company, 1958.

MORISON, SAMUEL ELIOT, *Builders of the Bay Colony.* Boston: Houghton Mifflin Company, 1930.

NUTTING, WALLACE, *Furniture of the Pilgrim Century 1620–1720.* Framingham: Old America Company, 1924.

———, *Furniture Treasury,* 2 Vols. Framingham: Old America Company, 1928.

ORMSBEE, THOMAS HAMILTON, *Early American Furniture Makers.* New York: Thomas Y. Crowell Company, 1930.

———, *The Windsor Chair.* New York: The Hearthside Press, 1962.

PARSONS, CHARLES S., *The Dunlaps and Their Furniture.* Manchester, N.H.: The Currier Gallery of Art, 1970.

PHIN, JOHN, *Hints and Practical Information for Cabinetmakers.* New York: Frederick A. Hodgson, 1884.

PLUMIER, H. R. P. C., *L'Art de Tourner ou de Fair en Perfection Toutes Sortes d'Ouvrages au Tour.* Leipsic: 1776.

PRIME, ALFRED COXE, *The Arts and Crafts in Philadelphia, Maryland, Etc: 1721–1785.* Topsfield: The Walpole Society, 1929.

Putney, Vermont, Fortnightly Club, *History of Putney, Vermont: 1753–1953.* Putney: The Fortnightly Club, 1953.

RECORD, SAMUEL J., *The Mechanical Properties of Wood.* New York: John Wiley & Sons, 1914.

RICHARDSON, M. T., *Practical Carriage Building.* New York: M. T. Richardson Company, 1892.

ROGERS, JOHN C., *English Furniture.* Garden City: Country Life Ltd., 1923.

SHERWOOD, MALCOLM H., *From Forest to Furniture.* New York: W. W. Norton, 1936.

SLOANE, ERIC, *A Reverence for Wood*. New York: Wilfred Funk, Inc., 1965.

SWAN, MABEL MUNSON, *Samuel McIntire, Carver, and the Sandersons: Early Salem Cabinet Makers*. Salem: The Essex Institute, 1934.

SYMONDS, ROBERT WEMYSS, *Furniture Making in 17th and 18th Century England*. London: The Connoisseur, 1955.

TUNIS, EDWIN, *Colonial Living*. New York: The World Publishing Company, 1957.

WILLIAMS, HENRY LIONEL, *Country Furniture of Early America*. New York: A. S. Barnes; London: Thomas Yoseloff Ltd., 1963.

WILSON, THOMAS R. C., "Wood Bending." Madison, Wisconsin: USDA Forest Service and University of Wisconsin, 1929.

WOODBURY, ROBERT S., *History of the Lathe to 1850*. Cambridge: The M.I.T. Press, 1961.

WRIGHT, LOUIS BOOKER, *Cultural Life of the American Colonies 1607–1763*. New York: Harper & Brothers, 1957.

Index

The majority of page references in this index are grouped in the following principal categories:

chair
chairmaking
furniture
furniture makers
inventories
joints
lathe, lathework
lumber
timber
tools
wood

Page numbers in **boldface** refer to illustrations.

Aldren A. Watson

is a book illustrator, designer, and author. His work reflects a long-standing interest in craftsmanship and the hand tool trades. He is the author-illustrator of *The Village Blacksmith, Hand Tools: Their Ways and Workings, Hand Bookbinding: A Manual of Instruction,* and the illustrator and co-author with Theodora A. Poulos of *Furniture Making Plain & Simple.* His studio and workshop are in North Hartland, Vermont.

Ⓟ Plume

COUNTRY LIVING